Reluctant Socialists, Rural Entrepreneurs

Class, Culture, and the Polish State

Studies in the Ethnographic Imagination

John Comaroff, Pierre Bourdieu, and Maurice Bloch, *Series Editors*

RELUCTANT SOCIALISTS, RURAL ENTREPRENEURS

Class, Culture, and the Polish State

CAROLE NAGENGAST

WESTVIEW PRESS

Boulder • San Francisco • Oxford

Studies in the Ethnographic Imagination

The map of Poland on p. xvi is reprinted from Jack A. Goldstone, Ted Robert Gurr, and Farrokh Moshiri, eds., *Revolutions of the Late Twentieth Century* (Boulder: Westview Press, 1991), p. 137. Copyright © 1991 by Jack A. Goldstone. Used with permission.

Published in 1991 in the United States of America by Westview Press, Inc., 5500 Central Avenue, Boulder, Colorado 80301-2847, and in the United Kingdom by Westview Press, 36 Lonsdale Road, Summertown, Oxford OX2 7EW

Library of Congress Cataloging-in-Publication Data
Nagengast, Carole.
    Reluctant socialists, rural entrepreneurs : class, culture, and
the Polish state / Carole Nagengast.
        p.   cm. — (Studies in the ethnographic imagination)
    Includes bibliographical references.
    ISBN 0-8133-8053-7. — 0-8133-1932-3(pbk.)
    1. Poland—Rural conditions.   2. Agriculture—Economic aspects—
Poland.   3. Social classes—Poland.   4. Poland—Population, Rural.
I. Title.   II. Series
HN538.5.N34   1991
307.72'09438—dc20   91-27458
                                                              CIP

Printed and bound in the United States of America

The paper used in this publication meets the requirements
of the American National Standard for Permanence of Paper
for Printed Library Materials Z39.48-1984.

10   9   8   7   6   5   4   3   2   1

*To my grandparents Michael and Katherine Malek,
who taught me to love "the old country"*

Contents

Preface

I FIRST VISITED WOLA PŁAWSKA, the small rural farming community in Poland upon which many conclusions in this book are based, in 1977. The purpose of this first trip was to ascertain if indeed anthropological research of the sort I had in mind was going to be possible in "Communist" Poland. Having found a positive response (at both the local and national levels), I returned with my three children, Mary Anne, John, and Claire Connelly, in fall 1978. We remained in the village, staying with a village family, until almost the end of 1979. My partner and friend, Michael Kearney, joined us for four months during the dead of winter 1979, rendering moral support and bringing welcome material resources, including replenishment for our already depleted supply of cold medicines and a shortwave radio that gave us access to the BBC, Radio Free Europe, Radio Moscow, and Radio Beijing, which caused us a certain amount of consternation when we compared contrasting versions of, for example, the Three Mile Island disaster, the incidents at Jonesville, and other major events of that year.

In Poland, I was witness to the election of Karol Wojtyła as Pope John Paul II and, more important for the purposes of this book, to the events and processes that led to the eruption of Solidarity onto the national and international scene less than a year after my departure. I made two subsequent visits to Poland, one in 1988 and another in 1990, during a period that was, of course, especially significant for Poland, indeed for all of Eastern Europe and the rest of the world. On the surface, this book is not about those events but about farmers—peasants, some might call them. These are people, however, whose history and whose lives figured in the dramatic events of the past decade in sometimes unexpected ways.

As a resident of Wola Pławska, I have been both participant in and observer of daily life in most settings, including parties, weddings, funerals, and births and one complete agricultural cycle: plowing, planting, cultivation, harvesting, and marketing. There is not an agricultural chore that I have not participated in: I have plowed, sowed, harvested, threshed, dug potatoes, spread manure, milked cows, and helped to slaughter more pigs than bear remembering in order to make sausage and smoke ham. I was not, in fact, especially competent in some of these tasks (I never did master milking), but people put up with me with amazing grace and, as time went by, I was able to render significant help. My children quickly learned basic Polish, attended the local school for a full academic year, and within months were incorporated into the social life of the children and adolescents. They were also my informal field assistants and collaborators, especially in producing accounts of the village school system and the social groups of children. As the parent of school-age children and perhaps because of my own Polish peasant ancestry, I was fitted into the social fabric of Wola Pławska and to an important extent into that of the adjoining and larger village of Rzędzienowice. In 1978 and 1979 I recorded agricultural statistics and did extensive oral histories and interviews and a complete demographic survey. I was given access to the archives of Wola Pławska (the church records of marriages, baptisms, and deaths), the complete records of agricultural sales to the local authorities, purchases of fertilizers and other inputs, and the bank records of loans and credits. I copied or photographed most of these documents. I also conducted a number of interviews with local authorities and a few with other officials of the state as I encountered them on my monthly trips to Kraków and two trips to Warsaw. Later visits to Poland, during which I was unaccompanied by my children, were necessarily briefer and only for gathering data; though done in a somewhat less formal style, these visits nonetheless provided historical depth and have been crucial to my understanding.

The research in Poland would not have been possible without the assistance of many people, most notably that of the people of Wola Pławska and Rzędzienowice. To those who prefer to remain unnamed but who gave me and my children a home in all senses of the word during 1978 and 1979 and hosted me again on later trips, I shall always be grateful for their hospitality and for their warmth and graciousness beyond what anyone could ever expect anywhere.

My official status as a visiting scholar at Jagiellonian University in Kraków, arranged by the International Research and Exchanges Board (IREX), opened doors that might otherwise have remained forever closed. IREX, the National Science Foundation, and the Chancellor's Patent Fund of the University of California–Riverside, financed my original fieldwork. Their help is acknowledged with gratitude. John Comaroff, Martha Lampland, and Jean Lave have read and commented on this and earlier versions of the manuscript, and Michael Kearney on more than he or I can remember. Special thanks to him and to Kellie Masterson of Westview Press, who guided this project through the shoals. The usual disclaimers pertain!

Carole Nagengast

Guide to Polish Pronunciation

THE POLISH ALPHABET comprises thirty-two letters, including nine vowels. Polish uses the Latin alphabet plus several special letters to represent sounds that do not exist in Latin. Other Polish sounds are represented by groups of letters. Spelling is basically phonetic, and stress is usually on the penultimate syllable.

The Vowels

a	as in *far*
e	as in *get*
i	approximates the *ee* in *feet*
o	as in *lot*
u, ó	like the *oo* in *good*
y	like the *i* in *pit*
ą	nasalized like the *on* in the French *bon*
ę	nasalized like the *in* in the French *matin*

The Consonants

The twenty-three consonants include soft and hard consonants, each having distinctive stem endings. Most have pronunciations similar to those in English, but several have pronunciations peculiar to Polish.

c	like the *ts* in *cats* or the *tz* in *blitz*
cz	approximates the *ch* in *choice*
ć, ci	approximates the *ch* in *cheese*
ch	as in *loch*
dz	as in *adze*
dź	like the *j* in *jeep*
dż	like the *dg* in *bridge*
j	equals a *y*
ł	equals a *w*
ñ	like the *ny* in *canyon*

sz	approximates the *sh* in *shelf*
ś	approximates the *sh* in *sheep*
w	equals a *v*
ż, rz	like the *s* in *measure*
ź	like the *s* in *amnesia*

Finally, Polish is a highly inflected language. All verbs are conjugated, and nouns, adjectives, and pronouns are declined; they must, of course, agree. Moreover, there are three genders: masculine, feminine, and neuter; and the masculine has two aspects: animate and inanimate. Syntactical relations are indicated by the declension of nouns (nominative, genitive, dative) rather than by the use of prepositions, although there are some prepositions as well. There are several conjugational verb forms, almost all verbs have a perfective and imperfective form, and the reflexive is common.

Reluctant Socialists, Rural Entrepreneurs

Class, Culture, and the Polish State

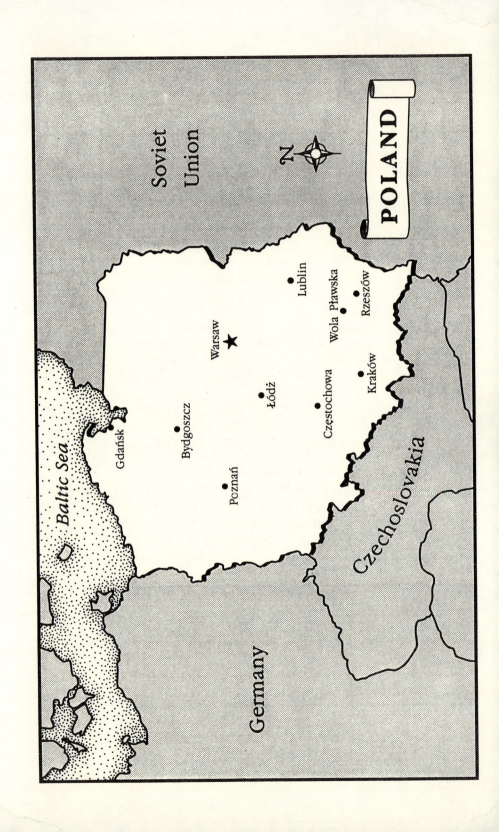

1

Introduction

IN THE PHYSICAL UNIVERSE, satellites do not just stray abruptly out of orbit; thousands, perhaps millions of small changes must first occur. Likewise in the social world. The Polish people removed themselves and their nation from the Soviet orbit in 1989 by the not so simple expedient of voting outspoken anti-Communists into parliamentary office. The new Parliament selected a prime minister who, with his cabinet, set about dismantling the command economy and the social services of communism and replacing them with the apparatuses and the economic and social relations of capitalism.[1] Triumphal explanations of this and similar occurrences elsewhere in Eastern Europe draw heavily upon the historical inevitability of communism's demise in the face of the "naturalness" of capitalism. Such accounts depend mainly upon the equation of free market with freedom. The centerpiece of this book is the argument that the reinstitution of capitalism in Poland was not the logical and inevitable victory of a superior system but rather reflects continuities in earlier, class-based *social* relations that masqueraded as *socialist* relations for four and a half decades. This new, old capitalism also reflects processes set into motion in the eighteenth, nineteenth, and early twentieth centuries.

Most Poles regard 1944 as a watershed, an abrupt break with the nascent capitalist social formation. In this view, the events of that and subsequent years inaugurated movement, for better or worse, along the dramatically different economic, political, and social path of communism, first under the influence and then the direction of the Communist party.[2] Within and without Poland, events and processes since the mid-1940s are measured against a yardstick of sorts, characterized as moves toward more or less social conflict, democracy, totalitarianism, or socialist democracy—the terms are dictated by the political and theoretical orientation of the commentator. Few argue, however, that a cardinal transformation did not occur.

1

When the new apparatuses of the state and the Communist party nationalized the industrial means of production in the years immediately following the end of World War II, they assumed direct ownership and responsibility for industry. In contrast, after dismantling large agrarian estates and farms, the party distributed appropriated land to smallholders and the landless. Agriculture, in other words, was never "socialized." Nonetheless, the official doctrine of the Communist party was henceforth that, although Poland was not yet totally classless, the "traditional" classes now played a small and diminishing role because they could no longer reproduce themselves. Sociological, political, and historical analyses of social identity thereafter followed directly from that premise, with undeniable inequality attributed to differences in status and occupation rather than class. For all Polish (and many non-Polish) analytic intents and purposes, before long Poland became a society in which there was neither class nor class conflict.

The theoretical and conceptual tools with which social science attempts to account for and explain the historical processes through and by which human action is coordinated pose certain conceptual problems. The historicization of continuity and the change in class composition, class relations, and social identity are among them. The problem of change entails accounting for and explaining transformations in class-based social formations such that class perhaps disappears, as many theorists claim it did in Poland. Historicizing continuity, in contrast, has to do with explaining, first, how an existing social formation is reproduced from one generation to the next with essentially the same forms of production and division of labor and, second, how the unequal class relations that result from that coordination are legitimated such that reproduction of inequality occurs with relatively little overt social conflict. How, in other words, is inequality rendered natural? In order to attend to the various dimensions of the problems of continuity and change in social and economic relations, of adequately conceptualizing a Polish ethnography, my research strategy draws on the insights and methods of recent critical social science and history as well as the conventional field methods of anthropology.

I was a participant-observer in a rural community of mostly small farmers on several occasions between 1977 and 1990. During early visits, I established a baseline for subsequent comparison and identified a series of trends in differential farm ownership, productive practice, rural culture, and both the reproduction and transformation of capital and power in its several guises. My most recent visit in summer 1990 and the well-publicized events of 1989–1990 confirm some of my original findings and give new salience to many of my earlier predictions (Nagengast 1982, 1985, 1990). My interpretations of these phenomena are contrary to those of theorists associated, however peripherally, with the project of the socialist state and who draw on the concepts of status and occupation as explanatory devices. They are also different from anthropological interpretations of Polish village life that invoke populist and Chayanovian theories of peasant economy (Hann 1985).[3] I elaborate here the argument that the appropriation and accumulation of capital in all its forms *continued* to be a class phenomenon in rural Poland during the forty-five years of putative communism and that these class relations and consciousness configure contemporary economic, political, and social relations in unexpected ways. What is more, and this is the crux of the matter, the events and processes of the immediate past both frame and highlight two class conflicts within the overall scenario of neocapitalism in Poland, the embryo of which was already apparent some years before the 1989 change in government that is so widely regarded as dramatically new and different. These conflicts were, in other words, woven into the very fabric of the socialist state. The first is a rift between the interests of emerging class fractions in the countryside. The second is a potential split between the interests of a nascent rural bourgeoisie and those of workers. I view these contests as an aspect of the relationship between the state and its power and rural communities, and within the context of the monopolization of capital and power on the part of the rural bourgeoisie. This monopolization is nourished and made to appear natural by a local and national intelligentsia. Thus, the formation, perpetuation, and transformations of rural class, class fractions, boundaries between fractions, indeed the culture of rural class, are at issue. In my treatment of them, I assume that the present cannot be understood as the culmination of a series of discrete events but that continuities and discontinuities in social relations are susceptible to processual analyses that are not necessarily teleological.

Wola Pławska,[4] the community in which I worked, is a small village in the southeastern part of the country. In spite of the historic vicissitudes of geopolitics and changing borders, it has been part of the Polish state since the tenth century, except for a 130-year period when it was incorporated into the Austrian empire. I take Wola Pławska to be more or less prototypic for this part of Poland as it is similar in size, essential structure, and history to a thousand villages like it. However, the subjects of this study—class and power, class consciousness, differentiation, and change—are incomprehensible if examined only at the local level and only in the contemporary era. The inhabitants of Wola Pławska order their lives, their economic philosophies and practices, and their social and political arrangements according to a set of conscious and unconscious strategies that are geared toward the satisfaction of material and symbolic interests. The goals they articulated (that is, their survival as ever more prosperous, landowning, independent, profit-making producers) were at odds with a long-term stated objective of the socialist state (that is, agricultural production primarily for social use rather than profit), but they were congruent with the socialist state's short-term aim of raising production levels to meet the immediate demands of consumers. They now are also decidedly in accord with the ideals of capitalist enterprise and a market economy articulated by the government that took power in 1989.

But not all farmers are equally successful in attaining their goals. One's position in an emerging hierarchy is predicated in part upon location within the historically constituted economic and social structure of the village. Differential ownership and access to land and other means of production, differentially available labor power, and contacts in the regional political arena, dominated by Communist party apparatchiks, also have contributed to differentiation among village households. The range of strategies is given by the social formation, organized with reference to a determinate set of political, economic, and social conditions. The strategies themselves, however, are the creative acts of human agents, producing and reproducing social forms. The following chapters turn the anthropological spotlight on the cultural, symbolic, economic, and some of the structural features of class, class identity, and differentiation as these processes have been historically elaborated in one village as well as nationwide.

Among other points that I discuss are the agricultural policies and practices of the state in the period immediately prior to 1989. The sociological theory of official (i.e., party) and nonparty planners and theorists alike that guided agricultural policy was informed by two seemingly contradictory but in fact similar development orientations: orthodox Marxism and Western modernization theory. One level at which to address this apparent anomaly is that at which theorists, politicians, and planners have hitherto addressed it—how to rationalize agricultural production, enhance the realization of surplus value, and account for inequality without overtly recognizing and consequently without addressing the existence of class, the possibility of class fractionation, or class conflict. Given the object of this study, their analyses must be viewed as part of the dynamic, a reflection of both the reality of the state of agriculture and a cause of it. The ways in which policies and political philosophy contributed to the reproduction of class distinctions are identified, analyzed, and placed in historical context. This analysis is woven together with that of the more subtle production, reproduction, and transmission of capital in all its forms in Wola Pławska. An essential part of the argument is that the image of a decisive rupture in 1944 in the reproduction of class and class relations and in the very nature and practice of the preceding capitalist state masks historical continuities that critically shape the present.

There then follows a description and analysis of the ways in which official policy and ideology partially penetrated the village and were transformed through the emergence of a countercultural oppositional logic and practice that engendered both the division and the cohesion of a farmer class.[5] The primary emphasis is on how the rural cultivators of Wola Pławska mediated, resisted, but in the end incorporated the logic of the dominant system of production. The irony is that for at least ten years prior to the 1989 announcement of a return to capitalism, the system the farmers were reproducing was essentially that of agrarian capitalism, atavistic to be sure but capitalism nonetheless.

The plan of the book is as follows: In Chapter 2 I review some recent events and processes that have been significant to the issues at hand as the socialist state moved in not so stately fashion toward self-destruction. In Chapters 3 and 4 I elaborate the themes introduced above in both general terms and with specific reference to Wola Pławska. These include the historical genesis of the rural sociocultural order and the development of social categories of inequality in the context of economic development, as well as the role of the state and other major actors in the creation, imposition, and enforcement of class identity. In Chapter 5 I sketch material conditions in Wola Pławska between 1978 and 1990, preliminary to the portrait of the village that will emerge in more detail in subsequent chapters. I assess, among other factors, the impact of forty-five years of a state socialist system of production and distribution on rural inequalities. In Chapter 6 I outline and analyze the metamorphosis of the socialist state's agricultural development theory by examining some of its philosophical, theoretical, and historical bases. In Chapter 7 I trace the transformation of material inequality in Wola Pławska into emergent class fragments under the aegis of the socialist state and the Communist party. In Chapter 8 I describe farming practices and the underlying ideology of emerging class fragments in Wola Pławska and further discuss the ramifications and implications of development theory in practice. Finally, in Chapter 9 I discuss the generation of oppositional logic and its effects on the process of the overall system in the context of alternative theories of the state and then conclude with potential long-term implications for class relations within the country.

NOTES

1. That this could not have happened in Poland and subsequently in Hungary, Czechoslovakia, and East Germany without the sanction of the Soviet Union is indisputable but not at issue here.

2. The "Communist party" in Poland has had several versions since 1944, the most recent but one of which was the Polish United Workers' party (Polska Zjednoczona Partia Robotnicza, or PZPR), which was formed in the late 1940s and ruled until 1989. The earlier permutations are not relevant to the discussion in this book; consequently, "the Communist party" refers to the PZPR unless otherwise noted.

3. Chayanov's theory treats peasant economy as qualitatively specific (see Thorner, Kerblay, and Smith 1966).

4. In earlier publications (Nagengast 1982, 1985), I call Wola Pławska Mala Wies; in later ones I give it its proper name (Nagengast 1990). My intention in using a pseudonym was to protect the long-term security of the residents because much of what I reported was at that time quasi-legal or even illegal. In my judgment, enough time has passed and the political situation has sufficiently changed so as to make the use of a pseudonym no longer necessary. Names have been altered, however, to ensure the privacy of those who told me things in confidence. Moreover, many of the actual situations described are composites and others have been changed enough in detail but not in substance so as to render individuals and families unrecognizable both to themselves and, more importantly, to others.

5. I do not take all forms of oppositional behavior as constituting resistance to the state.

2

Poles Apart

THE POLITICAL UPHEAVALS during the 1980s captured the imagination of the world, spawning a plethora of scholarly and popular analyses that addressed many aspects of the turmoil: the perennial and sometimes bitter rivalry between the Catholic church and the Communist party (Polska Zjednoczona Partia Robotnicza, or PZPR); the cleavage between workers and the party, as embodied in the formation of the once dissident trade union Solidarity; and the initial support and then full participation of the intelligentsia and farmers in what was originally a workers' uprising.[1] The complex and distinctly Polish scenario that unfolded was the prelude for yet more momentous events in 1989 and 1990: the election of former opposition figures to positions of national leadership, the legalization of Solidarity, the collapse of the Communist party as the leading force in the state and country, the demise of socialism, the advent of a market economy, and the overt reincorporation of the country into the international economy. In the view of most Poles, the very foundations of the Polish nation, Polish culture and the proper moral order, had been restored. These events, of course, took place as subplots within what later turned out to be the yet greater drama of the fall of the Berlin Wall and the restructuring of East-West relations. Indeed, the commander of NATO Forces in a July 1990 letter to Mikhail Gorbachev declared the cold war officially over.

The Beginning of the End

Although journalists, social scientists, and pundits have commented extensively on the democratic opening, the end of state communism, and the institution of a market economy, another story has gone largely unremarked, one that for forty-five years constituted an essential paradox in socialist Poland.[2] Industry and agriculture had been nationalized in the 1940s and 1950s in the political and economic system of the countries in the Soviet bloc, and all workers and farmers were officially incorporated into their respective proletariats as part of centrally planned and administered command economies. However, in spite of an intense collectivization campaign in Poland between 1948 and 1952, most Polish farmland and farm production remained privately owned. This was the result of the resistance of farmers themselves coupled with overall economic and political considerations at the level of the state. Consequently, 3.5 million individual families (45 percent of the population and 26 percent of the labor force) still own and operate in varying degrees some 75 percent of all farming land for autoconsumption and the market. Throughout the 1970s and 1980s, private farmers produced between 78 and 80 percent of the country's total agricultural and livestock output and between 72 and 75 percent of its marketed produce (*Rocznik Statystyczny* 1984, 1988; Sanford 1981).[3]

The persistence of private farmers in an overall political environment that could only be described as hostile had cultural and symbolic ramifications in addition to the economic impact. If we define culture as "the structure of meaning through which people give shape to their experience" (Geertz 1973:312), we must also consider the politics of that meaning and struggles over who imposes upon others a particular concept of how things "really are" and how, therefore, people are obliged to act (Geertz 1973:316).[4] The struggle over the meaning given to the persistence of private farmers and to extensive private ownership and production in an overtly Communist political economy by both its proponents and critics influenced the outcome of the events leading up to the "end of communism" in ways that are no less critical for their subtlety. Between 1956 (when the overt drive to collectivize ended) and the present, farmers became an icon of the values many perceived as lost to Polish political and economic culture, that is, democracy, independence, and individual enterprise. Private farmers, in other words, became near and dear to the hearts of urban Poles because their perceived independence from the control of the central state symbolized freedom and autonomy, especially to workers who have been acutely aware of those lacunae in their own lives. The emblematic place occupied by farmers is a manifestation of Raymond Williams's (1975) keen observation that urban perceptions of the country and its inhabitants alternate between positive and negative depending upon the social and political climate. In times of particularly severe stress, "the country" and by extension its inhabitants come to represent an essential core of "traditional" cultural values. In less conflictual times, the country is seen as a bastion of backwardness and ignorance. As symbols as much as individuals and collectivities, then, farmers had a role larger than usually remarked upon in the drama of "restructuring" that both ushered out the Communist party and brought central planning to an end.[5]

The commonsense explanation for the united opposition to the Communist party that culminated in its overthrow and the dismantling of the centrally planned economy coalesced around issues of political tyranny and consumer shortages, both laid at the feet of the PZPR because it and the state it directed were supposed to have provided for all the needs of the people, including democracy. Although not exactly wrong, such partial explanations raise as many questions as they answer. A quick look around the world, for example, reveals many socialist and nonsocialist states, less developed and advanced alike, with aspirations as lofty as those of socialism but even meaner achievements than those of the Polish state: These countries may have poor economic records, disparities between the haves and the have-nots that rival those in Poland, and equal or greater ferocity in repressing civil liberties and human rights, but the official administrations of such states have been challenged by far less vehement and cohesive opposition.

Because I assume human nature does not mandate devotion to private property and individual competitive enterprise, in the chapters that follow, I uncover some of the subterranean aspects of the apparent unity of everyday resistance with the aim of elucidating the virtually total failure of the hegemony of the official socialist ideology and identity and thereby accounting for the conflation of political freedom and free enterprise. I consider the proposition that the anomaly of extensive private ownership in a socialist economy formed the parameters of a series of contingent contradictions having to do with the processes of class transformation, consciousness, and differentiation not just in the recent past but over the last century and longer. These contradictions shaped the circumstances that united disparate sectors of Polish society in the groundswell for the dramatic political and economic transformations that occurred in 1989–1990.

There has always been a substantial opposition in socialist Poland, the politics of which spanned the political spectrum. The emergence of a national opposition united against the dominance of the PZPR, and against socialism and a socialist identity as well, was partially a result of the theoretical and practical incoherencies and ambivalences of the Polish version of socialism with respect to both the economy and political liberties. When workers had rioted in Gdańsk in 1970 the police shot and killed hundreds. The official response to worker demands was not, however, restricted to abuses of civil and human rights. Much of it also entailed progressive steps to "rationalize" socialized production and to tie some aspects of both it and private farming production to international markets in order to better address consumer demands. After 1970, for example, imports from the West were intended to expand industrial output and increase supplies of food, other agricultural products, and consumer goods, thereby arresting the political dissatisfaction that had led to open defiance in the first place. Yet the economic measures taken by the government actually contributed to ever more critical shortages as planners found that the technology offered them by the West was already outdated, that Polish products could not compete on the world market, and that inflation and recession in the West made capital loans impossible to repay. The result was further political upheaval exemplified by new violence in 1976, the formation of Solidarity in 1980, the proliferation of the underground and not so underground alternative civil society, and an out-of-control debt to Western capitalists. The debt, which must be paid in hard currency and which grew from $760 million to $28 billion during the 1970s alone, made Poland the first of what came to be a succession of so-called developing countries incurring stupendous and unmanageable foreign deficits in the 1980s.[6]

Although the PZPR and other institutions of the official state never overtly acknowledged or condoned it, an illegal black market that competed with as well as supplemented the state's allocation system became increasingly critical to the distribution of food and other goods and services after 1970, notwithstanding the inflation its existence entailed. The black market was organized on principles of supply and demand as determinates of price, and a major if not the major medium of exchange was the U.S. dollar, which was difficult to obtain but paradoxically legal. Foreign currency, especially dollars, was also exchanged on the black market at much above the official exchange rate and thus aggravated inflation. The need to service the foreign debt and the gaps in its own distribution system probably accounted for the state's toleration of the black market. As we shall see, inequities for both producers and consumers in such a contradictory system were inevitable. With respect to private farmers, of particular concern in this study, those with what turned out to be privileged access to the needed agricultural inputs from, ironically, state sources began to produce for the profitable black market in food, necessarily depriving the official market and thereby causing shortages in state-subsidized food. Not surprisingly, this further fueled discontent as ordinary workers and citizens were faced with long queues whereas the more affluent or those with access to dollars were able to make their purchases privately (or, until they were abolished in the early 1980s, at special state shops that catered to the wealthy by stocking only the best cuts of meats at highly inflated prices). In attempting to reform the system of socialism such that it would work better for more people (and of course, maintain themselves in power), planners, bureaucrats, and theorists only succeeded in promoting bourgeois values and practices. This fact has been largely unremarked or at best minimized, as has the fact that the failure of socialism was the result of the acts and omissions not only of Communist party bureaucrats but also of all the people.

By the 1980s, these circumstances combined with internal contradictions in the centrally planned economy were manifest. Food shortages were of grave concern to consumers and planners alike, consumer goods were in ever shorter supply, the much-touted industrial expansion had floundered, and exports were less competitive on the world market in terms of price and quality than authorities had hoped (and planned for). The foreign debt, on which the principal and interest payments amounted to between 30 and 92 percent of the country's export earnings between 1979 and 1986, could not be paid[7] and it grew to $40 billion by 1989 as interest and penalties accrued. Overt public expressions of dissension swept the country during August 1980, factory after factory went on strike, Solidarity was formed, and ten million workers, farmers, and intellectuals joined together in calling for economic reforms as well as for freedom and democracy. With the economy further disrupted by the strikes of 1981 and unable to control political events, the authorities declared martial law in December and outlawed Solidarity. The United States and other Western countries imposed embargoes on grains, livestock feed, and other goods, causing additional shortages and further production cutbacks, especially but not exclusively in livestock and hence meat. Centrally planned food distribution broke down altogether for a time, and barter temporarily replaced market mechanisms (see Steven 1982 for examples). Workers, farmers, and intellectuals alike were arrested, official censorship tightened, a draconian austerity program initiated, food and other consumer goods rationed, and prices immediately increased by 300 to 400 percent. Many dissidents emigrated to Great Britain, France, and the United States and were instrumental in producing alternative newspapers that, in spite of censorship, were widely though clandestinely distributed in Poland, augmenting *samizdat*, the domestic underground press. The official state was unable to control the thriving underground civil society, though dissidents continued to be repressed in a variety of ways, including arrest and imprisonment and several evidently politically motivated killings.

After a few years of surface quiescence, the government eventually rescinded martial law and released most political prisoners. In 1988, however, strikes began once again, and once again the opposition became publicly vocal. By early 1989 the opposition was playing a prominent role in the official affairs of the state, never having lost its cultural dominance and, if anything, having augmented its symbolic power. Public attention both within and without Poland shifted from political prisoners and the activities of Solidarity leaders to (1) the political opening symbolized by the 1988 roundtable discussions between the PZPR and the intelligentsia that had gathered around the union; (2) the subsequent formation of the Senate, a second chamber in the Sejm (Parliament) to which non-Communist party members could be elected; and (3) the election in which the Citizens' Parliamentary Group (Obywatelski Klub Parliamentarny, or OKP)—the political organization in Parliament made up of the opposition intelligentsia—was successful beyond the most optimistic expectations, garnering a number of Senate seats. Finally, in August of that year, the United Populist (or Peasant) party (Zjednoczone Stronnictwo Ludowe, or ZSL)[8] and the Democratic party (Stronnictwo Demokratyczne, or SD), both of which had been allied with the PZPR for many years, defected to the OKP. The ZSL and its pre-1944 predecessor, the Polskie Stronnictwo Ludowe (Polish Populist party), significantly, had long been a stronghold of the most prosperous farmers allied with many of the intelligentsia (Narkiewicz 1976:267–268). By breaking ranks with the PZPR, the ZSL paved the way for a move that startled much of the world and presaged similar events in East Germany, Czechoslovakia, Bulgaria, Hungary, and Romania. On 24 August 1989, the Sejm elected Tadeusz Mazowiecki, journalist, long-time adviser to Lech Wałęsa and Solidarity, and member of the Catholic Intelligentsia Club, as prime minister of the first non-Communist government in Poland since 1947.

In 1990 the opposition figures who became the government made immediate and dramatic changes in the politics and the economics of the state. One of Mazowiecki's first announcements was that he was going to steer Poland back to the capitalist path it was on in 1939 when the Nazis invaded—a statement greeted enthusiastically by a majority in the newly constituted Sejm. Furthermore, he was reported as saying that, "it is necessary to remove responsibility for social welfare from the state," a sentiment since widely expressed and more importantly implemented by the new cabinet. The cabinet contains nine members of the OKP (compared to four from the PZPR), most of whom are academics drawn from the Catholic intelligentsia. It also includes Tadeusz Syryjczyk, the leader of a small but aggressive organization of private entrepreneurs in the Kraków region, as the minister of industry.[9] The spirit of the West had far earlier "gone to the heads of the intelligentsia," as Daniel Singer put it, quoting a journalist who had hoped in 1988 that "market, money, and profit having found acceptance, maybe 'capital' will cease to be a class-alien concept" (Singer 1988:302). Just how capital might escape its class association is unclear. It is one of many ironies in recent Polish history that the anti-Communist and in many cases antisocialist project of the intelligentsia coincided with that of the Communist party bureaucracy itself in promoting bourgeois values.

After Mazowiecki's election, the tables were turned on the powerful, the upper echelons of the PZPR. Jails were emptied of political prisoners, censorship abolished, and restrictions of movement eliminated. The coercive measures of a repressive state seemed to disappear overnight. Some of the most illustrious figures of the opposition, advisers to Solidarity during its underground existence, are now cabinet ministers; the less powerful of only a year earlier are now in control, and the end of the "leading role of the Communist Party in the state" is hailed as a triumph for democracy. In fact, the PZPR voted to dissolve itself in late January 1990 when it became clear that it enjoyed the support of less than 5 percent of the population. It has since been bifurcated and reconstituted as the Social Democratic Union (Unia Socjaldemokratyczna, or USD) and the Social Democracy of the Polish Republic (Socjaldemokracja Rzeczpospolitej Polskiej, or SDRP).

With a new political system in place, history is being reinterpreted and the bad old days of pre–World War II capitalism are being reinvented as the good old days. During August, September, and October of 1989, numerous speeches in the Sejm and articles in the Solidarity daily, *Gazeta Wyborcza*, as well as in government newspapers all addressed the necessity of dramatic reforms in the economy. Declaring that "it is economically flawed to blend economic and welfare functions," the new leaders engaged the services of one Jeffrey Sachs, a Harvard Business School economist who had already presided over major restructuring in Bolivia (with results that most experts regard as disastrous for ordinary Bolivians), and set out to dismantle the command economy and convert it to one driven by the market. In their draft economic plan the new leaders proposed ending (they have since indeed ended) subsidies to food and to "unproductive enterprises"; eliminated regulations that hamper free economic activity; offered state enterprises for sale to private entrepreneurs, domestic and foreign alike; ended all monopolies in industry, agriculture, transport, mining, shipping, and others; eliminated all cooperatives; and liberalized foreign trade and investment.[10] With respect to agriculture, subsidies to all capital inputs (fertilizers, pesticides, machinery) have been removed, but retail prices are still partially determined administratively rather than by the free market. Thus far this has meant that many farmers are operating at a loss. Other measures taken by the new government include lifting all restrictions on farm size, mode of operation, inheritance of land, and so forth, and placing the approximately 25 percent of agricultural land hitherto incorporated into state farms on the block, presumably to be bought by individual farmers or, significantly, by the former managers of the farms. Experts expect and want the smallest farms, which they say have been receiving inordinately high incomes because of state subsidies, to be absorbed by the larger farms and their proprietors forced to seek other livelihoods. "Farmers have been accustomed to an economic setting in which even the smallest and least efficient of them have been provided for by the government," said the new deputy for agriculture; "this must stop, they must alter their profiles of production, or sell their farms."[11] They must, in other words, do what is necessary to acquire the necessary inputs at whatever price in order to produce and then figure out how to sell their products at a profit sufficient to maintain and reproduce themselves. Failing this, they must go out of business. To some extent, the country's agricultural sector is intended to be a model for what the future might bring to the production processes of the entire economy.

As recently as 1988, it was not at all clear that this vision was as widely shared as the present leaders imagine. In August 1988, a year before the formation of the Mazowiecki government, I attended an international human rights conference in Kraków in the midst of the most widespread labor strikes since the imposition of martial law seven years earlier. This conference, which was convened by two then illegal groups (the leader of one of which was a political prisoner in 1982 but is now an elected member of the Sejm), presaged the subsequent political opening of Polish society epitomized by the legalization of the opposition and the opportunity for open debate about the future. Over 1,100 human rights activists, all but 220 Eastern Europeans and most of them Poles, attended. There was also a sizable contingent from Hungary, at least one person from Romania and one from East Germany, several from Czechoslovakia, several from Yugoslavia, even a few from the Soviet Union. A number of Western European, African, and Latin American countries were represented, and there were a dozen or more delegates from the United States. In spite of the labor unrest, the conference participants were not interfered with by agents of the state nor was the conference itself proscribed, as had happened with a smaller gathering sponsored by Charter 77 in Prague earlier that year. Foreigners were prevented (by subterfuge) from traveling to a nearby mine where workers were on strike, but delegates from the Solidarity strike committee made daily reports to the conference and appeals for moral and material support. The attendance at the conference and the nature of the speeches, discussions, and resolutions were a sure sign that *glasnost* and *perestroika* were receiving widespread public response in Eastern Europe.

The debate about the possibilities and the nature of meaningful restructuring that would encompass respect for fundamental human and civil rights and that would entail dialogue and concerted joint international activity of people of similar viewpoints was one of the most striking and heartening aspects of the conference. Also striking was what appeared to me to be an implicit, subtextual, but fundamental political split among the Poles in attendance.[12] All were united in opposition to the policies if not the substance of the PZPR, but one contingent opted for a gradual reform of the existing economic and political system such that, as one person told me, "the Polish nation can be the master of its own destiny." He and others of more or less like mind did not envisage the dismantling of the system of socialized industry, at least not the major industries. Not only is this unnecessary, he told me, it is not desirable. Better to democratize the economic decisionmaking of major industry and allow small businesses and trade to be privatized like farming already is, so that a system of socialist democracy similar to those of the Scandinavian countries can gradually emerge. He was unclear as to just how this process might unfold, what role if any international or even national capital might play, or what role he foresaw for the Catholic church.

Another point of view, profoundly antisocialist, seemed more prevalent. It was also approximated in an opinion poll taken within the country in 1980 by the French daily *Paris-Match.* In this poll, published in France but not in Poland, 53 percent of the population surveyed supported political parties antagonistic to socialism; only 3 percent would vote for the PZPR in an open election, 27 percent for the Socialist party, 34 percent for the equivalent of the Christian Democrats, and 19 percent for the Conservatives.[13] The Christian Democrats are closely tied to the Catholic church, and both it and the Conservatives long favored close economic and political ties with the capitalist West. This was reflected at the conference, where many participants explicitly condemned anything and everything "Communist" or even mildly socialist or leftist as immoral, contrary to the teachings of the church and contrary to the interests of the Polish people. Everything associated with the undifferentiated West, on the other hand, was taken as emblematic of democracy and freedom,[14] with the free market and private enterprise the most celebrated aspects. Implicit and in some cases explicit was the projected reprivatization of the entire economy, with the help of capitalist governments and international lending agencies, and with the full sanction and assistance of the church.

Certain aspects of this project had already been under way for some years. Pope John Paul II, for example, pledged $2 billion in Vatican funds to aid small farmers in late 1983, Poland was accepted as a member of the International Monetary Fund (IMF) in 1986, and in 1987 David Rockefeller, in a joint venture with Poles and with the approval of Polish authorities, set up the Foundation for the Development of Polish Agriculture, also intended to help small farmers to increase their production and profits. The initial project of the foundation was to boost the export of high-quality ham to the United States—something of a contradictory project in light of the then critical domestic shortages of

meat. In 1989 Barbara Piasecki Johnson, heir to the Johnson and Johnson
fortune and a Polish-born U.S. citizen who is by all accounts "fiercely
anti-Communist" even by Polish standards,[15] put up $100 million for
55 percent ownership of the ailing Gdańsk shipyard, in danger of closing
because of outdated technology and the general decline in shipbuilding
worldwide. The idea behind privatizing the shipyard was to improve
production, in part by tightening labor control techniques, ostensibly in
order to prevent what would have been the layoff of some 10,000 shipyard
workers had the shipyard closed. Johnson let it be known in an article
in the *Gazeta Wyborcza*, that she does not approve of strikes (Margolick
1989:64). Workers objected—the Gdańsk shipyard was, of course, the
site of the earliest strikes in August 1980 and is the symbolic locus of
Solidarity—but the reason the deal later soured had more to do with
Johnson's inability to provide sufficient money to finance the bailout
than with the new government's sensitivity to workers' rights or their
political sensibilities.

The economic and, by implication, the political program of the
Mazowiecki government contradicts most of the principles put forth by
Solidarity in the early 1980s. These were typical workers' demands for
better wages and working conditions and for union rights. When the
Economic Reform Program was first presented in September 1989, experts
anticipated unemployment of approximately 500,000 as the economy
became "rationalized." That estimate, however, has been continually
revised upward as the recession deepens. By December 1990, there were
already some 1.3 million officially without jobs. The real figure is probably
much higher. Minimal "safety nets" have been devised, but in fact there
seems to be neither the money nor the political impetus for adequate
social welfare. The monthly unemployment insurance benefit is just
sufficient to pay for bread. Preliminary plans for food stamps intended
for the 4.2 million poorest people were scotched by Labor Minister Jacek
Kuroń, who said on 31 October 1989, "there will be no food stamps
for the poor because the National Bank refuses to issue them as a
security paper and the creation of a separate machinery would be too
expensive."[16] The finance minister has "appealed to the generosity of
the people," and Kuroń has called on local communities to organize
soup kitchens, emphasizing that "anything that stands for the state's
welfare function should be carefully and precisely divorced from wage,
which is the price for work."[17] In stark contrast to early Solidarity
demands for equal, across-the-board wage increases for workers in all
industries regardless of job description, wages are now regulated by
administrative indexing. New trade union legislation also contradicts
principles for which many went to prison. It prohibits strikes unless
two weeks have passed after a decision to strike is taken by more than

50 percent of the work force. It further stipulates that strikes cannot be in defense of trade union rights, assigns penal responsibilities to organizers of any such protests, and holds workers collectively responsible for them.

Meanwhile, Western banks were prevailed upon to temporarily suspend interest payments on the debt, foreign capital was invited in, the European Economic Community has pledged massive aid, and IMF and World Bank moneys have been granted to aid the transition to a capitalist economy, subject to the usual austerity measures. Poland "can only count on foreign assistance from the IMF, the World Bank and western governments if this kind of program is implemented," said the finance minister.[18] According to Minister of Industry Syryjczyk, "Either foreign capital flows into Poland and we work for a German, Frenchman, or Swede to the benefit of our country—for those capitalists will found factories and companies in Poland—or it does not flow in, and then we shall have to look for work abroad, to our own personal benefit perhaps but not to our country's."[19] Syryjczyk's statement reflects a stunning disregard for the experiences of the people of other less-developed nations with foreign capital, but more about that in due course.

Economic advisers anticipated inflation of 1,500 percent by the end of 1990 as so-called necessary adjustments were made. On 1 January 1990, the costs of basic necessities were increased by between 250 and 600 percent higher than inflation. By late July 1990, state-owned and operated shops in Mielec, the town nearest Wola Pławska, were rapidly being sold to private entrepreneurs. Every day, villagers told me, yet another store was converted. In general, the prices in the newly privatized shops were far higher than they had been in the state shops and, in small cities such as Mielec, the quality was inferior. Thousands were unemployed as factories cut back shifts and small enterprises went bankrupt. People seemed to me to be on the verge of hysteria and, aside from the absolute necessities that they bought in the smallest possible amounts, were doing little buying. "No," one of my friends from Wola Pławska told me, "there will not be any strikes like in 1980 and 1988. People are afraid to strike; there are already so many unemployed. For every one on strike, there would be one replacement."

Workers will benefit least of all from the capitalist restructuring, according to sociologist Jadwiga Staniszkis, who was an adviser to Solidarity. With the kind of "revolution" under way, that is, "a mutual accommodation of elites in order to stabilize reform, even a trade union is awkward ballast and we are witnessing a clumsy demolition of it. . . . It is not inconceivable," she adds chillingly, "that at some stage, trade unions will be suspended or disbanded, if there are strikes."[20]

Economist Piotr Aleksandowicz advises the government to stop avoiding the question of whether it should "maintain the kind-hearted system of employment regulations, the various welfare and trade privileges, etc. or rather approach Parliament to adjust legislation to the hard rules of the economic game in a market economy."[21] The neocapitalist strategy of economic development implied in steps already taken and those expected in the near future has proven a notable and disastrous policy for the poorest and least powerful inhabitants of countries throughout the less-developed world, including Bolivia, Peru, Mexico, and Brazil (to name only a few), where some version of neocapitalism has already been implemented. Polish planners claim that eventually people will be better-off than before as publicly owned enterprises are replaced by private property, the market system weeds out "inefficient and non-productive" enterprises and workers, new domestic entrepreneurs swing into action, private banks are chartered, the currency becomes convertible, foreign investors move in to take advantage of cheap labor, and Polish products become competitive on the world market, presumably earning greater foreign exchange. Which class of Poles exactly and how many of them will be better-off and when remains to be seen, but it is clear that in the short run many will be facing cold, hunger, and deprivation not seen in Poland for three generations. That this will be temporary and that greater prosperity for all will inevitably follow is an unverified assumption. Experience elsewhere in the world and, as we shall see, processes already under way a decade ago in Poland suggest the contrary.

Class and Conflict

Recent work on capital and power demonstrates that they appear in different guises (cultural, economic, symbolic, and social) depending upon the field in which they function. All, according to Pierre Bourdieu (1977, 1986), can be transformed into the others under specified circumstances, and all entail what he identifies as habitus.[22] Habitus has a logic of its own that is derived from shared material, social, cultural, and symbolic conditions and that regulates shared responses to those conditions and hence the daily practice of a set of individuals. Economic capital, the only sort usually categorized as capital per se, is directly and more or less immediately convertible into money and is ordinarily institutionalized as property relations. Cultural capital, embodied in individuals, may be institutionalized as education and is objectified in writings, paintings, and other "cultural" objects; under certain conditions, it is reconvertible into economic capital. Social capital, constituted by social ties, networks, and obligations, is also potentially transformable into economic capital and may be institutionalized in, for example, noble titles. In the late twentieth century, it is more subtly represented by the possession of a "good" name. Symbolical capital is primarily a relationship of knowledge and know-how.

The question of the arbitrariness of the appropriation and possession of capital in all its forms and the question of its reproduction becomes critical in the process of transferring it from one generation to the next. Every strategy of transmission is, of course, also an exercise in legitimation. What is being legitimated is the rightness of the exclusive ownership and control of capital and the resultant power. Even radical critics of unproblematic and arbitrary entitlements do not recognize much of the transmission of capital because it is so well disguised by convertibility. Thus, "the more the official transmission of capital is prevented or hindered, the more the effects of the clandestine circulation of capital in the form of cultural capital become determinant in the reproduction of the social structure" (Bourdieu 1986:254–255).

In Poland the political and economic processes instituted by the new Communist government of the late 1940s eliminated the links among class, urban manufacturing, and industrial ownership of economic capital and in part that between class and income. However (and this is a significant "however"), the association of education, prestige, and other forms of cultural, social, and symbolic capital, albeit sometimes ambiguous, did not disappear. Although social scientists do not deny the existence of inequality, even those critical of official institutions generally regard it as residual and primarily an individual or at most a family phenomenon that coincides more or less with status. For example, referring "to the distribution of people in terms of status dimensions," prominent sociologists explain that "the concept of social status is based on the socio-occupational structure" (Kolosi and Wnuk-Lipiński 1983:6–7). Commentators both in and outside of Poland note the importance of education to individual status, prestige, and occupation (Dziewanowski 1977:289; Majkowski 1985:128) but do not relate it to the possession of capital or to continuity in class or class membership.

A part of the argument that I make in this book is that, the redistribution of former large agricultural estates notwithstanding, much of the class stratification among peasant farmers in place on the eve of World War II still remains. In villages, the overt links of class to economic capital have been partially reproduced but have also been supplemented and transformed by other forms of capital, today as in the past. During the forty-five years after the advent of the socialist state, these relationships were disguised as simply natural differences among farmers in individual ability, ambition, educational achievements, and success in accumulating social, cultural, and occupational prestige. The veiled process of stratification, the political struggle over meaning, masks the symbolic nature of cultural capital. Further, it accentuates the necessity of examining the accumulation, transmission, and reproduction of all forms of capital such that social identity and class relations have been continuous even when they appear to have been disrupted.

Likewise, significant portions of the highly educated class fraction of professionals, though not always of the same social composition as the pre-1944 intelligentsia, maintained the same social location. Indeed, the ideas, ideals, and practices of the contemporary intelligentsia are similar to and even continuous with those of the prewar class fraction. Bourdieu (1977:81–87) contends that the intelligentsia is a segment of the leading class, the "dominated sector of the dominant class" in a capitalist society, its cultural capital supporting and rendering logical, legitimate, and inevitable the dominant fraction's possession of economic capital. The Polish intelligentsia has retained its cultural hegemony in the Polish state over the last forty-five years—albeit, until late summer 1989, in an underground, alternative civil society that simultaneously challenged and was incorporated into the official state institutions. In effect, for four and a half decades the intelligentsia held in trust the cultural capital appropriate to a class-based social formation. Even those members overtly associated with the formal institutions of the socialist state engaged, by and large, in intellectual endeavors that failed to challenge—because their very incorporation into the state structures made it impossible to recognize—the cultural and symbolic power of their own class fraction. As part of the project to redirect the economy toward the path it was on in 1939 (probably an impossibility, but that is a different question), they are rendering inevitable and therefore legitimate both a rural and a newly emerging national bourgeoisie (cf. Gouldner 1980; Konrad and Szelenyi 1979).

Thus, two points of departure I take in subsequent chapters are, first, the contention that a national intelligentsia because of its possession of capital/power has exercised hegemony since the nineteenth century but has its roots in the even more distant past. Second, a parallel process in village society, in which an emergent bourgeoisie exercises similar control at the local level (as well as economic power in this case), is linked to the first in a complex matrix such that the saliency of capital, class, and class domination has been upheld in a superficially altered but fundamentally unchanged fashion. Therefore, in spite of a split between the possession of economic and cultural/social/symbolic capital between 1944 and 1989, the apparent complete break with the pre–World War II class structure in Poland was largely chimerical.

The State

I have used "the state" a number of times without specifying the sense in which I am employing it. At one end of a definitional spectrum, the state is naked force and unbridled power (Lenin 1965; Althusser 1971). Social control is envisioned as a top-down phenomenon in which the ruling class, whatever its composition, manipulates and dominates the subordinate classes through the "apparatuses of the state" (e.g., the police, the army, the laws, courts, educational institutions, etc.). The Leninist state pretends no separation of political and civil society; indeed, the reified state, governing in the name of and at the behest of "the people" (or the proletariat in a revolutionary state), is supposed to explicitly determine the content and operation of both levels. At the other end is state power solely as consent, the unmediated, ahistorical operation of, in Weberian terms, legitimacy. To be sure, the establishing of legitimacy is a critical chore of a state but not a reified, objectified state. Philip Abrams notes that the state

> is not an object, akin to the human ear. Nor is it even an object akin to human marriage. It is a third-order object, an ideological project. It is first and foremost an exercise in legitimation—and what is being legitimated is, we may assume, something which if seen directly and as itself would be illegitimate, an unacceptable domination. Why else all the legitimation work? The state . . . is a bid to elicit support for or tolerance of the insupportable and intolerable by presenting them as something other than themselves, namely legitimate, disinterested domination (Abrams 1988:760).

Effective, that is, successful, legitimating state rule, as Abrams and others rightly note, is that in which the two moments of power—coercion and consensus—are in balance but consensus predominates. The struggle for consensus is waged on an everyday basis at the level of civil society and the realm of apparently private institutions: churches, scientific endeavors, agricultural institutes, trade unions, and the media. It is not ordinarily contested at the level of political society, the realm of coercion: the police, the courts, the military. A state that depends primarily on coercion may exercise political control; it does not have hegemony (Gramsci 1971; Williams 1977:108–114). In the capitalist state, civil and political society are ostensibly separate, but recent research on power, knowledge, and the state suggests that the effective exercise of power, that is, the legitimating of the illegitimate, cannot be divorced from, for example, social discourse on population categorization, tabulation, and control (Foucault 1973, 1977, 1980), nor can it be separated from the symbolic power of the intelligentsia or of the bourgeoisie. Most especially, it cannot be analyzed apart from consideration of the transmission of capital/power. The power of the state, in other words, does not proceed only from its official institutions downward or even from institutions alone, public or private. Hegemony and consent are also created, imposed, and enforced through social knowledge and cultural practices, the meaning of which are negotiated and contested, though not on an equal basis; they may but need not entail overt force. These practices and knowledge result in the identification, naming, and imposition of social identities that also become enshrined as national identities—as culture— as well as in the establishment of regulatory institutions. More than simply a set of ideologies, they constitute "cultural revolution" (Corrigan and Sayer 1985), such that force need only be resorted to in the breach. As an integral part of the project of the state, then, the intelligentsia, the dominated sector of the dominated class, constructs both itself and, in defense of its own material and symbolic interests, an ideology of its own intellectual and cultural autonomy from political and economic determinants (Garnham and Williams 1980:211). The intelligentsia, local and national alike, must also render natural and inevitable such historically constituted concepts as private property and the economic and social dominance of elite classes and class fractions over equally constituted and constructed identities such as "peasants." These identities, far from ontological, are created and maintained through "microtechnologies" of power through and by which the state constitutes them via bureaucratic measures (censusing, judging, taxing, marrying, and all other practices that document and so form the subject).

It is difficult to underestimate the role of the state broadly defined as both the ideological project implicit in the concept of consensus and the coercive action of specified institutions in formulating *and* regulating cultural knowledge and social identities. But there is always the danger of regarding, in this case, a small community and its inhabitants as more or less passive recipients of social engineering, technology, or the penetration of values, attitudes, and ideas originating from a more developed center, from elite classes, or from the intelligentsia. I neither underestimate the state nor underestimate the citizens; instead, I see social identity, class formation, and class fractionation as a process involving such historical realities as the institutions and practices of the state and its functionaries; the cultural, social, and symbolic hegemony and practice of the intelligentsia; as well as, of course, global economic and political forces. My analysis must and will also weave into the fabric the creative practice of rural dwellers as they resist the state (in all of its guises) while at the same time they are incorporated into it.

The New Populism

One final theme must be introduced, and that has to do with the nature of the opposition. Now that the opposition of the recent past *is* the government, who will now be the opposition and by what shall it be politically informed? One of the major problems is that for forty-five years the political spectrum, aside from the PZPR, has been artificially truncated at dead center. The Left has been so discredited that there is now the danger of right demagoguery, possibly in the form of right populism, the seeds of which have actually lain dormant for many years.

At the human rights conference in 1988, I had a personal conversation that struck me as odd in that context but that I gradually realized demonstrated a dominant viewpoint, at least among the Polish participants. A professor of philosophy at a major Polish university rehearsed to me the principles of natural law to deny Communists the right to even peacefully express their views, because communism, he said, is "demonstrably wrong" and the very antithesis of freedom itself. Moreover, he added, communism is anti-Christian, it threatens the unity of the Polish nation, and it is destroying Polish culture. These sentiments echoed the remarks made in the keynote speech of Jerzy Turowicz, the influential editor of *Tygodnik Powszechny*, the leading Catholic newspaper. That communism is foreign, alien to the Polish nature and to Polish sensibilities, was the sum and substance of a number of speeches. In the two years since the new government was seated, overt signs of anti-Semitism have appeared, beginning in 1989 with graffiti reading that "Jaruzelski is a Jew" and "Urban is a Jew." (Wojciech Jaruzelski, of course, was first secretary of the PZPR between 1981 and 1989 and instituted and presided over martial law between 1981 and 1983. Jerzy Urban was chief spokesperson for the PZPR throughout the 1980s.) Neither is Jewish as far as I know, but the equation of "leftist" with "Jewish" has become commonplace, as has the ubiquitous association of the Left with all that is alien. The subsequent explosion of public anti-Semitic xenophobia provoked a special bishop's letter in early 1991. It was the first time in history that the Catholic clergy in Poland took a strong stand against anti-Semitism.

Several other speakers at the conference summoned up the memory of Roman Dmowski, an extreme right-wing nationalist and political figure associated with the generally reactionary National Democrats between World War I and II, and that of Józef Piłsudski, dictator of a state that between 1926 and 1935 became increasingly oppressive under his direct leadership. Even after Piłsudski's death in 1935 the increasingly

Nazi-like state ruled by his "colonels" was strongly influenced by his personality and politics. A revered veteran of World War I, which restored the Polish nation-state to independence, and of the Polish-Soviet war of 1920, Piłsudski continues to be an heroic figure to much of what was the political opposition. Lech Wałęsa, for example, has his portrait prominently displayed in his home. Technically at the other end of the political spectrum from Dmowski, Piłsudski was also a de facto proponent of extreme nationalism and, in spite of his stated socialist principles, the politics of the state under his leadership was decidedly right-wing.

What turned out to be a fierce struggle between political camps of Wałęsa and Mazowiecki culminated in Wałęsa's election as president in December 1990. Some of Wałęsa's prominent supporters came from what emerged as a rightist political party known as the Center Agreement (Porozumienie Centrum). During the often bitter campaign, they linked what they called "left" politics with Judaism, commenting on the ancestry of Mazowiecki supporters Bronisław Geremek (leader of the OKP) and Adam Michnik (writer and editor of *Gazeta Wyborcza*), among others. Wałęsa himself made a number of remarks that were interpreted as anti-Semitic (but he has since repudiated anti-Semitism and established a special council for Polish-Jewish affairs).

The constellation of political views that provoked the left/Jewish brand included a willingness to honor the provisions of the roundtable agreements that provided for a power-sharing coalition with the PZPR until scheduled parliamentary and presidential elections, a desire to maintain the agreed-upon schedule, and a reluctance to accelerate the economic changes already under way—debatable but hardly leftist stances. One of the major concerns of the Center Agreement was that the *nomenklatura* (former PZPR bureaucrats) have an unfair advantage in acquiring possession of former state enterprises. Proclaiming their intention to replace the former elites with their own favorites, members of the Center Agreement hoped to depose all former PZPR officials from all positions and revoke privileges without regard to competence, honesty, or longevity. Foremost among those they wanted to oust was President Jaruzelski.

During the months preceding the election, the Center Agreement, which claims its support is among workers, alternately called for a general popular and immediate election of the president (which required a prior change in the constitution favored by a two-thirds majority) or immediate election by simple majority in the Sejm pending some later constitutional amendment. The former course was taken, and, as is well known, Mazowiecki was decisively defeated and Wałęsa forced into a runoff with the barely known Stanisław Tymiński.

As Tymiński's background was revealed, Mazowiecki supporters as well as many others began to regard him with suspicion: In 1960 he left Poland for Canada, where he apparently made a lot of money (he says millions; others say hundreds of thousands); he seems to have returned surreptitiously to Poland a number of times between 1981 and 1989 but has denied doing so; he has unspecified ties to Libya; he is the head of a tiny, right-wing political party in Canada that some have described as "lunatic fringe"; he is completely without practical political experience; and he has no discernible political or economic program for Poland. As these damaging facts about Tymiński were widely publicized in the weeks between the election and the runoff, Mazowiecki's backers rallied (uneasily) around Wałęsa, and in the end Wałęsa soundly defeated Tymiński. Nonetheless, even after Tymiński's past became known, one in four Poles voted for him.

Wałęsa quickly replaced some of the intellectuals who were long associated with Solidarity and who played leading roles in the Mazowiecki government with "more pragmatic people, smarter in the ways it counts," as one observer put it.[23] Several provisions of the roundtable agreements have subsequently been nullified, including the date of new parliamentary elections, which were moved up to fall 1991. Wałęsa did not change the pace of the economic program (Minister Leszek Balcerowicz was still very much in place) or remove many one-time PZPR bureaucrats from leadership positions. He presumably recognizes the impossibility of fulfilling all his campaign promises.

During the presidential campaign, Wałęsa's critics and the Center Agreement formed their own group, Citizen's Movement–Democratic Action (Ruch Obywatelski–Akcja Demokratyczna, usually known by the acronym ROAD). ROAD was drawn mostly from the (once again dissident) intelligentsia and included, for example, Geremek, Michnik, and Kuroń as well as members of the original Solidarity leadership who were disenchanted with what they regarded as Wałęsa's self-obsession, personal ambition, and political demagoguery. Originally formed to support Mazowiecki's candidacy, after his defeat the group organized itself into a political party, Democratic Union (Unia Demokratyczna, or UD). The UD is now formally led by Mazowiecki and fielded its candidates for the parliamentary election in fall 1991.

The UD and the Center Agreement are the two largest parties, but a number of smaller ones garner significant popular support. Tymiński has formed Party X, a mysterious and, according to some observers,[24] an unsavory group that nonetheless harnessed some of the popular discontent during the parliamentary election. The USD and the SDRP (former Communist party) still have supporters, and there are several other parties that represent all hues of the political spectrum.

As for the farmers, they were on strike during summer 1990, charging the new government with the same insensitivity to their needs as the old. The strike ended with but minor concessions to the farmers and, although they backed Wałęsa during the summer, that support ultimately went to either Tymiński or to Roman Bartoszcze, the candidate fielded by a coalition of peasant parties. The politics of the several branches of the various populist parties is suggested by reference to some of the events of the 1988 human rights conference I mentioned above. The conference took place, it will be recalled, during a period of intense conflict and strikes. In an impassioned speech, the farmer who spoke for Rural Solidarity invoked the church and the pope to dedicate the products of farmers' work to striking workers because, he said, the interests of workers and farmers coincide in forging a national identity that does not include communism. Each mention that the donated food was produced on privately owned land by the uncoerced labor power of the country's free farmers brought thunderous applause and tributes to the farmers as the backbone, the very embodiment of the nation and its traditional values. The farmers' most significant attribute seemed to be simply that they were not producing to the dictates of the state and Party. The reception farmers enjoyed is but one indication of their symbolic significance to urban people and workers, from whom most of the illusions of independence were taken. This is especially ironic because the stereotypic image of farmers as completely independent producers who work hard but reap commensurate rewards and, more importantly, are answerable to no one, applies only (and even then only partially) to the rural bourgeoisie—merely a handful of the largest and most prosperous of the landowners. That this essentially populist vision of bucolic country life is a fantasy has not prevented rural entrepreneurs from becoming a prototypic identity for the new Pole of the 1990s.

Significantly, Józef Slisz, the leader of Rural Solidarity, was part of a group of intelligentsia and activist farmers that in late 1989 reorganized a new Peasant (Populist) party, the Polskie Stronnictwo Ludowe, or PSL. Invoking the names of Wincenty Witos and Stanisław Mikołajczyk, populist political leaders on the right in the period between the two world wars, members of the recreated PSL National Council condemned what they called the "collaborationist" ZSL leaders for their decades-long accommodation with the PZPR and their "adoption of the programme for the building of socialism in the countryside."[25] The National Council organized a congress, and it and regional groups passed resolutions calling for a return to the program of the prewar PSL and for setting up a "strong, sovereign, and national peasant party"[26] that, as presidential candidate Bartoszcze, a deputy to the Sejm and member of the PSL leadership said, "gives more heed to agrarianism and the social teachings of the Church."[27] Presumably, the right populist nationalism of the prewar party has also been adopted. The ZSL subsequently reorganized itself as the Polskie Stronnictwo Ludowe–Odrodzenie (Polish Peasant Party–Rebirth). Other wings, the most influential of which is led by Bartoszcze, have also emerged. Although all support some of the government programs, they oppose others, especially the agricultural ones. In spite of the return of "peasant parties" to the national scene, many rural people seem to have voted for Tymiński rather than Bartoszcze in the general election; some but hardly all of that support was eroded before the runoff in the light of the well-publicized suspicion about Tymiński's background and the closing of ROAD and Center Agreement ranks around Wałęsa. Too little is yet known about the electoral process in Poland, but one possible explanation for Tymiński's unlikely support is simply that he is the embodiment of a messianic ideal. He went to "the West" as a young man, worked hard, made his "millions" (probably exaggerated), and came back to tell fellow Poles how they too can succeed as self-sufficient individuals and as a nation-state (become nuclear capable and independent).

The farmer from Rural Solidarity, the philosophy professor, and others with whom I spoke in 1988 each raised in only slightly different terms issues of freedom, national identity, and Polish culture. Consciousness of shared identity and a common discourse centered upon that identity is, of course, a social construction rather than an ontological given and is therefore achieved only through contest. Part of what was at issue for the professor, the farmer, and the others is just such a political struggle over the content and meaning of Polish, that is, national identity, culture, and tradition. Discussions of needed economic and political reforms, even the philosophy professor's willingness to restrict the rights of those defined as leftists to freely express their ideas, must be viewed in the context not only of the forty-five years of Polish state socialism but also of the long-term political struggles to define the salient social identities, the meaning of Polish political culture—the intersection of class and the nation, as it were, and how that intersection relates to the ideological project of the state and to the transmission of capital/ power. At issue, then, is how things really are in Poland—how, therefore, people should act, and who decides.

In fact, farmers have never been an internally homogeneous group of independent cultivators producing their own subsistence and surplus on their own self-sufficient plots of land. Internal differentiation and jural distinctions intensified by centuries of serfdom that ended only in the mid- to late nineteenth century and quasi-feudal and servile relations with former landlords that persisted until well into the twentieth century (for many right up to the Nazi invasion in 1939) rendered problematic

the very definition of "peasants" as well as their incorporation into the
nation until at least the 1920s. Even then, peasants were widely regarded
(and presumably treated) as affectively attached primarily to their villages
and immediate surroundings with little or no sense of nation (Thomas
and Znaniecki 1918, 1:159). In spite of intense and self-conscious efforts
on the part of the intelligentsia to politicize rural cultivators they helped
to categorize as peasants through the populist politics of the PSL beginning
in the nineteenth century, it is not at all clear that rural nationalist
sensibilities had been widely adopted by any but the upper stratum of
the most prosperous farmers prior to World War II. On the eve of the
Nazi invasion, some 70 percent of the country's rural cultivators had
less than 5 hectares of land and another 16 percent were totally landless.
Fifty years later, 58 percent still have 5 hectares or less, the generally
accepted minimum farm adequate to produce a living (*Rocznik Statystyczny*
1978:223).

What did seem to be well developed among at least the more affluent
of the prewar farmers were the economic and social values and practices
sanctifying private property, rational efficiency, and especially individualism. These values and practices were consciously and systematically
introduced into villages by large landowners and intellectuals, mainly
via the PSL, during the late nineteenth century. With but a handful of
truly independent "peasants" able to realize the material or the symbolic
and cultural attributes of independence, to invoke the self-sufficient rural
entrepreneur as the emblem of the historic nation is to nurture a sustaining
myth of what Benedict Anderson (1983) has called an "imagined community": In such a highly selective reading and construction of the past,
the presently constituted nation appears rather more historically inevitable
than it actually is or contains a vision of a projected future.

The contemporary populist social project to construct or resurrect a
partially mythical national identity—one that seems to have more appeal
than abstract and international identities—indeed the very rhetoric of
national identity obscures the demonstrable fact that long-standing rural
inequalities persist and are already being transformed into class fractions
with opposed interests. There is no available information on the composition of Rural Solidarity, but the head of the union who spoke at
the human rights conference owned a farm of about 15 hectares—not
huge by any means but still larger than those of all but 6 percent of
the rest. In fact, farmers with the largest landholdings are often defined
by themselves and others as "professionals," and in Wola Pławska and
Rzędzienowice they exert the greatest political power and economic
dominance in the village, power and dominance that ordinarily coincides
with cultural and social hegemony as well. In a very real sense, larger
landowners constitute a grassroots intelligentsia. What is more, my

research indicates that larger farms are appropriating labor power from smaller ones in order to increase production, albeit mostly through informal kin or neighborhood-based labor groups. These relationships are, by their very nature, unequal, and the increased production was, until 1989, sold on the black market at sometimes substantial profits. Even though the black market has since been eliminated by the simple expedient of linking the złoty to the U.S. dollar, recent developments in political and economic pluralism are likely to accelerate the process of differentiation.

NOTES

1. It would be impossible to list all the articles or even all the books published in English about Poland since the early 1980s. A sample includes Bielasiak and Simon 1984; Ash 1985, 1990; Singer 1981; Starski 1982; Woodall 1982; Staniszkis 1984; Steven 1982; Kolosi and Wnuk-Lipiński 1983; Michnik 1985; and Majkowski 1985.

2. I hold no brief for the socialist nature of PZPR-dominated Poland but use the term "socialist Poland" as a shorthand for distinguishing between pre- and post-1989.

3. The state and cooperative sectors employed 11.63 million people in the late 1970s, compared to 4.74 million in private enterprises. The latter figure includes the farmers and approximately 500,000 owners and employees of privately owned businesses (Sanford 1981:575). Nonfarmers, therefore, constituted a relatively small (but growing) part of the private sector well before the reprivatization that began in 1990. The total number of private farms fell to about 3.5 million during the 1980s whereas the number of nonfarm private entrepreneurs grew.

4. My concern with meaning and the politics of meaning begins with Geertz's injunction but also extends beyond it to a central concern with class and other forms of inequality that inflect peoples' understanding of the world and their and others' roles in it. Although Geertz is not especially interested in "the annalistic chronicle of what people did, but rather the formal structural patterns of cumulative activity" (Geertz 1980:5), I tend to identify more with the historical anthropological project outlined by Eric Wolf (1982).

5. The only book-length monograph in the past decade to address Polish farmers is Christopher Hann's *A Village Without Solidarity* (1985).

6. Brazil, Mexico, Argentina, and many African countries have since far surpassed Poland in the amount of their foreign debt and the proportion of export earnings paid in interest. In 1979, however, Poland held the record for both debt and debt service.

7. According to Cameron (1980:125), the 92 percent estimate came from the CIA. The *Christian Science Monitor* (14 July 1986, p. 13), however, simply gives a figure of "more than 25 percent" by 1986.

8. The *Ludowe* in Zjednoczone Stronnictwo Ludowe can be glossed as either "populist" or "peasant." The significance of the alternative rendering will become apparent in Chapter 3.

9. The underground activities of the dissident intelligentsia and a thriving alternative civil society long challenged official society. The Committee for the Defense of Workers (Komitet Obrony Robotników, usually known by its Polish acronym of KOR) was founded in the 1970s by such well-known intellectual dissidents as Jacek Kuroń and Adam Michnik in order to provide financial and legal help to the workers arrested in the wake of the

1976 uprisings and their suppression by government forces. The formation of KOR was the first conscious successful attempt at a worker-intelligentsia alliance in Poland. In time, KOR demands became more generalized and included free expression and the right of workers to strike. The organization was integral to Solidarity, and many of its members were advisers to the union. After the 1989 election, many of them, including most notably Tadeusz Mazowiecki, prime minister until December 1990, and Jacek Kuroń, minister of labor under Mazowiecki, became part of the government. No member of KOR served in the administration in 1991.

10. See *Uncensored Poland* 15–19/89, for details and an outline of the government's draft economic program (19/89:9–10) and *East European Reporter* 4 (Winter 1989-1990):66–67, for the version submitted to the European Community in Brussels and to the IMF and World Bank in Washington, D.C.

11. Quoted in *Uncensored Poland* 21/89 (17 November 1989):4.

12. This split also characterized other Eastern European delegations, but only the Poles are at issue here.

13. Quoted in Majkowski 1985:208, n. 39. Majkowski does not indicate—or perhaps the *Paris-Match* did not say—how many people were surveyed, how they were chosen, or other details of the study, but the results of the actual June 1989 election bear out the results in general contours if not in detail.

14. Even the British army killing of suspected Irish Republican Army operatives in Gibraltar and the official U.S. aid given to the *contras* in Nicaragua—both issues of considerable controversy and debate within Great Britain and the United States, respectively—were endorsed uncritically by participants as unproblematic means of creating and preserving democracy and freedom, though it was less clear that this perspective was as widely shared.

15. Johnson reportedly condemned fellow Poles Zbigniew Brzezinski and John Cardinal Krol for shaking hands with Wojciech Jaruzelski (Margolick 1989:65).

16. Quoted in *Uncensored Poland* 21/89 (17 November 1989):4.

17. Ibid., p. 8.

18. Ibid.

19. Quoted in *Uncensored Poland* 8/90 (26 April 1990):15.

20. Quoted in an interview by Professor Czabanski, originally published in *Tygodnik Solidarność* and reproduced in part in *East European Reporter* 4 (Winter 1989-1990):80–81.

21. Quoted in *Uncensored Poland* 10/90 (29 May 1990):22.

22. Habitus is "a tendency to generate regulated behaviors apart from any reference to rules"; it is "the social inscribed in the body; a system of dispositions; a feel for the social game"; it is, in other words, "an interpretive device" (Bourdieu 1977:81–87). Habitus is not an individual phenomenon, though the practices and values of a specific class derive from an individually acquired class habitus. Thus, rather than regulating only individual activity, habitus configures critically social, economic, and political interaction. In a capitalist social formation, it is a family, a group, but most of all a class phenomenon, "a system of shared social dispositions and cognitive structures which generates perceptions, apperceptions and actions" (translator's note, Bourdieu 1988:279, n. 2). Re class habitus, see Bourdieu 1977:81–87.

23. Andrzej Koźmiński, professor at the International Business School in Warsaw, in a presentation to the Pacific Coast Sociological Association in Irvine, California, 13 April 1991.

24. Namely, Timothy Garton Ash, who describes the headquarters and manifesto of "party X" in "Poland After Solidarity," *New York Review of Books* 38 (13 June 1991): 46–58.

25. Sejm Deputy Roman Bartoszcze in a speech to the Sejm on 29 September 1989, read on the T.V. news. The full text appears in *Uncensored Poland* 19/89 (18 October 1989):16.

26. See *Uncensored Poland* 19/89 (18 October 1989):14–17.

27. Bartoszcze, ibid.

3

History, Class, and Identity

THE SYMBOLIC SIGNIFICANCE of "peasants" to the construction of a national identity is an aspect of the Polish paradox. First of all, the jural relationship and obligations of rural cultivators to the landed aristocracy changed when serfdom was finally abolished in 1807, 1848, and 1861 in Prussia and the Austrian and Russian empires, among which Poland had been divided in three separate partitions between 1772 and 1795. The history of serfdom is, among other things, a history of class formation in the Polish commonwealth during the late medieval and early modern periods, the enserfment of formerly free peasants by magnates and by the noble and gentry class (*szlachta*) that defined itself as the Polish nation,[1] and the daily practice of resistance by serfs to the appropriation of their labor and surplus value. Second, both jural and material differences among small cultivators themselves emerged during the same period. Indeed the very term "peasants," even "serfs," obscures material contrasts, manifest dissimilarities in self-perceived identities and consciousness, and varying ways of relating to landlords.[2]

The circumstances surrounding successive transformations in economic, political, and social relations; the genesis of class formation; the creation of a serf system of labor control; and the cultural legacy of that system were the most salient social and economic characteristics of Poland from the fifteenth until well into the twentieth century. In certain respects, the ideology, consciousness, and identity of contemporary farmers and the nature of their relations to other sectors of society are rooted both in the structure and practice of the constituent elements of the decentralized feudal state that preceded the partitions and in the experience of serfdom and serfs' resistance to exploitation. By the same token, ideas about the nature of Polish identity and from whence it derives, and the relationship of Polish identity to "freedom" can be located also in the historical experience of peasants and nobility, and most especially in versions of that experience that have become part of current everyday life. The attempts by the PZPR to identify the ideological project of the socialist state with agreed-upon, public, and "correct" forms of expression of contemporary life and the organization of historical experience had their counterparts within the Polish state over the centuries. The difference, or at least a difference, is that the early state (as defined in Chapter 2) was successful in imposing its version of social reality whereas the socialist one was not. The socialist state, in other words, was never an organic part of society and culture.

The Second Serfdom

By the sixteenth century, magnates and the szlachta had strengthened their position vis-à-vis the monarchy. This increased power came about by their establishing and maintaining regional and national Sejms in which they passed laws limiting the sovereignty of the crown (especially preventing the monarchy from becoming hereditary), their electing monarchs from outside of Poland, and, finally, by their control of taxes and revenues. A repertoire of rituals and routines of rule organized the fundamental divisions within society and became the media through which gentry democracy was expressed. At the same time the rituals and routines celebrated "democracy," legitimated the power of the szlachta, and authorized modes of control. The political position of the szlachta resonated with and set the stage for the reenserfment of formerly free peasants and the economic de-development of the country at more or less the same time capitalism was emerging as the dominant economic, social, and political system in the West. By the sixteenth century, serfdom was in decline in western Germany and France and had already virtually disappeared in England, the Low Countries, Switzerland, Scandinavia, Italy, and Spain. To the east of the Elbe River, however, serfdom was firmly entrenched. The dichotomy is all the more striking because labor corvée was gradually being replaced with money rents in the East as well as the West until the fourteenth century.[3] How had the Polish commonwealth so diverged economically and politically from Western Europe?

The depreciation of currency throughout Europe in the fourteenth and fifteenth centuries had reduced the value of fixed rents while the wages of workers were increasing—to the detriment of the revenues of landowning classes everywhere. Moreover, the still fluid eastern frontiers to which Polish peasants often fled to escape rents and further their opportunities, and the declining numbers of colonists arriving from the

West because of the economic contraction and population losses there caused increasingly acute labor shortages in the commonwealth, analogous to those in western Europe (Malowist 1959:182). Reorganization of estates, labor control, and the recultivation of abandoned land became a necessity to the survival of landowning classes. There were two contrasting ways in which the szlachta could reorganize: by improving the working conditions of the peasant cultivators or by intensifying coercion of the labor force. They took the second path. In theory, Eastern landlords could have commercialized agriculture by commuting remaining labor services and payments in kind, evicting superfluous peasants, and—as was done in England and elsewhere on the Continent—turning to activities such as sheep breeding that require less labor than does grain production.

It was the international grain trade, at first slowly growing and then rapidly accelerating from the now Polish-controlled port of Danzig (Gdańsk), that provided the rationale for the szlachta's strategy (and that allowed the English to continue their concentration on sheep). In spite of falling prices, grain shortages resulting from the reduced acreage devoted to agriculture in the West assured landowners east of the Elbe large profits for export production if certain conditions could be met (see Schoffer 1959; Kay 1975). They had to put deserted land and virgin forest under cultivation, establish better (i.e., more restrictive) management of the labor force, and bypass the monopolistic Hanseatic League ports to become the direct suppliers of western Europe (Malowist 1958). Their success can be measured by the dramatic increase in the export of grain, timber and other forest products, livestock, and hides. In the 1460s, Polish folwarks (agricultural domains organized primarily for the production of grain as a cash crop for export) exported 2,500 *lasti* of rye (1 last = 60 bushels); by the end of the century, the figure had grown to between 6,000 and 10,000 lasti, and in 1618, 75,000 lasti of rye and "a considerable quantity of wheat" left Danzig for ports in Holland, Flanders, England, and elsewhere (Malowist 1959:184).

The szlachta's political success in controlling local laws via regional diets and the Sejm allowed them to consolidate its economic position by creating new folwarks, by exerting pressure on freeholders' labor power, and by further weakening the burghers. Legal restrictions on the physical movements of peasants were of prime importance. Statutes of 1496 stipulated that only one child of a peasant was allowed to attend school or learn a trade; others were henceforth legally bound to the soil. Burghers were forbidden to own land outside city limits, and other laws exempted nobles from import and export duties. The difficulty of enforcing legislation preventing the movement and personal freedom of peasants and limiting their recourse to the courts is attested to by passage of additional and harsher measures in 1501, 1503, 1510, 1511, and 1518. These deprived urban centers of new migrants and contributed to the cities' decline.

The results of producing grain for export and concentrating economic assets and political power into the hands of the nobility include the irreversible decline of cities—the potential haven of runaway serfs— and the undermining of the money economy. The nobility was subsequently to force peasants to purchase necessities in manor stores, mills, and inns rather than from urban merchants, further contributing to the collapse of internal markets. Moreover, commercial relations were confined to those between landlords and foreign merchants while the indigenous bourgeoisie were squeezed out altogether, effectively preventing them from politically challenging the power of the nobility, as they were able to do with considerable success in western Europe. Landlords populated abandoned land with peasants whose personal and economic freedom they truncated. The landed nobility was further able to gradually increase compulsory labor dues so that by 1520 corvée labor of six days a week was allowed by law and, during the course of the next two centuries, was more and more often exacted (Rutkowski 1950:443; Malowist 1959:181).

At the time of extensive German colonization of sparsely occupied Polish territory between the thirteenth and fifteenth centuries—Wola Pławska was probably settled at this time—the typical peasant was a *cmethone*, one who had been given a farm large enough to be worked with at least a yoke of oxen and to provide for a family (Rutkowski 1950:444, 1956). The average farm of a cmethone was 1 *hufe*, between 17 and 20 hectares, a size that could be cultivated by a single person with two horses or four oxen. The typical holding of a headman who was granted sovereignty over a new village and was entitled to collect rent from settlers was between 6 and 12 hufen. In exchange, the tenants were obliged to render military service to their lords. These "village nobility" (*szlachta zaściankowa*) adopted coats of arms and came to share the political rights of the nobility but were distinguished by their relative poverty (Aubin 1942:366–367). By mid-sixteenth century, fewer than 20 percent of the peasants farmed even a hufe of land. The number of *hortulani*, peasants with only a garden plot, had increased, and two new strata had appeared, *inquilini*, or landless agricultural laborers, and *subinquilini*, those who didn't even have cottages but lived in stables or corners of other peasants' houses (Rutkowski 1950:442–443). Not only had the growing class of village gentry managed to appropriate peasant land and labor power,[4] the appropriation enhanced internal differentiation in villages.

A former serf described conditions just before emancipation, when conditions had actually improved somewhat:

No worse punishment could be found for men and women than serfdom was. People were treated worse than cattle are today. They were beaten both at work and at home for the merest trifle. . . . it is unbelievable how men could thus torture their fellows. Every farmer had first to do his dues at the manor house, whether with team, or on foot. Only then could he work his own land, sowing and reaping at night. No excuse as to pressing needs at home was of any use. If one did not appear as ordered, at once the overseer would come. If he found the wife busy cooking, he would throw a pail of water on the fire, or in winter he would carry off the windows or the doors. In case that didn't work, and men were needed for service, the overseer would come with his foreman and eject the farmer from home and homestead. Another would be put in his place. Nor was there any appeal anywhere, since that was the usage and at bottom, the lord of the manor was owner of everything. His was both land and water, yes even the wind; since only he was allowed to build a wind-mill to grind corn (Słomka 1941:14–15).

Except for a prolonged but intermittent and geographically limited uprising in the mountain region of southern Poland (1623–1633, 1651), there were no overt peasant rebellions against the szlachta during their consolidation of land and power in Poland proper. Jacqueries, however, were common in the Ukrainian portion of Lithuania, which had been incorporated into the commonwealth in the fifteenth century. Janusz Tazbir (1968:222–223) suggests the difference lies in two circumstances: First, increases in labor dues in Poland were only gradually imposed over the course of a hundred years, but in the Ukraine resistance was fueled when corvée was inflicted during a single generation; second, Ukrainian peasants, unlike their Polish counterparts, spoke a different language and practiced a different religion from the Polish Catholic lords and were therefore united by shared ethnicity and ideology in opposition to the foreign nobility (cf. Nagengast and Kearney 1990; Comaroff 1987).

The ways in which serfs resisted were not by any means always obvious or manifest in physical violence. Folwarks required two kinds of serfs: one group that provided only labor and hence had small plots sufficient only for meager subsistence and another with plots large enough to provide subsistence *and* to reproduce the domain's productive capacity—the maintenance and reproduction of the work animals used to plow the fields of the lord and the preservation and repair of farm equipment. Thus, variation in the size of peasant plots was due to the uneven distribution of functions on the folwark, with serfs responsible for draft animals and equipment—having more land but owing more labor.[5] Landlords kept the services serfs had to render and the amount of livestock and equipment they had to maintain at a level calculated to prevent them from accumulating any surplus (Kula 1976:73–74).

Although there is evidence that smaller plots were burdened with corvées proportionately greater than the larger plots (Kula 1976:73–74), serfs with larger pieces of land and absolutely larger obligations also often managed to make good at the expense of the lord. Households of the better-off serfs had the most members, but they were not larger because they were rich, but rich because they were larger. Families with additional workers could fulfill their labor obligation and cultivate the family plot for subsistence but also have sufficient labor power to purloin land from the margins of the landlord's forests, pastures, and uncultivated land; evidence suggests they did so regularly (Kula 1976). Furthermore, if conditions were right, they might also rent a plot of abandoned land from the lord, but always for money, never for additional labor dues. Surplus greater than immediate familial needs was marketed, with the proceeds adding to the consumption fund. Serfs consequently fought fiercely to keep family members together and to produce a salable surplus, the lords just as vehemently to prevent them from so doing. An eighteenth-century author observes that: "The peasants who live together with their children, and not separated . . . provided they are many in number and even if they are weak, will farm the land better and will bring in better harvests than a peasant . . . without the aid and assistance of other hands" (quoted in Kula 1976:72–73, n. 66). Kula adds that "it is precisely for this reason that the instructions for the estate at Ros order the 'steward,' in 1775, to settle 'serious young people' on the abandoned plots, 'separating sons from fathers and brothers from brothers.'" Family size and family solidarity are hence an aspect of both survival and of resistance, the importance of which cannot be overemphasized. The struggle over control of labor and surplus from the sixteenth to the nineteenth centuries resonates with the contemporary contest over the same control.

There is another way in which serfs with larger landholdings, who were given responsibility for the lord's draft animals, had an advantage over their fellows: In a poor year they could pass on losses to the landlord because they controlled key elements in the productive process. Thus, they could feed draft animals (more valuable to the lord than to serfs) less grain in order to maintain the familial consumption level, forcing the lord to help provision livestock because their loss would prevent tilling of the folwark. Serfs could even eat the seed grain, again forcing the lord to replenish it as the price of sowing the next year. The aphorism that "if you don't steal from the manor you are stealing from your family" was as common in Poland as in Hungary during the same period (Lampland 1987). The critical point is that compulsory labor inherent in serfdom implies unremunerated labor power for the domain if and only if serfs are in physical condition to provide it and have the wherewithal to maintain the draft animals and implements—serfs had to be helped through hard times. Making a virtue of necessity, a moral imperative demanding assistance to the destitute developed, what E. K. Hunt (1979:31–33) calls the "Christian paternal ethic" characteristic of feudalism.

As serf plots became smaller and declined in productivity during the seventeenth century (hastened by the devastating wars of midcentury), hard times came more often. Withheld aid meant the starvation of the lord's animals or even the death or flight of serfs; all inimical to folwark production. Kula notes that eighteenth-century attempts by landlords to create "insurance funds" into which each serf had to contribute a measure for the relief of fellow serfs, were ill-disguised and unsuccessful attempts to transfer the burden of disaster relief to serfs themselves. A serf understandably adopted the motto that "I belong to your Lordship; let your Lordship take care of me" (Kula 1976:65). This is an attitude not unlike that many Poles had toward the socialist state; it contrasts with the capitalist notion that everyone should take care of herself or himself.

Agricultural production did initially grow, primarily because new land was brought under cultivation; increases in labor productivity were slight and little technology was introduced. As Karl Marx notes, increases in labor productivity leading to greater surplus product (cheaper goods and a larger total product in circulation using the same labor force) can be accomplished in two ways: by increasing either relative or absolute surplus labor power. An increase in relative surplus labor is achieved through technological innovation and is characteristic of the capitalism of western and northern Europe. Increased absolute surplus labor, on the other hand, is realized through the extension of the working day, intensification of the workload, and decreasing living standards. Both may lead to a greater total output from a given work force, but the limits of increased absolute labor power will be quickly reached because of physiology and resistance alike. This is what happened in Poland, to the detriment of the development of the production forces.[6] Polish agricultural techniques remained at the medieval level while they were advancing rapidly in the West because production in Poland was limited by the degree to which workers could be exploited. Kula (1976:43) asserts that Polish folwarks, producing grain for export, would have operated at stupendous losses if labor power had been compensated.

At the same time the nobility in general was assuming preeminent political power in the realm, economic assets were also being redistributed among aristocratic fractions. Monastery and church estates remained at the same level, but elected monarchs, kept chronically short of cash by the Sejm, were forced to use royal domains as collateral against loans from magnates and upper nobility. Revenues from royal holdings thus became important sources of income for the upper nobility (Mączak 1968:457). Monarchs also used outright grants of crown land and villages to purchase the loyalty and services of important magnate families. Thousands of gentry villages were transferred from the crown into magnate estates in this manner.[7] Thus, an already politically weak monarchy also lost economic sovereignty to the magnates and the political independence of the smaller gentry faded in proportion to its waning economic position. None of the szlachta zaściankowa, which numbered about 400,000 by the seventeenth century, owned serfs any longer. Retaining full political rights and jural equality with the nobility, many became economically indistinguishable from peasants.[8] Yet the magnates, comprising no more than two dozen families in the seventeenth century, occupied all the highest offices, kept their own armies, directed all the affairs of the realm, and were essentially in almost sole control of all aspects of the state (Lindsey 1957:57).

Thus, during the course of the sixteenth and seventeenth centuries, the power of the upper nobility eclipsed that of the monarchy, the gentry, the burghers, and the peasants. Economic development was retarded by restrictions on the indigenous merchant class; as towns and local and regional markets declined accordingly, small producers had relatively few opportunities to sell surpluses whereas the largest domains produced primarily for the export market. Moreover, the squeeze on the labor power of peasants prevented the development or import of technology, placing absolute limits on productivity. Not only did the power of the nobility bring about economic ruin, its concentration contributed to the political demise of the country. This early "democracy," epitomized by the *liberum veto*, by which a single dissenting vote in the Sejm could prevent any legislation from being enacted,[9] was a source of pride to Poles. In fact, it was rule by the aristocracy in the guise of democracy, and it was to deteriorate to oligarchy in the latter part of the seventeenth century and to chaos by the eighteenth. Not only had the szlachta rendered the monarchy impotent, it managed to neutralize the legislature. By the time attempts were made in the mid- and late eighteenth century by a progressive segment of the nobility to repeal the *liberum veto* in favor of majority rule, to emancipate serfs, and to institute agrarian reform, albeit limited, it was too late. The commonwealth had fallen prey to more powerful, centrally organized states. Between 1772 and 1795, Poland was forcibly dismantled by Austria, Prussia, and Russia in three separate partitions. Each incorporated portions of the commonwealth into its own territories so that by 1795 Poland no longer existed as a separate state. The political economy of Poland at the time of the partitions was such that an anonymous writer was to observe:

The large quantity of grain that Poland exports every year would give the impression that this country is one of the most fertile in Europe. But those who know it and its inhabitants will judge otherwise. . . . The truth is that the nobles are the only landowners there and the peasants are slaves, and the former . . . appropriate the toil and products of the latter, who form at least seven-eighths of the population and are reduced to eating bread made from barley and oats. Whereas the other peoples of Europe consume the major portion of their best grain, the Poles retain only a small portion of their wheat and rye so that one might say they only harvest it for foreign lands (*A Dictionary of Commerce*, 1797, quoted in Braudel 1973:84).

Perry Anderson (1974) argues that the power of the szlachta in preserving an atavistic, fragmented feudal state for its own benefit by inhibiting the formation of a bourgeoisie and a free labor force but also (and for his purposes, especially) in preventing the formation of an absolutist state left it prey to the imperial designs of the highly centralized and bureaucratically efficient absolutist states that had developed on its borders. These countries were dependent upon the fusion of the interests of the nobility and the monarchy in ruling militaristic states predicated on mercantilism, but, he points out, absolutism was a "redeployed and recharged apparatus of feudal domination," not an instrument of a nascent bourgeoisie (Anderson 1974:18). Nonservile peasants and plebeians were pinned down into new forms of dependency and exploitation through taxes and ground rents. The existence and persistence of autonomous towns prevented the nobility in the West from tying peasants to the manor. Anderson may be correct in observing that the political order may have remained feudal while the economic gradually became more bourgeois (1974:23), but the central institutions and cultural practices of a capitalist state, the "legitimization of the illegitimate," were laid in western Europe very early, though not in Poland until the nineteenth century.

New Relations, New Identities

There was, then, no Polish state [in 1795], but the literary and historical traditions tell us there was still a Polish nation. But who comprised the Polish nation? Before the partitions, the state was divided into clearly established classes: the gentry, who were the nation, and the peasants, who were serfs, without rights. The nation was Polish, the peasants were peasants (Narkiewicz 1976:9).

The ideal of szlachta, gentry, lesser nobility, and magnates alike, was a genteel rural life, disdain for business and trade, and a quixotic glorification of Poland's history of anticentralism, democracy, and freedom that romanticized its own role and alternately ignored peasants; invented for them an idyllic, Rousseauean existence; deplored their primitiveness; or sought to imbue them with bourgeois values.

Transformations in social identity, class relations, national identity, and attempts to construct a harmonious, shared community between 1795 and 1918—when a Polish state reemerged as a discrete political entity—were inflected by the French Revolution, the effects of which spread all over Europe (see Hobsbawm 1962); the subsequent Napoleonic Wars; and the politics and economics of the partitioning powers, the latter of which represented varying shades of the absolutism so feared by the szlachta. Although the Austrian state was somewhat more enlightened than the Prussian or Russian in the latter part of the partition period, none was initially intent on eliminating serfdom in its new Polish colony but simply to remodel it in accordance with its own political and economic structures. Even though the Polish nobles were stripped of much of their political power within territory that was once theirs to rule, the partitioning states averted their immediate insurrection by the simple expedient of maintaining serfdom as the base of szlachta wealth and privilege.

The seeds of liberal reform, however, had been sown in Poland during the brief enlightenment just before the partitions. During the early and mid-nineteenth century, a new generation of Polish reformists saw within the struggle for the abolition of serfdom and the extension of personal freedom to peasants the potential for uniting all classes to overthrow the foreign powers and for instituting much-needed economic reform. The terms of abolition, however, and the role of nobility and gentry versus peasants in the projected revolution were a source of dissension among noble conspirators, helping to ensure the failure of the uprisings they planned and led in 1831 and 1863. Gentry alone "made up the nation"; it treated the "agricultural class as property indivisible from the land," comments Kalembka in his analysis of the Great Manifesto, published in 1836 by the Polish Democratic Society (quoted by Narkiewicz 1976:9). The twenty-five or so families of the great nobility generally supported neither reform nor the conspiracies; with marital and other ties to the ruling classes of Europe, they were not overly encumbered with nationalism nor did their immediate interest lie in changes in the economic and political structures. For the most part, the rebels were middle and lesser nobility, dispossessed gentry, and students who con-spired among themselves and advocated national revolution among villagers.

An intelligentsia, a new social identity drawn mostly from the same ranks, also emerged as a vital force in the social and political life of the dismembered country. Those not actually descended from the szlachta appropriated most of its manners and ideals (Polonsky 1972:31). The intelligentsia, which regarded itself as the conscience, the directing force, the very embodiment of the Polish nation, bearing responsibility for motivating national liberation and for preserving Polish culture, became the most influential sector in creating a quintessential Polish identity. From exile in Paris, to which many fled after the failed rebellion of 1831, poets such as Adam Mickiewicz (1798–1855), Juliusz Slowacki (1809–1849), and Zygmunt Krasinski (1812–1859) were among the creators and spokespersons for this intense nationalism. Although they took part in the romantic movement in the arts that characterized much of Europe at that time, their literature was also unique in that they used a model of crucifixion and resurrection to describe the dilemma of Poland and to give voice to the sentiment that Poles were people chosen by God to fulfill a specific democratic destiny. Even as Christ rose so would Poland, and "the day of its resurrection would usher in the day when justice, liberty, and love would rule the whole world—the Kingdom of God on earth" (Orvis 1947:59). The specifically Catholic imagery resonated with the suppression of that religion in much of the old commonwealth.

Mickiewicz, Slowacki, Krasinski, and others inspired several generations of conspirators against the partitioning powers. The version of Polish culture and Polish social relations they sought to preserve and resurrect, however, embodied a highly idealized past. The portrayal of peasants by the next generations of intelligentsia is especially revealing. The art of Apoloniusz Kedzieriski (1861–1939), Władysław Benda (1873–1948), and Alfred Wierusz-Kowalski (1849–1915), to name just a few, depicts an essentially homogeneous "peasantry"—sturdy, independent cultivators of the land dedicated to centuries-old traditions, atavistic and "primitive" in many respects, to be sure, but partaking of essential "Polishness." Much is still made of the importance of the intelligentsia as the arbitrator of manners and distinction in Poland. Polish sociologist Helena Lopata, for example, asserts in a 1976 article that "the role of developing and disseminating culture is universally valid for the intelligentsia of all countries" (quoted in Majkowski 1985:209, n. 48; cf. Bourdieu 1984).[10]

Few peasants participated in the orgy of messianism or in the revolts—and why should they? In fact, they turned against the conspirators in the 1846 Galician rebellion by sacking and burning over 400 manors, killing 90 percent of the resident nobility (Kieniewicz 1969:486–488)—possibly (though the evidence is controversial) with the connivance of the Austrian emperor, who had an interest in turning peasants against their Polish landlords.

The details of conspiracies and rebellions need not detain us except to note the response of the partitioning powers to the liberation movements. Their primary motive for the gradual abolition of serfdom in the old Polish commonwealth was to eliminate its inefficiencies and increase production. But the secondary motive of undermining the political power of the nobility by winning the sympathy of peasants cannot be ignored. It is no accident that rural reforms, intended to satisfy the aspirations of peasants as well as limit those of the nobility, were earlier and more radical in the Polish territories than in the central provinces of Prussia and the Austrian and Russian empires. In retrospect, however, peasants gained little, and though the upper nobility did not emerge unscathed, much of its power was maintained.

Largely in response to the uprisings, the traditional estates of Polish society were partially dismantled and the legality of aristocratic privilege was eroded by the imperial powers, especially that of Russia. Only a handful of the wealthiest and most powerful magnates were taken into the Russian nobility; Austria and Prussia were somewhat more generous. The former nobility, however, kept all its land and, although most nobles were now legally commoners, much of its status, albeit on a less formal basis. In other words, even though the institutional form of its cultural capital disappeared, its habitus as a socially constructed category of privilege and prestige apart from any rules remained mutable into the varying forms of capital. This relationship persists to some extent to this day.[11] The more numerous gentry and especially the remaining szlachta zaściankowa did not always fare as well. Deprived of legal standing in the nineteenth century, by the beginning of the twentieth many had disappeared into the ranks of the bureaucracy, proletariat, and peasantry whose economic fate they shared; others managed to cling to the lifestyle of their former estate (Davies 1982:182–185); all, however, retain to this day their sense of separateness from ordinary people and especially from peasants (cf. Skreija 1973).

During most of the partition period, the priests and clerical magnates did not support the independence movements in any of the three sectors, but after the final defeat of insurrection in 1863 much of the struggle, especially in the Prussian sector, came to focus on a few radical priests and Catholic journalists. The German Kulturkampf, for example, banned the use or teaching of the Polish language. When some ninety priests from the Polish provinces of Prussia were exiled to Rome for attempting to use Polish in church schools, the German state succeeded in fostering a sense of ethnic identity among common people where little had existed before. Davies notes that "Bismarck ensured that Polishness and Catholicity . . . should be permanently identified" (1982:127). Repression of language and culture intensified in Russian Poland after 1863 as well.

Much of the nobility were both Polish and Catholic,[12] whereas over half the peasants and almost all workers, classes with little sympathy for noble aspirations, were neither. Peasants spoke dialects of Polish, Lithuanian, Ukrainian, and Byelorussian and were Orthodox and Unitates as well as Catholics; workers spoke mostly German and were Protestant or Jewish. Thus, only in Prussian Poland did Catholicism become a synonym for Polish national identity. This joint identity persisted there until independence in 1918, spread throughout (though not uniformly) the new state in the interwar years, and took on new stature beginning in the 1950s as an expression of nationalist and ideological opposition to the socialist state. The Solidarity-church coalition against both the PZPR and the socialist state, which emerged in 1980, had deep roots.

The Prussian Legacy

Prussia expanded its territory by more than 50 percent with its Polish acquisitions, making their integration essential to its national unity and economy. In order to establish control over the new provinces of Silesia, Pomerania, and (after 1815) Poznania, the Prussian state confiscated royal estates and those of participants in the unsuccessful liberal revolution led by Tadeusz Kościuszko, which had intervened between the second and third partitions and represented a last-ditch effort to save the commonwealth. These estates were sold to Prussian Junkers, who evicted Polish serfs and resettled German agricultural workers. The state encouraged all landlords to replace three-field systems with annual crop rotation, oxen with horses, and to introduce other new technology—all financed with inexpensive state credit. In theory, the centralized Prussian state controlled the activities of the landlords such that serfs were not to be overburdened; compulsory labor was reduced but was to be more rigorously defined and strictly enforced. In practice, enforcement devolved to landlords, whether Junker or Polish, and neither was inclined to uphold laws that curtailed production. Moreover, local judiciary custom was followed, meaning Polish serfs had no legal rights and were left to the justice of the landlord.

During the Napoleonic Wars, Prussia temporarily lost a share of its Polish territory to the French—a circumstance with lasting effect for the Poles. When serfdom was immediately abolished in the new French-controlled Duchy of Warsaw in 1807, Prussia, as a vassal state of France, was forced to concede personal freedom to resident serfs. In Silesia and Pomerania, however, only self-sufficient serf farms performing labor services with draft power or capable of providing requisite oxen or horses were given land rights and only *after* their farms had been reduced by one-half or one-third, depending on whether they had "strong" or "weak" rights to the land.[13] The lower limit of such a farm was set at 25 *morgi* (17 hectares), meaning that only a small minority benefited. The numbers of rural laborers employed on Junker and Polish domains continued to swell as smallholders were regularly turned off the land. The sum total of Prussian reforms between 1811 and 1836, when the regulations were finally extended to all provinces, was the creation of two peasant-class fractions: a small, relatively affluent group of proprietors and a much larger rural proletariat that was de jure free of compulsory labor dues but in fact had no alternative but to pay them (Kieniewicz 1969:58–71).

The *Encyclopedia of Domestic and Agricultural Economy* (cited by Hobsbawm 1962:182) does not even mention the existence of rural laborers in Prussia in 1773, but by 1849 there were almost two million landless or virtually landless agricultural wageworkers. By the second third of the century, 2,000 huge estates covered 61 percent of the land; 60,000 small and medium farms accounted for most of the rest. Kieniewicz (1969:66–67) notes the absence of rural resistance to Prussian reform and suggests its cause lies in the bifurcation of a peasant class previously more or less united in opposition to the landlords. Historically led by the most affluent peasants—those with draft animals and larger holdings—whose interests now lay in accepting the prejudicial terms of the regulations, the poorest segment was left without leadership and was unable to develop its own.

The deliberate divide-and-rule strategy of the Prussian state provided the basis for the transition to agrarian capitalism in the latter nineteenth century via the "Junker Road." By this system, land reform is legislated from above, the state provides the means through which technology is introduced and adopted, and the landlords themselves, rather than a bourgeoisie, become the agrarian capitalists using the labor power of peasants simultaneously liberated from both serfdom and their land (Lenin 1956:32–33).

Galicia: The Stepchild of the Habsburg Empire

Galicia, the Austrian share of Poland, was annexed in the first partition in 1772, when Maria Theresa and her son, Joseph II, after an initial repressive period sought to reform and restructure the economic and political life of the empire. Reform intended to more equitably distribute tax burdens among peasants and lords prohibited some abuses of serfdom:

Beatings, torture, and the requirement that serfs purchase specific amounts of vodka at the manorial inn were proscribed. Although compulsory labor was eliminated and crown land was distributed to peasants in some parts of the empire, Galicia was not included. There, royal estates were sold to the highest bidder without regard for the fate of the serfs living and working on them. On the positive side, weak rights to land were made strong, it was stipulated that "rustical" land could not be converted into manorial and vice versa, and serfs were given the legal right to bring suit against landlords. The Robot Law (1786) explicitly defined compulsory labor and stipulated what was to be expected in a day's work. It also limited the maximum number of compulsory labor days to three a week, a boon to serfs with larger landholdings (as only those with draft animals were obliged to work more than three days) but of little help to the majority with smallholdings. Joseph II also resettled in Galicia some 64,000 German-speaking colonists familiar with more advanced techniques of production (Polonsky 1972:40). Most colonists went to the Ukrainian-speaking areas, but many settled in the region around Wola Pławska, especially in two adjacent villages, Czermin and Orłów (called Schönanger until 1946)—circumstances relevant to contemporary socioeconomic relations, as we shall see.

The Austrians also instituted village "self-government," with a *wójt* (mayor) selected by the landlord and two *ławnicy* (aldermen) chosen by villagers themselves. The wójt was charged with administering village justice, according to the dictates of the landlord, one would assume. Jan Słomka, former serf who in the late nineteenth century was appointed wójt of a village only 30 kilometers northeast of Wola Pławska, makes his sycophantic relationship to the local lord clear (Słomka 1941). Finally, the Austrian state instituted a comprehensive rural census and mandated the keeping of records of births, deaths, and marriages that always included the "status" of the principals—effectively regulating relations of responsibility and subordination and providing for more effective tax collection. The subjects of the census were thus objectified by the process of division and, through objectification and categorization, serfs and free peasants were given both a social and a personal identity by the state. Dividing practices, Michel Foucault (1977) reminds us, are modes of manipulation that combine the mediation of science (statistics) and the practice of exclusion, usually in a spatial sense, always in a social one. Notions of legitimacy and respectability, already part of the habitus of Polish gentry and noble classes, became part of the "civilizing project" of the late eighteenth and early nineteenth centuries.

If anything, peasant-landlord relations deteriorated as the wójt and the ławnicy were made responsible for the collection of taxes and the army recruitment made urgent by continent-wide war. As the author of reforms, however, Emperor Joseph II enjoyed growing prestige among peasants. Far removed from their daily life, he represented the benevolent because distant father figure whereas Polish nobles were the immediate oppressors. The Austrian state cultivated this perception as it aided the peasants in their conflicts with the indigenous nobility (Wandycz 1974:11–13). But in the end, reforms were a dead letter as protest by Polish landlords, allied with the Austrian nobility, forced Joseph II to rescind many of them.[14] Austrian involvement in the Napoleonic Wars and reaction to the French Revolution prevented any further reform in Galicia for more than fifty years. Peasant rights of appeal, prohibitions on eviction from rusticial land, and the three-day limit on compulsory labor remained on the books but were poorly enforced; the landlord privilege of beating recalcitrant serfs was restored. It was not until the aftermath of the 1846 peasant revolt that serfs finally won their emancipation in Galicia (Kieniewicz 1969:35–40).

Meanwhile, the political, economic, and social apparatus of Galicia was brought into conformity with the rest of the empire. Noble tax exemptions were canceled, provincial diets disbanded, and Polish officials replaced with Austrians. In contrast to Prussia's acquisitions, which became central to Prussian economy, Galicia was intentionally made a backwater of the Habsburg empire. It was stripped of many of its resources and labor power to fight the wars, tobacco and salt monopolies and heavy taxes were introduced, its few factories neglected, and its currency devalued. Moreover, cut off from its former trading territory to the north and particularly from the mouth of the Vistula—which led to the Baltic and to England—its exports declined, its few towns became even more moribund, and its economy stagnated.[15] Thus, the course was set that was to make Galicia the poorest of the three areas of the former commonwealth.

The Russian Sector

The largest share of the commonwealth, in terms of both territory and population, went to Russia. Magnates did particularly well under the tsars at the expense of peasants, gentry, and lesser nobility. Because there was no Russian analogue to gentry, the noble status of that Polish stratum was denied in Russian Poland and its land often given over to magnates or royal estates. Under Russian rule, local self-government was left to the upper nobility and the lot of the peasants quickly deteriorated to that of native Russian serfs who could be bought, sold, loaned, given away, beaten, tortured, raped with impunity, and sent off to the army for service of twenty-five years (see Robinson 1960). In

Russia, corvée was determined on the basis of the number of males in the household rather than on the amount of land cultivated. A head tax was levied for each male owned, and landlords then extracted labor power for work on manorial land as compensation. Thus, nineteenth-century increases in population meant that compulsory labor automatically grew in proportion (Kieniewicz 1969:403). Unlike their counterparts in Galicia and the Prussian provinces, serfs in the Russian sector did not see reform until the 1860s.

After the defeat of Napoleon, the Congress of Vienna (1814) created the Congress Kingdom from most of the short-lived Duchy of Warsaw. The kingdom was united with Russia but had a separate sejm, staffed by Polish nobility. The *kresy*, the remainder of the commonwealth in the east that fell to Russia, populated mostly with Lithuanian, Byelorussian, and Ukrainian peasants, remained under direct Russian rule (Wandycz 1974:17). Polish serfs living in the Congress Kingdom had been granted their personal freedom by the Napoleonic constitution of 1807 but were still liable to compulsory labor until 1861. The provisions of 1807 had allowed landlords to evict peasants who were not permitted to take implements, livestock, or draft animals with them. Under the threat of expulsion, peasants had little choice but to accede to the continuing corvée demands of the landlords.

1848: Hastening Emancipation

The Galician jacquerie of 1846 strengthened peasant class consciousness throughout the old commonwealth. It inspired a peasant revolt in Prussian Poland that led to the inclusion of smallholders in the earlier settlements; they were henceforth permitted to buy the land they worked and to spread payment over a number of years. Some dues were even abolished without compensation. Significantly, the Polish members of the Berlin Parliament (the so-called Polish Club) voted against granting property rights to smallholders. As Kieniewicz points out "class interest came before national duty" (1969:133). With the creation of a free working class, capitalism in Prussia advanced and the Prussian provinces of Poland became the most highly developed of the three portions of the former Polish state, having the highest productivity, the most widespread incidence of bourgeois values, and, concomitantly, the most polarized rural class structure.

Although the Galician peasant movement failed, the Austrian government responded to the strikes by abolishing serfdom by fiat in 1848, giving all peasants their land, theoretically without compensation to the lords and with retention of servitudes (access to forests and pastures).

Thus, the imperial government profited politically at the expense of those Polish landlords trying to gain the support of peasants for independence. In fact, the Austrian state promised them compensation, to be paid from state funds, but the post-1848 reactionary Austrian government reneged. It was the peasants themselves who ultimately bore the burden of recompense through taxes that had been levied on the province as a whole but that landlords invariably transferred to peasants.

An increasingly liberal Austrian state in the latter part of the century gave considerable autonomy to the Polish nobility and to Galicia. Semi-independent sejms and a judiciary composed of native Poles, some of them peasants, were largely free of Austrian interference. Polish art, literature, and education flourished, and Kraków became the major center of intellectual activity and eventually liberal reform. The net result of emancipation in Galicia, however, was the retention by lords of 90 percent of the forests and 43 percent of the arable land. Compared to Prussian and Russian Poland, there were proportionately fewer landless peasants, thanks to the 1790 ban on evictions, but two-thirds of the peasant holdings were less than 5 hectares and dependent upon servitudes. With few rural proletarians, manors were faced with labor shortages. Blanket servitudes were rescinded in the face of reaction as each landlord negotiated agreements individually through the judiciary. With courts controlled by landlords, however, peasants lost most of their servitudes and villages remained economically dependent upon the manors. Because peasants had no alternative to work on the manors, the landlords' labor problem was solved (Kieniewicz 1969:139).

By the late nineteenth century, aspirations for national liberation had faded considerably. A new generation of intelligentsia, formed largely by the ideology of populism, turned its attention to the needs of industrial progress and capitalism as a small but wealthy middle class began to emerge from a core of former nobility. Among the tasks it undertook was to extend the ideas and practices of economic liberalism into the countryside. Accordingly, they encouraged the formation of independent, rural cultivators by introducing agricultural circles, cooperatives, credit facilities, and rural banks into villages. The explicit intent of the intelligentsia was to increase productivity by promoting land consolidation, new technology, and bourgeois values. Słomka (1941) describes temperance societies, reading rooms, and other "cultural" benefits that enlightened landlords also provided to villagers in order to further their education. The mayor castigated those unwilling or unable to take advantage of these benefits, characterizing them as lazy, improvident, and worthless drunkards. Peasants, in other words, in order to advance their welfare, were to forgo historic means of resisting the dominance of landlords, and to adopt the cardinal virtues of a middle class by becoming sober, thrifty, hardworking, utilitarian, rational individual producers of surplus value. What is more (to paraphrase Corrigan and Sayer 1985:132), they were to acquiesce in their regularization as part of an expected, acceptable and legitimate social order, policing their own errant members. The role of the intelligentsia in the service of the dominant class and as part of the state in creating and enforcing these cultural values cannot be overemphasized.

The Russian sector was the last in which serfdom was legally abolished. Decrees of 1846 had allowed peasants to appeal to authorities in case of dispute with the lord, and all extra tribute and labor not appearing in a written contract were forbidden. The result was a decline in obligatory labor but a dramatic increase in the number of landless or almost landless peasants, who numbered some 40 percent of the total by 1859 (Kieniewicz 1969:145). The final defeat of the insurrection of the gentry in 1863 and the ruthless repression of Poles and Polish culture and language that followed signaled the demise of overt national conspiracy. However, hastened by Russia's defeat in the Crimean War, the ascension of a more liberal tsar, and widespread peasant agitation—there were 474 outbreaks of peasant violence in the last years of formal serfdom (Hobsbawm 1962:352)—the end of the uprising also marked the end of compulsory labor in Russian Poland. Peasants were given the land they cultivated and landlords were in theory to be compensated from the state treasury; the result, however, was similar to that in Austria and rural differentiation intensified. Moreover, nothing was done to indemnify the already landless peasants or to restore the land illegally taken from them and smallholders.

Thus, the partitioning of the Polish state had various net effects on agricultural development and class structure in the three sectors. In Prussian Poland, where capitalist production was most advanced, where reforms had been the earliest, and where their terms particularly favored peasants who had already had larger landholdings, villages became more polarized. Even though Junkers owned 55 percent of the most fertile and productive land in 1882, their share was to shrink to between 46 and 30 percent by 1907 as "affluent peasants" purchased manor land and bought out debt-ridden smallholders. By 1907, 6.6 percent of the peasant farms accounted for between 40 and 60 percent of all peasant-owned land, depending on the area (Kieniewicz 1969:214). Smallholders with larger farms could afford to keep pace with manors by purchasing machinery, replacing oxen with horses, applying chemical fertilizer, and breeding cattle and pigs. For the remainder, however, farming remained labor intensive, and the owners of the dwarf farms of less than 2 hectares (67 percent of the total) were agricultural wageworkers on noble and large peasant estates. The number of rural proletarians quadrupled between 1870 and 1891, so that by the end of the century, 80 percent of those who depended on agriculture for their livelihood worked as wage laborers (Kieniewicz 1969:182). These circumstances persist to a certain degree today in the form of still larger than average private farms in the former Prussian territories, some of which continue to be worked with hired labor. We will return in due course to the circumstances surrounding this apparent anomaly in an erstwhile socialist state. For the moment it is sufficient to observe that many of the large estates of western Poland were incorporated into the state farms that still constitute some 25 percent of the arable land but that are slated to revert to private ownership in the near future—whose ownership, of course, remains to be seen.

Nineteenth-century conditions in the Russian Congress Kingdom and Austrian Galicia were variations on the same pattern we saw in Prussian Poland. In the kingdom, medium-sized peasant farms of between 5 and 20 hectares were more important than elsewhere, primarily a result of measures taken by the Russian government to restrict the economic power of the Polish nobility after the insurrections of 1831 and 1863 (Polonsky 1972:4). Nonetheless, the nobility still owned 37 percent of the arable, 65 percent of peasant farms were still smaller than 5 hectares, and productivity per unit of land was decidedly lower than in Prussian Poland (Kieniewicz 1969:222–225). Disparities were even more marked in Galicia, where in 1900 more than 80 percent of peasant farms were smaller than 5 hectares, each divided into numerous small plots—the infamous checkerboard of Galicia (Kieniewicz 1969:204). With the highest population density of the three areas, the least industry, and lowest land yields, the province was the most underdeveloped and suffered the most endemic rural poverty of the areas that constitute modern Poland, although in terms of political and cultural autonomy, it was the most advanced.[16] Thus, even after emancipation and (limited) land reform, many, perhaps even most peasants were still forced to surrender their land and labor power to the manors. Vast numbers, between 3.5 and 4 million, emigrated in the forty-year period prior to World War I, over 2.5 million to the United States alone. Rural population had, however, increased fourfold in the nineteenth century and emigration was only able to "drain off" 28.4 percent (Berend and Ránki 1974:18–20).

The Polish Republic

Only in the aftermath of World War I was a geographic and political unit called the Republic of Poland (unexpectedly) reconstituted from the ruins of the defeated imperial powers. It fell to the leadership of the new Polish state, drawn for the most part from the intelligentsia, to construct a nation from the hodgepodge of ethnic, linguistic, and religious groups that crosscut class identity in the new state. The new Poland, whose geographic center was well to the east of the present center, was made up of a central core of Catholic Polish speakers with the eastern territories comprising huge national, religious, and language minorities, primarily Ukrainians and Byelorussian peasants who were either Orthodox or Uniates. Largely as a result of the expansion east after the formation of the commonwealth in the fifteenth century, the landlords were either Polish or polonized. Even all Polish speakers in the post–World War I republic did not necessarily want to be part of the new Polish state (Polonsky 1972:52). Economic and political divisions among the three disparate sections of the new state were compounded by varying social identities and class relations that often crosscut ethnic boundaries. In 1921, 63 percent of traders and some 40 percent of artisans were Jewish, and Germans and Jews were significant minorities among industrial workers (Polonsky 1972:31–35). Intense anti-Semitism on the part of Poles of all classes prevented them from allowing Jews a place in the Polish nation. Moreover, it is sometimes asserted and regretted that "peasants," constituting 70 percent of the total population in 1931, had a poorly developed sense of nation, identifying more with their land, village, and its immediate surroundings (Thomas and Znaniecki 1918, 1:159; Polonsky 1972:26; Majkowski 1985:124). This was an overstatement in light of the growing politicization of peasants between the wars and their increasing participation in national politics, though small peasants and rural laborers were no doubt the least likely of rural inhabitants to elaborate a specifically Polish identity. Peasants with larger farms, however, were integral to the interwar republic to the extent that they were participants in national peasant/populist political parties.

During the late nineteenth to early twentieth century, populism became increasingly widespread among both the better-off peasants and some strata of the intelligentsia. Polish populism never developed the intensity of the Russian *narodniki*. But with its extreme apotheosis of the undifferentiated "people," after an initial period of complementarity with socialism, it did eventually become antisocialist, especially once conservative quasi aristocrats, intelligentsia, and large landowners began to see the utility of populism as a means of influencing peasants. By the years just prior to World War I, the Polish Peasant party, which had formed in Galicia under the Habsburgs in the 1890s, had split into a left and a right wing. Having early dissociated itself from the Socialist and Communist parties, the left wing, ultimately smaller and far less influential, had no coherent leftist stance but, according to one observer, appropriated the left end of the populist spectrum simply because it was vacant (Narkiewicz 1976:140). Another wing, PSL-Wyzwolenie (Liberation), headed by a nonpeasant follower of Piłsudski, had progressive politics but also never captured large numbers of peasant supporters, in part because the village clergy regularly condemned it as "communistic" and threatened its adherents with excommunication. The right wing of the PSL, the Piast, was strongly influenced by the Catholic clergy (though not to the same degree as yet another wing, the radically religious Christian Peasant party, which had been formed in opposition to the original PSL in the 1890s). PSL-Piast was closely linked and loyal to the most conservative elements in the country: the National Democrats, the large landowners (including, for example, prominent Galicians Count Henryk Potocki and Prince Adam Sapieha), the business community, and a reactionary lobby known as Podolak (Narkiewicz 1976:142). Olga Narkiewicz asserts that Wincenty Witos, a peasant and the longtime leader of PSL-Piast (and prime minister of independent Poland in 1920–1921 and in 1926), allied with the National Democrats, landowners, and other right-wing elements less because of his own conservative politics than because they, like he, were anti-Ukrainian and tended to be Slavophiles and hence pro-Russian. With Ukrainian (and to a lesser degree Byelorussian and Lithuanian) nationalism in the east threatening the economic interests of the predominately Polish landlords as well as the ethnically Polish peasants in those territories, Poles of all classes opposed minority calls for autonomy. Whatever the motivation of Witos's political conservatism, the PSL-Piast incorporated large landowners and the more prosperous peasants into its fold and represented their interests throughout its history, including in its latest-but-one manifestation as the United Peasant party. (The ZSL announced in August 1989 that it would no longer support the PZPR as it had since the 1940s but would support the Solidarity coalition in order to form a non-Communist government.)

Populist politics in Poland—though perhaps to a lesser degree there than elsewhere in Eastern Europe—was characterized in the late nineteenth and early twentieth centuries by a romantic peasant mystique. A fundamental assumption of this myth was that "the peasant had been the repository of all the virtues of man [sic] throughout the course of history" (Jackson 1966:41) and that peasant farming in its traditional form would persist well into the future only if, to paraphrase the program of the PSL when it was formed in 1893, peasant farms were defended from ruin, overburdening, abuses, and exploitation. It is significant to note that the "Ludowe" in "PSL" is alternately translated as either "Peasant" or "Populist." That the two are synonymous to many theorists as well as participants in the PSL suggests that the identification of undifferentiated peasants with the equally undifferentiated people was and is commonplace. The initial demands of the early PSL had mostly to do with alleviation of heavy taxes and other burdens (Narkiewicz 1976:67). But after independence and the restoration of the Polish republic in 1918, it called for the appropriation and redistribution of land. The Land Reform Act of 1920, however, which was supported by PSL-Piast, restricted itself to a maximum annual appropriation with compensation of 200,000 hectares of mostly state and church lands and estates of Germans. Even this minimal reform was poorly implemented: Between 1931 and the end of 1934 a total of less than 300,000 hectares were actually distributed; the record was no better and sometimes worse in other years (Polonsky 1972:351). The interwar land reform, opposed by the Right as too radical and by the Left as too conservative, only succeeded in transferring a small proportion of land from the largest estates to small farms. Because the already better-off peasants were the only villagers who could afford to obtain credit for the purchase of land, rural class relations were not substantially affected (Narkiewicz 1976; Dziewanowski 1977:155).

In the face of the deepening depression and the increasing authoritarianism of the Piłsudski dictatorship, the several wings of the populist party united in an uneasy alliance in 1931 under the leadership and domination of the right-wing Witos and PSL-Piast. One source says the combined membership of the united PSL was 120,000 in 1933 (Polonsky 1972:37); another claims it grew from 300,000 to 400,000 "in the early 'thirties'" as "relations between the village and the manor became more tense than at any time since serfdom" (Narkiewicz 1976:225). Regardless of which figure we accept, the percentage relative to the number of peasants (between fifteen and sixteen million) was minute, even if all members were peasants, an assumption that cannot be sustained in light of the evidence of large landowner and intelligentsia membership. The only concerted action of the populists that even appeared to actively defend the interests of peasants throughout the interwar period (1918–1939) was a short-lived peasant strike in 1937, called by a conspiracy known as the Front Morges, of which Witos was a part. The strike was encouraged, it has been alleged, by the French, who were interested in overthrowing the pro-Nazi government of "the colonels" that had succeeded Piłsudski in 1935. Put down with killings, brutality, and armed repression, the strike failed to bring about any change in the government, the policy or practice of the state, or the otherwise quiescent program of the PSL.

The program of the PSL and populist politics in general was based on the assumption that rural economic development could proceed without differentiation. In fact, it implicitly assumed the fundamental unity and equality of all landowners, a symbolic link by virtue of a common tie to the soil that made kin of all, regardless of the size of the farm or estate. Apologies, explanations, and justifications notwithstanding,[17] populists were individualistic, subscribed to fundamentalist Catholic ideology that justified and rationalized the status quo—and despised and excoriated "nonbelievers," (Jews and Orthodox) and all ethnic minorities (Lithuanians, Ukrainians, Germans, etc.). Populists were also antisocialist and anticapitalist alike because of the preeminence socialism and capitalism give to the working and bourgeois classes, respectively. Socialism in particular, because of its assertion of the essentially social rather than individual nature of property, was anathema to landowning peasants (as well as to quasi-aristocratic landowners, of course).

Holding aside the class differences between nobility and peasants, populists also often failed to recognize, in spite of abundant evidence, the significance of stratification among peasants. Instead, they maintained that the status of rich or poor peasants depended on whether they were hardworking or lazy, an ideology of individualism and "blaming the victim" analogous to that of the middle class in capitalist society (Ryan 1976). Exemplified in the memoirs of Jan Słomka (1941) and those of other Galician peasants, including Witos himself, the ideal was the independent, wealthy peasant who was admired, emulated, and looked to for village leadership and advice by the poorer peasants and was also the person from whom they rented farm implements and obtained loans, or if related, cooperated with in reciprocal but unequal labor exchange. Independent peasants, though they were the exception rather than the rule, were targeted when large landowners and well-meaning intelligentsia sponsored the formation of agricultural circles, schools, cooperatives, credit unions, and the like. The right-wing National Democrats were responsible for founding numerous such institutions, ensuring that education would regulate the distribution of both social and cultural capital and hence that of symbolic power. Social and cultural capital can, of course, be translated into economic capital. The leader of the National Democrats, Dmowski, in particular emphasized developing the national sentiments of peasants, whom he characterized as more energetic and enterprising than the szlachta, which, in spite of his overwhelming support for magnates, he often reproached for its political passivity and lack of national feeling (Polonsky 1972:55). Thus, part of the reforms introduced into villages were appropriate bourgeois values, practices, and strategies that, among other things, valorized cooperation with rather than resistance to the manor. Such reforms consequently enhanced class fragmentation.

Disparities between noble and peasant farms were extreme, but the differences between peasant strata were also a dominant feature of the rural landscape. In 1921, 0.9 percent of all holdings but 47.3 percent of the arable was in farms of greater than 50 hectares. Of the 10.5 million hectares owned privately, well over half were in estates of 1,000 hectares or more, but aside from a handful in the former Prussian territory, few peasants had large farms. They shared the remaining 42 or 43 percent of the land, and only 31 percent had farms of between 5 and 20 hectares. Another 20 percent were landless and the remainder had tiny, often insufficient holdings, forcing them to work on manors or to migrate seasonally. Except in the western area, yields on peasant farms were 20 to 50 percent lower than in Germany, and there were few tractors, other technology, or fertilizer in use. Yet agricultural products, especially sugar, wheat, livestock, and timber, made up almost 60 percent of Polish exports between 1928 and 1930, making small producers especially vulnerable to falling prices during the worldwide depression of the 1930s.

The effects of the depression were severe throughout Poland, but agriculture was hardest hit. On the farms of 2 to 50 hectares, the net return per hectare fell from 214 złoty in 1928–1929 to 25 in 1930–1931 and to 8 by 1931–1932. Recovery in the succeeding years was minimal, net income per hectare only reaching 26, 35, and 18 złoty in 1932–1933, 1933–1934, and 1934–1935 (Polonsky 1972:280, 350). These figures, moreover, do not include the 34 percent of all farms that were less than 2 hectares, which were even harder hit. With state policy favoring large landowners and heavy industry, large portions of which were dominated by foreign capital, onerous taxes (26 percent of the small farmers' income in 1933), monopolies in marketing, and a well-developed system of intermediaries that prevented rural cultivators from realizing the profits on the export of their produce, most villagers were poverty-stricken, the smallest landowners and the totally landless the poorest of all (Polonsky 1972:12–16). In spite of some reforms and political representation after Poland achieved independence in 1918, the bureaucratic state had not changed but only transformed the old rural class structure. Poor peasants remained dominated by the old landed class, and a middle village fragment emerged as all peasants were forced to compete with one another for land and other scarce resources.

What is more, numerous denizens of the eastern portions of the country identified themselves as of Ruthenian, Byelorussian, Lithuanian, or Ukrainian *nationality* in the 1921 census, even though census takers encouraged them to list Polish because of the "pressure to obtain politically satisfactory results" (Polonsky 1972:35). Categories were changed by the 1931 census to eliminate the nationality question and replace it with one that asked for language and religion. Compulsion to conform to Polish unanimity continued, but still only 69 percent agreed that they spoke Polish as their first language—a statistic that Antony Polonsky (1972:35) suggests is surely too high. In the very categories it devised and the constitution of those categories, the seemingly neutral and purely administrative census defined and delineated social identity (Hakim 1980). The ethos of unmediated tradition, the key ideas of national identity and historical experience, need not be shared by everyone for them to have a certain material force. Statistics, the science of the state, constructed shared identity from geographic contiguity while at the same time reinforced no longer jural but still social and economic differences in villages. Inquilini, hortulani and *rustici* (rustics) were replaced in the rural census with *rolnik* (farmer) and *robotnik rolny* (farm worker). Not incidentally, the intellectual worker, largely coterminous with intelligentsia, appeared for the first time as a kind of person to be counted.

In spite of a liberal constitution guaranteeing full rights to ethnic, linguistic, and religious minorities, the conservative bent of influential sectors of society in the Republic of Poland—intelligentsia, bureaucrats, and large landowners—ensured that in practice minority rights were not enjoyed. Dmowski, head of the Polish National Union, which, as the National Democratic party, maintained a plurality in the early interwar Sejm and was an important political force throughout the interwar period, was a vehement critic of liberal democracy. With its emphasis on individual rights of free speech, assembly, and so forth, it "conflicted with his idea of a coherent national community with a common will" (Polonsky 1972:55). The conservative view itself was not uncontested. In fact, the ideals and philosophy of nonrevolutionary socialism as well as liberalism were also common, but neither the Polish Socialist party, important in the opposition, nor liberal parties played a significant role in governing the country after 1922.

Government between 1926 and 1935 was dominated by the personality of one-time socialist Józef Piłsudski. The only clear ideological content of Piłsudski's semidictatorship was a vague personality cult that persisted even after his death in 1935. In spite of occasional prolabor, propeasant, and pronational rhetoric, the Piłsudski coalition was more conservative than socialist or even liberal.[18] The state became increasingly repressive during the 1930s, jailing, abusing, and forcing into exile opposition members and, in the face of the depression, first cutting back on and then rescinding social welfare. Fascism, centered among the intelligentsia and university students, also became an important social force, especially after 1935. The lesser members of the intelligentsia were hard hit by the depression and tended to blame competition from Jewish intellectuals, who predominated in law and medicine as well as in trade. Vicious anti-Semitism swept the universities as students demanded variously that the number of Jews admitted be limited, that all Jews be expelled from Poland, and that all Jewish traders, artisans, and shopkeepers be boycotted. The social and economic ramifications for the country's six to seven million Jews were devastating. Moreover, the effect on the overall economy was negative. Dmowski, who had always blamed his country's economic difficulties on "Jewish-Masonic" influence, branded the left opposition as a "Jewish Front." The state made efforts to repress anti-Semitism in the universities (it closed them several times following "incidents"), but some members of the cabinet and Sejm, followers of Piłsudski, were avowed Fascists, and press censorship intensified after Piłsudski's death in 1935. The National Democrats themselves became overtly fascist. Although the state was authoritarian and a quasi dictatorship in the 1930s, the continued existence of a centralist and socialist opposition minority did prevent the development of the kind of fully fascist state that evolved in Germany and Italy.

The penetration of bourgeois values, the ethos of liberal political freedom, even the national strength of the Socialist and the PSL parties in the 1920s and 1930s notwithstanding, the smallholder peasants and landless agricultural workers remained destitute and unincorporated into the national fold in meaningful ways. Although some progress was realized, the promised land reform was not fully implemented in the face of the resistance of the same landowners and other conservatives who were so much a part of and an influence on the state and its institutions. Few peasants could afford the necessary compensation to the landlords, and continued rapid rises in rural population rendered even the limited land redistribution ineffective. It has often been estimated that between two and four million peasants could have left the land without a decline in productivity, but few justifications for these figures have ever been made. Even if there was substantial underemployment in the countryside, there was no place for surplus workers to go. Industrial production recovered somewhat after 1936, but by 1939 it had not exceeded that of 1913.

The tension between the conservative intelligentsia that would construct and preserve an image of a past that never was and liberal reformers—also mostly of the intelligentsia—who sought a future in capitalist development was not to be resolved. The Nazi invasion in 1939 followed by the Stalin-Hitler pact that dismembered Poland and divided it between Germany and the Soviet Union, the rigors of the war itself, the slaughter of most of the Jews, new national frontiers that awarded most of the minority-inhabited areas of the east to the Soviet Union after the war, the forcible relocation of Germans from newly acquired western territories, and the appropriation of the large estates of the landed classes along with peasant holdings over 50 or 100 hectares (depending upon the section of the country) and their distribution to small cultivators and landless agricultural workers—all contributed to the creation of a rather more homogeneous community, overwhelmingly Catholic and Polish-speaking. More than anything else, however, it was the advent of a government and a state directed from hated Russia, which advocated (and attempted to enforce) internationalism, social revolution, and atheism, that mediated social and economic class distinctions. Old antagonisms were muted as Poles of disparate classes united in hitherto unrealized ways. The church hierarchy, as the only vehicle of opposition, gained additional stature, and the remnants of the old intelligentsia rallied to the church, soon to be joined by novices drawn partially from the ranks of workers and peasants. Just as the nonnoble nascent intellectuals of the nineteenth century copied the ideas, manners, and culture of the earlier szlachta, so did the post-1944 intelligentsia assume those of the earlier intellectuals. As one critic put it, "they share the benefits of social wealth by acquiring knowledge which is social capital but they fail to disseminate this knowledge in a social manner and moreover appropriate all benefits from the exercise of their profession" (Starski 1982:21).[19]

The new intelligentsia no doubt appropriates socially derived benefits. But, pace Starski, the intelligentsia—or at least that portion of it that never aligned itself directly with the project of the socialist state—did assume its historic role of defining Polish identity; of setting the standards against which all else must be measured; of asserting its cultural autonomy vis-à-vis what was, for the next forty-five years, the economically dominant class fraction (the party's upper bureaucrats, planners, and leaders); and of upholding the autonomy of the Polish people with respect to the Soviet Union. The sense of identity the intelligentsia defines is opposed to the Soviet Union and to everything Poles have come to understand communism and the Communist party to represent. It is paradoxical that while they resist the incursion of Communist ideals, the intelligentsia in general (including those who are or were associated directly or indirectly with the PZPR) reproduces the habitus and associated strategies of its class fraction, thus reproducing the constellation of prewar classes, albeit in a somewhat transformed configuration.

There has emerged a split between the holders of various forms of capital, especially between holders of cultural/symbolic and political/economic capital. In the latest shift, the intelligentsia, rather than legitimating socialist relations of power is now *de*legitimating the recent power-holders, that is, party bureaucrats, and legitimating other social actors. We must explore how this is being worked out as the definition of the nation and control of the state are once again contested.

NOTES

1. The term *szlachta* (*slechta* in Czech) derives from the Old High German *Slahta* (modern German *Geschlecht*), meaning "race," according to one authority (Portal 1962:122) and "family" or "lineage," according to another (Subtelny 1986:15). The distinction between magnates and the rest of the nobility and gentry had more to do with relative power and wealth than difference in kind. Magnates, no more than two dozen families, were probably descendants of the earliest military leaders and numbered their land in the tens or hundreds of thousands of hectares. Szlachta came to see themselves as a race apart from the common people, a distinction they reinforced by adopting in the late thirteenth and early fourteenth centuries the German custom, hitherto unknown in Poland, of family crests (Portal 1962:127–128).

2. For a general discussion of the highly problematic category of "peasant," see Kearney n.d.

3. The reasons for the persistence of serfdom (or its reemergence as "second serfdom") and its relation to the underdevelopment of eastern Europe have been the subject of lively debate (Malowist 1958, 1959, 1966; Blum 1957; Wallerstein 1974, 1979; Anderson 1974; Brenner 1977; Stavrianos 1981; Kay 1975; Schoffer 1959; Laclau 1971).

4. When the szlachta adopted family insignia, entire kin and client networks rather than just individual families adopted them (Portal 1962:122ff.). In the sixteenth and seventeenth centuries, the szlachta thus numbered at least 700,000, perhaps as much as 10 percent of the population compared to 2 or 3 percent in France at the same time. Middle and upper nobility numbered 300,000 and village gentry the remainder (Lindsey 1957:57).

5. According to Lampland (personal communication), less labor was required of Hungarian serfs when draft animals were owned.

6. Greater productivity because of technological innovation does not invoke the physical limitations of workers, but there is nothing to prevent the concomitant use of absolute and relative methods of increasing surplus labor; both were and still often are used simultaneously.

7. The estate of Chancellor Jan Zamoyski, for example, grew from four villages in 1572 to 200 in 1605. He also oversaw and collected revenue from over 600 royal villages encompassing 10,720 square kilometers. The appropriation of minor gentry holdings in payment for debts was as important as the acquisition of royal estates. The holdings of the Lubormirski family, prominent in the region near Wola Pławska, grew from four villages and parts of two others to ninety-one villages and stewardship over twenty-three royal properties in less than fifty years. The ninety-one villages had belonged to forty-three separate gentry squires. And Jermi Wiśniowiecki had 616 households in 1630 in the eastern provinces, where estates were measured in "hearths"; by 1647 the figure had grown to 38,460 (Mączak 1968:459–461).

8. The village nobility devolved into an economic hierarchy; thus there were also *szlachta zagonowa*, or bed nobility (a term that referred to their bed-sized plots of land), and *szlachta szaraczkowa*, or gray nobility (Thomas and Znaniecki 1918, 1:128), who are presumably those with ambiguous status.

9. The liberum veto was introduced into the Sejm in 1606. Not only did a veto end the discussion, it nullified any and all previous decisions of the body, and the delegates were forced to disband (Willetts 1968:267). The veto was never or rarely used until 1652; afterwards its increasing employment in the Sejm and the regional diets alike paralyzed

the operation of the legislature, eliminating the possibility of reform. Seventy-five percent of the meetings between 1652 and 1764 were thus disrupted. Although veto power was invoked by both gentry and magnates, its use came to primarily benefit the latter (Willetts 1968:267).

10. Bourdieu notes that any given cultural competence derives its scarcity value from its position in the distribution of cultural capital and yields profits of distinction for its owner. That the popular classes cannot afford to keep their children in school in order to realize the profits from the accumulation of cultural capital and cannot, of course, realize the social capital inherent in the valued networks, clubs, and marriage and other alliances means that they cannot participate in the "culture of distinction." They may in fact only be able to keep children in school long enough to acquire the skills for the least valorized forms of labor (Bourdieu 1984, 1986:245).

11. During our initial encounter, my first instructor in Polish, Magda, a native speaker and exchange student in the United States, identified her family as "nobility." In subsequent meetings, she would often distinguish between literary Polish or "beautiful" Polish, which she spoke, and "ugly" Polish, which, she often warned me, would be spoken by the villagers I would be living with. University students I knew in Kraków during my stay in Poland would tease me about the village Polish I spoke, a dialect that clearly had little cachet with them. Magda often told stories of her family's relationship to "the count," who, though long deprived of his jural status as nobility, remained part of the social and cultural elite in his area. Magda's own father was a mining engineer and also part of the former nobility, now intelligentsia, a class fraction with which she also proudly identified. I later met a number of other Poles who did not hesitate to trace their aristocratic ancestry for me.

12. The former commonwealth tradition of religious tolerance meant that many gentry in outlying regions were probably Unitate, Orthodox, or Protestant but still regarded themselves and were regarded by their Catholic counterparts as Polish.

13. Peasants with weak rights were settled for indeterminate periods of time and were always subject to eviction. Their rights to land and the servitudes (forest and pastures) were a favor from the landlord rather than payment for labor. Those with strong rights, which were more advantageous in that the peasants could not be easily evicted, probably acquired them under the terms of German law in earlier centuries (Kieniewicz 1969:60–61).

14. The Josephine reforms were canceled in Austria and other colonies of the empire as well.

15. See Wallerstein (1974) and Malowist (1959, 1966) for an account of the additional and devastating effects of, for example, British corn laws and Prussian and North American grain production on international grain trade, including that of Polish lords.

16. The kresy was even less economically developed than Galicia, but, as most of it passed to the Soviet Union after World War II, I will not consider it here.

17. Narkiewicz devotes an entire chapter to explaining that landowning peasants were essentially always out for themselves and this is why they scuttled principle whenever expedient in order to assure their own individual survival (1976:271–293). Her treatment is intended to be a defense of peasants' politics and a criticism of what she calls "intellectual" theories of populism, yet she in fact substantiates the essential point that populism is an ideology, a set of beliefs about the nature of the world deriving from a particular class location in that world.

18. The Non-Party Bloc for the Support of the Government was made up primarily of a core of former Polish Military Organization legionnaires (men who had served under Piłsudski in the Soviet-Polish War of 1920), the Party of the National Right, part of the Christian National party, many of the wealthiest and most prominent landowners, the

Polish Industrialists' Association, the Christian Democrats, and the most conservative of the several peasant parties, the Christian Populist party. Some members of Piast, the most conservative of the remaining populist parties, also joined as did the center-left Party of Labor, the National Workers' party, and the League for the Reform of the Republic. The radical Right and the remainder of the Center and Left, including the Polish Socialist party and most of the parties of the national minorities, constituted the opposition. Polonsky (1972) covers the politics of the interwar period admirably.

19. Starski's book, *Class Struggle in Classless Poland* contains many useful ideas and insights, but, like so many dissident Polish writers, his passionate anticommunism prevents an even-handed analysis.

4

The Production and Reproduction of Differentiation

LAND HAD VALUE in nineteenth-century Poland not only because of its immanence (it inherits the heir that inherits it, as Marx said) but also and perhaps mostly because it symbolized the independence manifest in control over one's time, work, and especially the disposition of one's own labor and surplus value. In describing this relationship around the turn of the century, William Thomas and Florian Znaniecki point out that

> there is hardly . . . an economic distinction so profoundly rooted in Polish consciousness as that between independent work on the person's own property and hired work. . . . hired work, before the development of industry, meant almost always "service," including personal dependence of the employee on the employer; hired work in whatever form has the character of compulsory work as opposed to free work (1918, 1:132).

Land was thus and continues to be at once material and symbolic. Its economic value and cultural significance derives, first, from its status as both concrete product and the sentimental embodiment of an order of meaning and social relations; second, from its capacity to reproduce a social system; and, finally, from the manner in which it links production and distribution. The degree to which land symbolizes the control and disposition of labor rather than land as an object per se, then, is a crucial aspect of rural social location and consciousness of that position.

In spite of the unambiguous inequalities among serfs that were based on land and labor obligations, these did not constitute realized class differences before emancipation because landlords had the means to exert strong extra-economic influence on stratification within villages. Landlords could and sometimes did unilaterally evict some serfs, commute the labor obligations of others, and otherwise affect the livelihood and status of all. Groups tended to be somewhat fluid; after emancipation, however, the boundaries dividing them solidified.

In the village where Jan Słomka lived, in the Austrian part of partioned Poland, there were forty-one cottages just before emancipation in 1848. Twelve of them belonged to "owners" of their own land, whereas twenty-three housed tenants of the lord and seven housed day laborers. The twelve owners had about 7 hectares each and did their labor dues on manor land six days a week with their teams or yokes of oxen, wagons, plows, and harrows and disks. The twenty-three tenants had temporary-use rights to 2-hectare plots and did labor dues three days a week with hand tools—flails, sickles, hoes, and spades. The seven laborers had only huts and no land or tools at all. Members of these families worked as servants and field hands for the owners (Słomka 1941:14). Słomka tells us that after emancipation, every owner kept a minimum of four servants: a hired man, a hired woman, a farm boy, and a herd boy or girl—not necessarily or even usually all of the same family. The children of the day laborers and tenants whose parents had little land or lost what they had went into service, that is, they hired out their labor power to those who could support them and pay them an annual pittance. Adult servants received room and board, three sets of clothing, and a few dollars per annum. The hired man was sometimes paid in kind rather than in money, with the amount dependent upon his responsibilities. Herd boys and girls received only their clothing and food (Słomka 1941:52–53). Other sources describe similar conditions. Serving women and girls usually slept in the cow shed on wooden benches covered with straw; laborers slept in the stable. The young women were often sexually abused by the master, his sons, or the other workers and were frequently required to leave service pregnant and in disgrace, not even knowing who the father was (original source cited in Narkiewicz 1976:34). Although owners generally ate the same food as servants and indeed worked alongside the hired help (Słomka 1941:52–53), families of day laborers were often separated, and servants were at the mercy of those who hired them, treated well or badly depending upon their employers' whims and resources. Regardless of how they were treated, servants were of a different socioeconomic group than peasants or even tenants because they did not have any productive property.

In describing his Galician village near Łancut in the postemancipation period of the late nineteenth and early twentieth centuries, the peasant Roman Szuberla notes that the rich peasants monopolized all the political offices and were the initiators of all economic and political enterprises. Narkiewicz summarizes Szuberla's account of village politics by observing that

The rich peasants were initiators of most social and political schemes. They ran cooperatives, and were electors to the rural council. Under the system of electoral colleges, each village was divided into rich, medium, and poor peasants. Each group had the right to elect six councillors. Since the rich peasants were the least numerous, this system meant that the richer farmers had a majority on the council. However, it was habitual to give rich peasants a chance to become councillors, since it was generally held that a landless peasant would not know how to behave on the council. So the system . . . merely underwrote a state of affairs which was already in existence. The headman (*wójt*) was always a well-off farmer. He may have been illiterate; a minor detail (1976:35).

These unequal relations are captured in the folk terms that placed people with sometimes daunting exactitude into their respective categories and instructed others as to how they were to be treated. One level, for example, was that of the *gospodarzcy* (the equivalent of earlier cmethones), who possessed land, oxen, or horses and employed farm laborers. These were the quintessential peasants (*chłopi*)—serfs or, later, heirs of serfs who worked with draft animals. Gospodarzcy contrasted with *małorolni*, or smallholders, in that the latter "used exiguous lots of land (not always the same every year); they did not have their own horses and oxen; they performed compulsory labor only as 'workers on foot'—and above that, they were expected to perform some obligatory work for hire, because otherwise, they could not support their families" (Kieniewicz 1969:53).

Of some fifteen million peasants in 1921, after the Polish republic had been restored, almost 3.5 million were landless (i.e., had no farms) and of them only 43 percent had their own houses. The remainder worked for the most part as seasonal wageworkers or lived and worked on the manors of the landlords or on the farms of more prosperous peasants (Polonsky 1972:27). By this time, małorolni formed an ordered hierarchy in any given time or place. An *ogródnik*, for example, had a house and farm buildings but only land enough for a garden (*ogród*); a *zagródnik* had a house and outbuildings but not even a garden; a *chałupnik* had nothing more than a cot (*chałup*); and *kormorniki* lived in a *kormora*, the smaller room of another's house; the *kątnik*, poorest of all, lived in a *kąt*, the corner of someone's room. *Bezrolni* (literally, without holdings), those who fell outside the peasant hierarchy altogether but were agricultural laborers who sporadically lived in rural villages, also formed a hierarchy made up of two levels: Farmhands, or *parobcy*, were permanently employed on manors or by gospodarzcy on an annual contract, and itinerant journeymen were hired only for harvesting or other short-term, labor-intensive tasks.[1]

The abject poverty and inequalities among peasants did not escape the attention of liberal reformers of the day, including sociologists and economists. Their complaint between 1900 and 1939, however, was less that most peasants had insufficient land to produce adequate surpluses (though this was one of them) than that they were ignorant and overly tied to "primitive" traditions that impeded "modernization." For example, after mentioning briefly extractions of labor and appropriation of surplus by the economically and politically more powerful, the steady loss of land to the same more powerful neighbors and landlords, and onerous taxes demanded by the state, the historian J. Feldman continues his assessment of Galician peasants: "Above all, [because of] prevailing ignorance, helplessness and use of primitive methods in agriculture, the Galician peasant had only bread for a few months, living for the rest of the year on potatoes, and, on the eve of the harvest, partly on grass and bark" (1951:337).

Sociologists with a rather more romantic view of "the peasantry" decried the breakdown of what they described as "the traditional family" (all blood and law relatives to the fourth degree, according to some) in the face of industrialization, migration to urban jobs, and immigration to the United States. Thomas and Znaniecki, the best-known and still widely cited sociologists of Polish peasants,[2] lamented the decline of familial solidarity and an increase in "the egotism of the nuclear family," noting that "when the social and moral side of familiar solidarity began to weaken, those who were the most efficient began to feel that familial communism was an injustice"; thus the "family was more of a burden than a help" (1984:75, 90). The spread of market relations engendered "the substitution of the principle of exchange for the principle of help and encouraged new individualistic values such as profit, travel, and personal pleasure, all of which further loosened the ties that bound individuals to the family group" (1918, 1:181). The rise of individualistic values is the key to what the authors call the "social disintegration" of the peasantry; their analysis is incapable of recognizing that an imputed familial solidarity was in reality of more value to the relatively better-off stratum than to the poor or the landless. The "traditional" extended family enshrined by Thomas and Znaniecki could have been characteristic of but a minority of serf families. Nor did Thomas and Znaniecki, exponents of a strong current of functionalism in Polish sociology, recognize the historical genesis of the large, tightly knit, hierarchically organized serf family, which could brook no horizontal solidarity or individualism because it would have been inimical to the survival of the unit. Consequently, it was natural, though mistaken, for them to characterize the emergence of individualism and utilitarianism in the face of new emergent capitalist relations of production as social pathology, a retreat from a mythical golden age of the past. The hierarchical family was *not* a reflection of some past pristine historical stage in which parental and elder authority was sacred; it was a response to the exploitation of feudal landlords and a form of resistance to appropriation of the family's labor power.[3]

Wola Pławska Today

When I did research in Wola Pławska (1978–1990), land was still the manifest criterion of true value and the estimation of rural community standing and social validation. The relationship among land, control, and identity, in other words, did not change dramatically between 1900 and the late twentieth century, even after decades of attempts by the socialist state to mandate new, more egalitarian social relations. In order to illustrate this, some elementary descriptive material of a contemporary village is needed.

In most respects, Wola Pławska is today a typical agricultural village, comparable to other contemporary communities throughout south-central Poland. Located in the northwestern corner of Rzeszów province, part of old Galicia that was incorporated into the Austrian empire between 1795 and 1918, and situated on the fertile flood plain of the Wisłoka, which joins the Vistula (Wisła) River about 10 kilometers to the north, Wola Pławska is geographically within the Kotlina Sandomierska, or Sandomierz Depression. This is a part of the country that has been ethnically identified as Polish for 1,000 years. The terrain in the county in which Wola Pławska is located is flat, and the soil, though not the best in the country, is far from the worst. Characterized by agricultural geographers as "low efficiency, medium productivity and medium commercial value" with a post–World War II production orientation of "rye-wheat-cattle with potatoes and a commercial orientation of cattle-pigs with poultry," the county is similar to many parts of Poland (Kostrowicki and Szczesny 1972:108). By the late 1960s the historic region of "Old Poland" (i.e., the central-west and central-east provinces that include Wola Pławska), was providing 47 percent of the country's marketed agricultural produce (Franklin 1969:207). Because the area lacks commercially exploitable mineral and other natural resources, most of its inhabitants have been, until recently, farming exclusively for generations.

Wola Pławska, in continuous existence for at least two and probably for four or more hundred years, is now and apparently always has been composed of small and medium farms of between 2 and 20 hectares. All of the farming households now own their own land and other means of production and farm independently. Situated as it is about 10 kilometers by road from Mielec, the nearest town of any size, Wola Pławska is neither uncommonly isolated and remote nor so close to a major urban center to be atypical. Mielec itself, with some 40,000 inhabitants in 1975, is neither especially large nor small by modern Polish standards. Finally, although there was a brief period between 1948 and 1956 in which the government attempted to force farmers to turn their land over to the creation of collectives or state farms, none was formed in this area.

Three hundred fifty-five people lived in Wola Pławska when I took a census in 1979, making it small by contemporary standards but still far from the smallest village in the vicinity. Most of its seventy-eight farmhouses are arranged along both sides of a paved road that bisects the village. Long, narrow fields extend from behind the houses to the river on the east and to the village boundary on the west—the ancient *Waldhufen* pattern, suggesting that the village may have been settled according to German law, probably between the fourteenth and fifteenth centuries (see Chapter 3). A second, unpaved road, a quagmire when it rains and dusty when it doesn't, forms a crossroads more or less in the center of the village. About fifteen houses are located to the west of the main road on this and another dirt road; only the school and one farmhouse are between the main highway and the river to the east. The riverbanks are lined with willows, birches, poplars, and lindens; the latter three are pollarded to provide kindling wood for cooking fires. Except for the trees along the riverbanks and the roads, there are no forests or woods left in Wola Pławska, these having long since been cut for firewood. Firewood was generally used for cooking and heating until the 1920s, when coal became available; the poor used wood exclusively until the 1950s and in 1990 had begun once again to cook with it. Village electrification was complete in 1956. Although not all houses have indoor plumbing, it ceased to be a novelty by the mid-1960s. Several new farmhouses were constructed during a period of especial prosperity during the early and mid-1970s. Houses constructed during the 1980s were largely the fruit of circular migration to the United States.

A pasture of about 25 hectares (probably a vestige of an earlier servitude), on which all households have the right to graze livestock, lies on the floodplain between the levee and the river. This is the only communally owned land in the village. The pasture also serves as a soccer field, volleyball court, and general playground for adolescents and children, including those who are tending livestock. The elderly also congregate there during fine weather. Perched on the banks of the levee, they offer comments on the skills of farmers working in nearby fields and the morals of adolescents who got drunk the previous night and otherwise engage in gossip—mostly about local affairs, often about state policies that directly affect farming, and occasionally about national and international politics.

No one denies that the socialist decades brought considerable positive material change to the area and village. In 1990, however, there were still only minimal consumer goods and services, even those necessary to farming, available in Wola Pławska itself or in Orłów, Czermin, or Rzędzienowice, the villages immediately adjacent to it. For all but a handful of amenities, villagers must take the bus to Mielec or to the much smaller town of Borowa, the *gmina*, or commune headquarters, where most agricultural services, including the procurement and selling agencies of the state, are located.[4] Aside from its agricultural and administrative services, however, Borowa is not very different from other villages in the unit, although it is somewhat larger.

Before World War II, Mielec consisted of little more than a few streets of houses clustered around the central plaza, local administrative offices, the courthouse, a Catholic church, a Jewish ghetto, a synagogue, the homes and businesses of small merchants and craftspeople and professionals, a few inns and taverns, and a small factory built in the 1930s. Most significantly for the inhabitants of Wola Pławska and other nearby villages, the *jarmark*, or market, at which produce, livestock, other necessities, and handicrafts were brought and sold was and still is located in Mielec. Until the road was paved, a new bridge built, and inexpensive and regular bus service provided, nonfarm employment opportunities for villagers in Mielec were limited. Nobody from Wola Pławska, for example, worked there until 1947. The factory, Wytwornia Spizeta Komunikacyjnego (WSK), which manufactures airplanes, buses, and electric golf carts, was considerably expanded after World War II. Its army contracts, in particular, make it analogous to U.S. defense plants in many ways, including its susceptibility to changes in the international political climate. With perhaps 18,000 employees in 1979, it draws workers from Wola Pławska and dozens of surrounding villages as well as the town itself and is far and away the largest employer in the area.

The population of Mielec almost doubled between 1960 and 1978, and today the town is headquarters of the gmina that adjoins Borowa. It is also the county seat, making it the center of political as well as commercial life. It contains the local Communist party headquarters, now presumably renamed the headquarters of the Social Democratic party; other political centers; county administrative offices; and a hospital and medical center. There were two movie theaters, three hotels, several restaurants, numerous small shops, a department store, a "house of culture" with an auditorium, a sports stadium, a museum, and a number of schools in the late 1970s. By 1990, a new shopping area with additional stores had opened up, and the population had clearly grown, but all in all, the continuities were more noticeable than the changes. Villagers do most of their shopping in Mielec, all middle and high schools are located there, and young people in particular do much of their socializing there.

Wola Pławska and Orłów share a branch office of the Panstowowy Osrodek Maszynowy (POM), the state-owned and -operated agricultural machine station. The POM provides tractor and other machine rental, pest control, and the like to the two villages. There is also an experimental cattle ranch on the road to Czermin on which breeding bulls are raised and that provides artificial insemination and other veterinarian services. The state dairy, located in Rzędzienowice, services Wola Pławska as well. Full milk cans are placed by the gate of each house every morning and collected by a horse-drawn wagon. Measured and tested for cream content by the few employees of the dairy, credit is posted to each household; funds are dispersed to producers once a month. Refrigerated trucks take the milk to the city of Rzeszów for processing and bottling.

In addition to its farms and the few farm supports, Wola Pławska has an elementary school (grades one through eight). None of the fifty-three village residents older than sixty-one in 1979 (that is to say, those born before Polish independence in 1918) had more than three years of schooling when I censused in 1979, and a number of them were without formal education altogether. Forty-five percent of those born in the interwar period had less than seven years of schooling. It is worth noting that the Nazis closed down all Polish schools between 1940 and 1945; some of those born in the mid-1930s who should have entered school during these years were also almost completely without an education. In contrast, more than two-thirds of the villagers born since 1945 had completed at least ten years. Ten years of education were made compulsory in 1980.

Among the few other services in Wola Pławska is a tiny convenience store located at the crossroads. A single employee keeps the store, which stocks little more than some canned goods, candy, cookies, soft drinks, beer, and cigarettes (and not much of any of them) and is open just a few hours in the forenoon and late afternoon. A fire station with its single engine is housed near the center of the village. A public meeting hall with kitchen facilities (dom rolniki) was completed in the mid-1970s but is only used for special occasions, such as dances, village meetings, and once in a while a wesele (wedding reception).

Everyone who professes a religion in Wola Pławska (almost everyone) is Roman Catholic. A church, which was built in 1927 on the boundary with Rzędzienowice, seats 200 to 300 persons. All the residents of Wola Pławska and many from Orłów and Rzędzienowice attend this church, old women daily, others weekly and on holy days. There are three masses every Sunday morning; during all of them there is standing room only. Prior to 1927 Wola Pławskans drove their carts or walked along a now abandoned field road to the then closest church in Czermin (about 6 kilometers). One old woman told me,

> We didn't have a horse, we walked, and we carried our shoes too, so they wouldn't wear out. When we were almost at the church we would stop at the stream, wash our feet, and put our shoes on. I had the same ones for three years. At first they were too big and I had blisters, then they fit for one year. When they were too small I had blisters again. . . . There were others who were poorer. . . . They didn't have shoes at all.

Many people still walk to church (though they invariably wear shoes); others ride in horse-drawn wagons, and those from the farthest parts of Rzędzienowice and Orłów take the bus or drive motorized golf carts built at WSK or, in a very few cases, cars. Few would think of missing mass. After the service, people gather in knots outside the church, usually in age- and gender-segregated groups, gossiping and discussing politics. With the exception of the generation now in its teens and twenties, which frequents Mielec on a social basis, a large part of the village's social life centers on the church and church-related activities. Sunday afternoons are spent visiting neighbors or kin—the only time villagers regularly entertain in any formal, non-work-related way aside from the occasions marking religious rites of passage, for example, weddings, baptisms, first communions, and funerals.

The Historical Production of Inequality in Wola Pławska (1848–1939)

Although some villagers told me that *their* ancestors were never serfs, historical records belie their assertions. Indeed few Polish villages escaped serfdom after the sixteenth century. By 1900 only one nonpeasant landholding was listed on the tax records of Wola Pławska. Judging by the amount of tax paid that year, this holding was small, and it was owned by the village's "first" family—a far from wealthy but nonetheless gentry family (of the szlachta zaściankowa) who lived in what by village standards was clearly a mansion. The only dwelling of its era built of plastered-over brick, this house still stands out among the log cabins of the same vintage, even among the later houses built after World War II but before the era of new brick structures. Nearby Rzędzienowice, in contrast, contained one *obszar dworski*, or large, probably noble-owned

TABLE 4.1   National Land Tenure in 1921

Hectares	Farms (%)	Arable (%)	Mean Size
0–2	33.9	3.5	1.0
2–5	30.7	11.3	3.4
5–10	22.5	17.0	7.9
10–20	9.6	13.8	13.4
20–50	2.4	7.1	28.6
50–100	0.3	2.5	67.6
> 100	0.6	44.8	718.4

Source: Antony Polonsky, *Politics in Independent Poland: 1921–1939* (Oxford: Clarendon Press, 1972), 521; Andrzej Korbonski, *Politics of Socialist Agriculture in Poland, 1945–1960* (New York: Columbia University Press, 1965), 20.

estate in 1900.[5] It included ten buildings, had 72 horses and 230 head of cattle (compared to 120 horses and 362 cattle for the rest of the village), and employed 184 persons. In 1900 this property consisted of 811 hectares compared to a total of 443 hectares owned by the 138 peasant households of that village. The average peasant farm was thus 2.4 hectares. The ratio of large- to smallholdings is consistent with turn-of-the-century nationwide averages, a disparity that had, if anything, been growing between emancipation and 1944 (see Table 4.1).

The proportions did not change dramatically after the land reform initiated by the government of the newly independent Polish state during the 1920s. According to the census of 1931, the last before World War II, 64 percent of the peasant farms were still under 5 hectares (Vaughan 1971:350, n. 2). Over half the large estates were still more than 1,000 hectares each; some of them were truly enormous. The Zamoyski estate of 191,000 hectares and the Radziwill holdings of 177,000 are representative of the largest; the relatively modest estate of the Potockis of Łancut (not far from Mielec) was "only" 19,000 hectares in 1931 (Polonsky 1972:12–13).

At the same time, conditions for peasants were desperate and, in the face of the depression, getting worse:

> Sugar no longer exists in the villages. The majority of children—in the Rzeszów district—have seen it only in the form of sugar cakes at the Kermis. At present, the gray type of salt is used and sometimes even the red type intended for cattle; in spring before the harvest, because of the lack of ready cash, even this worst variety is used over and over again, salted water being saved from one meal to cook the next meal's potatoes. The medium peasant goes about today shod in the same boots, patched and re-patched many times, in his one shirt, which is laundered at night. From his others, clothes were long ago made for the children. . . . They have one garment apiece, and feel most painfully their lack of clothes. It

is easier in the summer, but in winter in the northern part of the district [where Wola Pławska is located] one can meet in huts children who are bundled up to the neck in bags filled with chaff, since without clothing they would freeze in the cold, unheated dwelling.[6]

The Rzędzienowice estate, like all others over 50 hectares, was broken up by the socialist land reform, its acreage distributed to local smallholders and agricultural workers in an attempt to raise their holdings to the point at which they could support a family without resorting to wage labor. Although it was far from successful in meeting its objective of equalizing peasant landholdings, the terms of the land reform helped to temporarily mitigate long-standing inequities and to reduce the stability of strata that were already in place.

The estate was a major source of seasonal agricultural employment for peasants from several villages between World War I and II and the permanent place of employment for many others. Many of the families of Rzędzienowice were no doubt serfs owing labor to this property before emancipation. Although I do not have historic data about the Rzędzienowice estate in particular, similar properties all over Poland, particularly those located on navigable rivers as this one was, engaged in large-scale production for international markets using serf labor as early as the sixteenth century (Malowist 1966).

That most of the inhabitants of Wola Pławska were małorolni, land-poor, and forced to supplement the living provided by their farms with wage labor during the decades immediately prior to the socialist era is clear from estimates based on available data and the stories older residents related to me. All during the nineteenth century, families had been growing progressively larger, in part because of changes in mortality rates and longer life spans. At the same time, the average size of landholdings was decreasing—a factor that would tend to retard the formation of strata based on land ownership alone. However, a large family, it will be recalled, was primarily advantageous to serfs with draft animals and large labor obligations but not to those with small plots or to free peasants. I have calculated that by the beginning of the twentieth century, 44 percent of the farms in Wola Pławska had shrunk to less than 2 hectares and 81 percent were 5 hectares or less. This estimate is based on the *Skorowidz Gminy Galicyji* (1907), the official Austrian census, and the Wola Pławska church records for 1900. At that time there were 232 hectares of land in Wola Pławska, sixty-seven houses, a tavern, and a post office. Of the total population of 389, 375 were Roman Catholics, 6 were Jews, and 8 were "other," possibly German-speaking Lutherans (see Kersten and Szarota 1970:448–450). According to the parish documents, there were at least five landless

TABLE 4.2 Estimated Landholdings in Wola Pławska, 1900–1921

Land[a]	Mean	No. of Households	Percentage of Households	Hectares	Percentage of Total
< 2	1.0	27	44	27	12
2–5	3.4	22	37	77	36
5–20	10.2	11	18	112	52
> 20	na	< 1	< 1	0	0
Total		61	100	216	100

[a]Farm size in hectares.

families (called "inquilini" in the Latin used in all church records). The six Jews were probably all members of the same family, innkeepers without a farm who seem to have been residents of the village for many generations. (People simply said they "left" during World War II.) Eliminating the Jews and the inquilini, there could have been no more than sixty-one landowning families in 1900. Also, according to the *Skorowidz*, there was only one gentry family, which owned 124 *sazen* of land. This archaic measure glosses as "fathom," about 2 meters. If I am correct in assuming that a sazen is equal to 4 square meters, then the landholding of the resident gentry family was about 5 hectares. There were no obszar dworski or great properties listed in the Austrian census for Wola Pławska. My interviews with elderly residents of the village also suggest there were no large farms, that is, farms larger than 20 hectares.

Of the 232 hectares within the confines of the village in 1900, 217 were taxable (arable, orchards, pastures, and forest), with the remainder taken up by roads, wasteland, and public buildings. By using the average land size for Galician peasant holdings listed by Kieniewicz (1969:214) and the averages within category size for Poland as a whole in the early 1920s (Korbonski 1965:20), I have calculated the probable number of farms of a particular size in the village at that time. Although rough, the estimate of 216 hectares is close to the actual number of 217 available hectares in the village (see Table 4.2).

Church records for the parish also indicate that Wola Pławska contained forty-one households in 1800 (see Table 4.3), and there is no reason to think the total amount of available farmland was different than in 1900. The average farm in 1800 must have been about 5.3 hectares, considerably larger than the average 3.4 hectares a hundred years later, even without allowing for the existence of a number of landless households at the earlier date. Table 4.3 shows the progressively increasing size of families in Wola Pławska, suggesting that during the nineteenth century growing numbers of children survived to claim a portion of their parents' land

TABLE 4.3 Household Size in Wola Pławska, 1800–1979

Date	No. of Houses	Total Population	Average Household
1800	41[a]	185–200[b]	4.5–4.8
1869	63	305	4.8
1880	63	325	5.2
1890	63	338	5.4
1900	67	389	5.8
1979	80	355	4.4

Note: Figures for 1869, 1880, and 1900 are from official Austrian census data; the 1979 figure is from my own census of the village.
   [a]Estimated from church records of births, deaths, and marriages from 1787 to 1816.
   [b]Because church records show the rate of death exceeded the birthrate during this period, the population may have been declining unless there was net immigration. My calculation may be high in light of I. Berend and G. Ránki's estimate of a fourfold increase in Galicia between 1810 and 1900 (*Economic Development in East-Central Europe in the 19th and 20th Centuries* [New York: Columbia University Press, 1974], 18–19).

in the partible inheritance system typical of Poland prior to the 1960s. Increased fragmentation of the land was clearly occurring each generation. Thus we can see that the nationwide trend during the nineteenth and early twentieth centuries toward the greater pauperization of rural cultivators is reflected in the figures for Wola Pławska. Demographic factors such as population growth coupled with the cultural ideal that land and other means of production be divided among heirs might have tended to act as a leveling mechanism, or it might have lowered all strata equally if all had a more or less equal number of children and if the practice of dividing the land corresponded to the dictates of custom (ordinarily an inaccurate measure of the usual routines of daily life).

Land was available for sale in 1900 in Galicia, but few peasants had the money to buy it. Serfdom had only been abolished fifty years earlier, but the new legal status of the former serfs did not alter the economic and political relations between them and their former lords. The land the peasants had farmed for centuries was not given to them; they had to compensate their former lords. Although credit was available, it was expensive. The majority therefore continued their former relations with landlords. Sharecropping or tenant farming on the lands of the lords or working on their large folwarks (by the nineteenth century, capitalist estates run by means of wage labor) as laborers, they were no better-off and in some cases even worse-off than before. The *odrobek* system, in which a peasant borrowed seed grain, money, or even food from the manor in the spring and worked it off at harvest time, at the lowest possible wage, was common (Kieniewicz 1969:204–205). Heavily in debt, Galician peasants were often forced to borrow to meet daily needs, sometimes at interest rates of from 50 to 100 percent per annum

(Kieniewicz 1969:105). Almost 25,000 holdings were forcibly sold off at auction in a single nine-year period between 1875 and 1884, often for debts totaling the equivalent of ten bushels of grain (Kieniewicz 1969:204). The number of smallholders who lost all their land and their identity as even małorolni quadrupled in some parts of Poland between 1870 and 1891 (Kieniewicz 1969:182). By 1900, 80 percent of village farms had less than 2 hectares whereas in 1850, just two years after emancipation in the Austrian sector, the average had been 8 hectares (Kieniewicz 1969:203).

The Development of Class Stratification

There is no reason to expect rural economic structures or class membership to be stable over generations. Lenin (1956) has theorized the beginning of class differentiation and capitalist agriculture in prerevolutionary Russian villages. It has been widely noted (Shanin 1979)—even by Lenin himself, according to Anderson (1974:349)—that Lenin overstated, possibly dramatically, the capitalist nature of agriculture in turn-of-the-century Russia. Nevertheless, the process he highlighted—the reconstitution and coalescence of rural hierarchies into emerging class fractions under the pressure of capitalism—is relevant to Poland from at least the late nineteenth century to World War II. Lenin named these fractions petit bourgeoisie, middle peasants, and rural proletarians. At the top of the new emerging hierarchy in Lenin's scheme were the few families who had or managed to buy or lease additional land enabling them, usually with the use of hired labor power, always with draft animals, to market commodities commercially. These rural petit bourgeoisie also often had cash income from small craft or artisan businesses in which additional labor may have been employed. At the other extreme were the rural proletarians who owned no land of their own or had only the smallest plots on which they were unable to subsist. These were the poor villagers who were almost completely dependent on wage labor. Leasing their land to the larger owners if they were not actually employed by them, they would pursue a livelihood by migrating in search of wage labor, by working on the large estates, or even by entering into domestic service. Between the well-off and the impoverished were the middle peasants, villagers who neither regularly hired nor sold labor power and did not usually have their own draft animals but managed to subsist chiefly on the produce from their medium-sized holdings. There is an equivalent set of Polish terms that more or less correspond to Lenin's categories: the *bogaci* or gospodarzcy—the rich, the *średniki*—the average or ordinary (most of the małorolni), and *bedniki*—the poor (the rest of

the małorolni and bezrolni). Villagers, especially the elderly, still sometimes apply these terms to kin and neighbors to describe their relative
standing in Wola Pławska.

Lenin also theorized the two earlier mentioned roads to agrarian
capitalism, the first of which he called the "Junker Road." The prototype
was the Prussian Junker who owned a large latifundia farmed by hired
labor. Lenin, however, regarded the American, or kulak, road as more
revolutionary. He speculated that its development would break the
domination of the capitalist landowner of the Junker type. The model
for the kulak road was the small independent farmer, who produced for
the commodity market using both family and hired labor power and
capital investments. Lenin predicted that these new farmers would
eventually swamp the small and most of the middle peasants, buying
up their land and forcing them off the land altogether or into the status
of agricultural worker. Middle peasants would attempt to emulate the
successful farmers. Although a few might succeed, the majority would
in time be unable to compete and be forced to leave farming altogether.
Through this process Lenin foresaw the transformation of relatively
unproductive subsistence peasant farming to highly productive capitalist
farming that, according to orthodox Marxist formulations, must necessarily
precede socialist development.

This model provides some useful insights into the transformation of
Polish peasants prior to the socialist period. For example, Warriner
(1964:70–71) estimates that, given the level of technology in the early
part of this century and the quality of soil in Galicia, it would have
required a minimum of 0.9 hectares per person to maintain a family at
a bare subsistence level such that it could reproduce itself. From figures
calculated for Wola Pławska (see Table 4.2), it appears that half the
households (six landless and twenty-seven households with less than 2
hectares) were among the poorest of the poor (bedniki) in 1900 and
probably had to depend on income from wage labor. Those at the lower
end of the 2-to-5-hectare range may have also had to hire out family
labor power on a regular basis, whereas those at the upper end might
feasibly be characterized as średniki, or middle peasants. The eleven
households with between 5 and 20 hectares were the solid middle
peasants, subsisting on their own land, probably with hired hands on
a seasonal basis. Perhaps the ones with the largest holdings were the
gospodarzcy of the village, leasing land from the poor or employing
them on a regular basis.

Although this scenario is admittedly speculative for Wola Pławska,
it is consistent with national figures for Poland, with what older residents
of the village recall about presocialist land ownership and how families
supported themselves, and with Słomka's account of his village in the

years around the turn of the century (Słomka 1941). To be sure, the differences between the rich and poor of the village were not of any large magnitude (there were probably no farms larger than 20 hectares, for example, and there were assuredly no truly rich peasants at any time); nonetheless, the relatively better-off had more options to reproduce their social standing than the poor had to improve theirs.

A family seeks to keep its position, its standing in the social world through various strategies: procreation, education as a tactic of cultural placement, or more purely economic measures, such as investments, savings, and so forth. Immigration is one such strategy of investment. Between roughly 1885 and 1920, the opportunity of emigrating to the United States was one of those options that may not have been available to the bedniki, as in general European emigrants did not come "from the depths of their respective societies but occupied positions somewhere in the middle and lower-middle levels of their social structures. Those too poor could seldom afford to go, and the very wealthiest had too much of a stake in the homelands to depart" (Bodnar 1987:13).

In Wola Pławska, as throughout minimally industrialized Galicia, many peasants emigrated during the late nineteenth and early twentieth centuries to escape poverty and the lack of urban opportunities. Between 1895 and 1914, over one million left Galicia alone, most of them to go to the United States or Canada, and most never returned. By 1908, two-thirds of the men emigrating from Galicia were agricultural workers (Bodnar 1987:21) but "enough evidence exists to suggest that . . . those at the bottom, in abject poverty, remained fixed to their homes" (Bodnar 1987:22).[7]

The exclusionary immigration policies of the newly isolationist United States precluded further immigration from Poland after 1922. At best, emigration had absorbed less than 30 percent of Poland's population increase of the nineteenth century. The population density in rural Galicia remained among the highest in Europe. Population pressure made it imperative that land be cropped three years in succession without fallowing or manuring, causing yields to decline dramatically (Warriner 1964:132–134). The high population and excess labor kept the prices for agricultural products low while the cost of manufactured goods continued to rise. All but the wealthiest cultivators (the term is relative!) were thus effectively eliminated from participation in the marketplace.

Through a judicious investment in the immigration of family members to the United States or Canada, Wola Pławska families often found themselves with the social capital that such networks imply. They were thus in a better economic position with respect to other villagers if and when their new American kin started to send remittances, as most did, at least initially (Thomas and Znaniecki 1927). In the context of the economy of the present, maintaining close contact with U.S. or Canadian relatives is still important. As the years have passed, however, most of the original immigrants have died and genealogical distance between the survivors and their Polish kin has increased, making the maintenance of old ties problematic. Only a handful of contemporary Wola Pławskans have been able to keep these associations viable. Maintaining relations with foreign kin has certain consequences for economic and social success in the village. A brief history of the Nowak family will illustrate the importance of past immigration to present residents. Just as importantly, it will show that incipient class differences associated with economic and social differentiation occurring two generations ago have been maintained to this day through the elaboration of various strategies of reproduction. Further, the method of family case studies reveals some of the mechanisms by which families keep their place in the community over time.

The Nowaks

The Nowak family, descendants of German-speaking Catholic colonists relocated by the Austrian Emperor Joseph II between 1780 and 1790, owned 15 morgi (about 9 hectares) around 1900. Twelve children were born between 1885 and 1902, all but two of whom lived to adulthood, an unusually high survival rate for the time and place. According to Helena Nowak, age seventy-seven in 1979 and youngest of the twelve, even though her father had substantial nonfarm income from his black-smith shop in addition to revenues from the farm, it was difficult for the family to maintain its standard of living on this holding as the children reached adulthood and required dowries or inheritances in order to marry. Nonetheless, the family was far from impoverished. On the contrary, its landholding was 2.5 times larger than the village average when Helena was born, and the Nowaks had one of the few orchards in the village, at least one *parobek*, or hired hand, and a team of horses that, after their own fields were plowed, they used to plow those of kindred or neighbors for a share of the harvest. Dorota, the second oldest daughter, described the farmhand, whose name she did not remember, as "a dumb chłop [peasant]—too dumb to have his own farm." As proprietors of one of the larger farms and one of the few village enterprises with a cash income from a nonfarming source as well, all the Nowak siblings as well as their parents considered themselves comfortable. The younger generation was subsequently able to acquire additional land. What is more, they have internalized the attributes of a rational, thrifty, and hardworking "middle class."

Dorota accompanied a "rich" family from Czermin to the United States in about 1909, when she was fifteen years old. She traveled and worked as a babysitter and companion to the children, primarily (she says) to avoid betrothal to a man she disliked but who had close ties to her family and could not have been easily turned down. The nucleus of a social network was in place as her father's sister, with husband and children, was already in the United States. After a year of such employment, Dorota took a job as a presser in a shirt factory in upstate New York and was subsequently able to help finance the passage of two older brothers. Another brother, Michał, left for Chicago not long after. Much later, two more sisters emigrated, one to France and the other first to Canada and then to the United States. The sister who went to France and her husband were said to have been involved in politics and were forced to flee to France with their young son after the Nazi invasion in 1939. The entire family was killed by a hand-grenade attack before the war ended. All the emigrating children but this woman sent remittances to their families for many years after they left Poland, Dorota until her husband died in 1963 and Michał until his death in 1977.

It is probably not coincidental that the Nowak siblings became independent small entrepreneurs rather than working class in the United States. Dorota, for example, in 1915 or 1916 married a man who had himself emigrated from a nearby village on the far side of the Wisłoka River and whose średniki family was acquainted with hers. The marriage was arranged via an intermediary who knew both families and was empowered to negotiate suitable terms. Within five years Dorota and her husband bought a small butcher shop, later a tavern and restaurant that they operated throughout the depression. Dorota's daughter in the United States recalls,

> We weren't wealthy by any means, but our family had the nicest house on Sheridan Avenue [in the Polish neighborhood]. Even during the depression, we had plenty to eat and our clothes were better than those of my friends. My parents used to feed people all the time, and my mother invited people to supper if she thought they were going hungry. Ma would sew five dollar bills, a lot of money in those days, into the seams of dresses or the hems of coats and send them to her family in Poland. My grandmother would then send us sacks of goose down for pillows and comforters. We each had one on our beds.

By the mid-1940s, Dorota and her husband owned the building in which the tavern was located and two adjacent tenements containing three flats each, all of which they rented to other Polish immigrant families. By the time of her husband's death, Dorota and he had amassed a considerable estate. Dorota lived comfortably on the interest and rent until her death in 1988.[8] It was a matter of considerable pride to her that after her initial stint in the shirt factory, none of her immediate family, including her children and sons- and daughters-in-law, were blue-collar workers.

Of the nine children of Dorota's generation, only three remained in Wola Pławska: Helena, Krystyna, and Wincenty. Each of the daughters was endowed with nearly 3 hectares of land when they married in the 1920s and 1930s. This land, together with that brought to the union by their respective spouses, allowed them to reproduce the economic and social standing of the family. In addition to the largest share of land, Wincenty also received the house and his father's blacksmith and tools; a couple of cows each and various household goods were part of the daughters' dowries. Each Nowak offspring married at approximately the same economic and social level as that of their parents, and the solid gospodarzcy standing of the Polish branch of this family has been maintained.

Wincenty is long dead, but his son Karol and his grandson Stanisław are still smiths in Wola Pławska, although they farm as well. A respected political leader in the village, Karol was elected *sołtys* several times in the 1950s and 1960s. His brother Lech married both exogamously and "up" to a woman from Orłów. She is also from an ethnically German family, but one more affluent, an incentive perhaps for Lech to marry outside the village, a practice generally avoided by gospodarzcy because of the desirability of marrying into a family whose land was contiguous with one's own. As a result of his marriage and a substantial inheritance received in 1977 (from Michał, the Chicago uncle) that Lech used to purchase additional land and modernize farm equipment, Lech has become one of the more prosperous dairy farmers in Orłów. As sołtys (a position once held by his wife's father and grandfather), he is also influential in local affairs. He is not at all shy in showing off and talking about the experimental automated milking equipment he purchased in 1979 from the agricultural cooperative, on reportedly very liberal credit terms. His farm was a showcase in 1979, and the head of the county agricultural station sometimes brought dignitaries to tour it. Lech pursues woodworking as a hobby and has a well-outfitted shop; he is the only farmer I knew of in the three adjoining villages of Wola Pławska, Orłów, or Rzędzienowice that could afford the luxury, in terms of both time and money, for such leisure activity. Other members of the family imply that Lech exerted unfair influence on Michał, who returned to Poland to visit his family several times between 1950 and 1975, in order to secure the largest share of his estate. Lech is not as well integrated into the kin network as others and does not participate in all the usual kin activities, especially work-related reciprocity. He and his nuclear family seem to be regarded as part of a different stratum from their cousins in Wola Pławska.

Helena, who was widowed in 1972, lives in Wola Pławska with Katarzyna, the elder of her two daughters; her son-in-law, Adam; and her three grandchildren. Although she legally still owns her 3 hectares of land, Katarzyna and Adam now farm it. (An additional 3-plus hectares, which Helena's husband brought to the marriage, was bequeathed to their other daughter, who lives in Rzędzienowice.) In terms of the amount of land they have and their farm income (but not in terms of living standards as measured by ownership of consumer goods), Helena's is one of the most affluent families in the village. With several cash gifts and their 1977 inheritance from Uncle Michał, (which was, though, smaller than Lech's inheritance), Katarzyna and Adam bought a tractor and a thresher and built a new brick stable to house their expanding dairy herd. In 1978 they bought an electric milking machine, the first in the village.

Along with Helena and her husband, Michał also helped to support his sister Krystyna after her husband was executed in 1946 for collaborating with the Nazis during the Occupation. Krystyna's house and farmland was confiscated by the Polish state (along with that of all other traitors), and she was left destitute. All but her youngest child subsequently left Poland and eventually were given war refugee status in the United States. Michał bought a small house (but no land) for Krystyna in the 1950s and regularly sent money. Her one remaining son, a small farmer in Rzędzienowice, also contributes to her support.

Ryszard, the husband of Ewa, yet another Nowak sister, was similarly accused of Nazi sympathizing and was imprisoned by the Polish government for several years after the war. When Ryszard was released in 1948, he, Ewa, and their children made their way to Michał in Chicago, where Ryszard died shortly thereafter. Ewa, who later lived in New York City with one of her daughters, wrote to Helena and Krystyna, her sisters in Wola Pławska, and occasionally sent small gifts of money until her death.

The Nowak family considered themselves średniki in the period between the first and second world wars. In fact, they seem to have been what Lenin might have called rural petit bourgeoisie. Even though their landholdings were not large, they marketed more farm commodities than necessary to simply pay their taxes and provide for what they could not produce themselves; they were able to accumulate; they had a full-time hired hand who lived with them in exchange for room and board and a small annual salary; they had income from the blacksmith; they owned draft animals and other livestock and a small orchard; and they had one of the most modern farms in the village in terms of machinery and technology. Nowaks never were forced to work for wages themselves on the farms of others. Those who went to North America contributed to the well-being of their Polish kin. Ultimately, the improvement of the productive capacity of some of the next generation of Nowak farms was enhanced by the contributions of their American kin.

Many rural cultivators responding to the pressure of rural underemployment as well as political dissidents have periodically emigrated to the United States during the past century, with the last wave of dissidents leaving after martial law was declared in 1981. Most of these emigrants became permanent residents or citizens of the United States. Another, less well known phenomenon is temporary migration, which has occurred over the last twenty years or so. This migration was neither politically motivated nor a direct response to economic deprivation when I began this research in the late 1970s but rather consisted mostly of farmers or members of farming families seeking to take advantage of what was then the nationwide demand for foreign currency in order to make their farms more viable. This demand continued until the złoty was allowed to float against the dollar beginning in January 1990, effectively ending the black market in dollars. By July 1990 people were already seeking to migrate to the United States (and to a lesser degree to West Germany) out of economic necessity, just as they had done almost one hundred years earlier. I will return to this phenomenon in the final chapter, which focuses on events of 1990 and their probable ramifications.

Even though Polish currency still does not trade on the world market, it has never been illegal to possess foreign currency in Poland. In fact, there were (and still are) special accounts available in state banks that deal only in hard money and at which dollars could be, until 1989, exchanged for złoty at better than tourist rates. The government also operates foreign currency stores, called PEWEX, which proliferated during the 1970s. Every town of any size has one or more, including Mielec. The PEWEX stores specialize in imported foods and luxury domestic items that are otherwise nonexistent or in short supply, all to be paid for in the hard currency the state so desperately needs. All during the 1970s and 1980s the government of the PZPR closed its eyes to or, some would argue, actually incorporated a flourishing black market into official planning in order to obtain both hard currency and certain consumer goods. It was possible, for example, to buy a Polish Fiat with dollars in the PEWEX store in 1979 and to take almost immediate delivery, whereas paying for the same car in złoty meant as much as an eight-year wait. More importantly for the farmers, the same was true of tractors suitable for use on small farms, other farm equipment, and building materials to improve houses, barns, and so forth. What was not available from PEWEX was surely obtainable on the black market if payment could be made in dollars. These contradictions persisted until the change in the economic system. Now it is easier to obtain these items with złoty, but few can afford the new prices on Polish salaries. The motivation to travel to the United States (or, less frequently, to Canada) to work was and is compelling.

The migration strategy, however, has always been impossible for most. First, one needs a network in an American city with a large, Polish-speaking population, without which the enterprise is doomed. Then it is necessary to obtain the proper documentation from both the Polish and American authorities, necessitating several trips to one of the American consulates as well as to Warsaw for the passport. Not only must one travel to often distant cities, usually several times, but in 1978–1979 the round-trip airfare from Warsaw to New York was about $600 or Zł 60,000–70,000, a small fortune in a country where the average monthly salary was at that time Zł 4,500.[9] It is ludicrous that the fare in złoty seemed tied to black market exchange rates (about Zł 100 to the dollar in 1978–1979) rather than the official rate of 33:1. In 1990, the round-trip fare of $775 is still between one- and two-and-a-half-years' salary for an average worker. In some villages in southern Poland where the incidence of temporary migration to the United States is apparently much higher than in Wola Pławska, there are money lenders who specialize in financing American migrations. Interest rates are high, however, and only the relatively well-off seem able to afford it (Bloch 1973). There are no such money lenders in Wola Pławska.

Because the Polish government under the PZPR was concerned about brain drain, skilled workers and those with a higher education were usually denied passports to prevent defections, skewing the frequency of temporary migration toward semiskilled and unskilled workers and farmers whose skills are not highly valued, all of whom usually have low levels of formal education. Farmers who have maintained contact with U.S. kin more easily obtained passports to go to the United States than did workers. If they can produce a written invitation from U.S. relatives and other evidence of close family ties, they will apply to the U.S. consulate in Kraków or Poznań or to the embassy in Warsaw for a visitor's visa, valid for no more than six months. Evidence of family connections in the United States, some indication that the visitor will return to Poland (e.g., a spouse or dependent children and ownership of a house), and a dollar bank account are required by the U.S. authorities. Prior to 1990, the passport was validated by the Polish government only after the U.S. visa was obtained. Now all citizens may possess a valid passport at all times, but, I am told, it is far more difficult to obtain a visa from the U.S. government in this post–cold war era. Judging by conversations I had with prospective "tourists" outside the U.S. consulate in Kraków in 1990, far more are turned down than receive visas.

Once in the United States, migrants often jump the visa, remaining for a year or two working illegally, usually at an unskilled job for a Polish-speaking employer who is careless about the formalities of work permits and deductions. Staying with relatives in cities with enclaves of Polish residents (few migrants learn English), living frugally and saving every penny, the migrant accumulates a nest egg used, upon the return to Poland, to build a barn or a new house in the village or to buy a tractor and other farm equipment.

The U.S. consulate in Kraków issued 6,000 visas to Polish citizens in 1978, most of them to farmers, according to the assistant consul whom I interviewed in 1979. Presumably, approximately the same number were issued in Warsaw and Poznań. Although the consular staff screens applicants carefully, attempting to eliminate those who are likely to overstay the visa, they concentrate on limiting the number who may intend to stay permanently in the United States. Therefore, single men or women with no obvious motivation to return to Poland and entire families will ordinarily be denied. Married men and women, especially if they have children under eighteen, obtain papers only if one partner and the children remain in Poland. The consul estimated that as many as 60 percent of those who actually obtain visas overstay them and work illegally, bringing back to Poland between $5,000 and $10,000 each. According to the consul, the Immigration and Naturalization Service does not make a priority of apprehending Polish "illegal aliens," preferring to concentrate on what it perceives as the far greater problem of hundreds of thousands, perhaps millions, of Latin Americans who cross the U.S.-Mexican border every year to look for work or to escape political violence in their own countries.

Only three households in Wola Pławska had been able to muster all the resources to send a recent temporary migrant to the United States by the late 1970s. Two of them had already left before I arrived in the fall of 1978; the third departed shortly thereafter. Several others went between 1983 and 1990. I do not have information as to how migrants raised the money for the trip, but the possibility of migration was a topic of considerable village interest, and many questioned me closely about the opportunities available in the United States and the pitfalls involved in going there. Many expressed regret that I live in a part of the country (California) in which there is no substantial Polish-speaking community and could not, therefore, be of much help. The younger members of the Nowak family, including Katarzyna and Adam and Helena's younger daughter, Anna, and her husband, Jerzy, for example, would like to establish even closer contact with their U.S. relatives with the aim of being invited to the United States. A number of families asked me to translate letters to non-Polish-speaking descendants of aunts, uncles, and cousins who had left Poland sixty and more years ago. The crux of these often painful letters was that "here we are suffering in Poland and you, dear cousin, aunt, or uncle, have it within your power to help by inviting us to come to the United States for a visit." No one was so explicit in these unsolicited communications as to say they planned to work illegally, but it was made clear that the distant relatives would be expected to help with room and board as well as other services, such as finding their visitors "something to do." Replies were rare and usually equivocal. Nevertheless, there are thousands of undocumented Poles in cities such as Chicago, where in 1986 people told me that in the face of deteriorating economic conditions and political repression, the numbers arriving were, if anything, increasing.

In addition to the three Wola Pławska families that had actually sent migrants, there were nine others who have been in contact with their U.S. relatives between 1965 and 1979. A few kin, such as Michał Nowak, have visited Poland from time to time, leaving behind varying sums of money. Others have occasionally sent small sums (none more than a total of a few thousand dollars over a period of years), much of which was used, as far as I could determine, to purchase goods on the black market, particularly building materials and machinery.

Viable foreign networks, particularly in the United States, are an aspect of both fragmentation and social standing in rural Poland, one paradoxically fostered by the socialist state's involvement in the capitalist world economy. Another aspect of the mounting contradictions, not directly relevant to Wola Pławska, were the incentives given by the socialist government to Americans of Polish descent to retire with their Social Security income in Poland. Retirement checks that barely provided the necessities in the United States guaranteed a luxurious existence in Poland. The government allowed Social Security checks to be mailed directly to special foreign-currency accounts, and withdrawals could be made in either złoty (at a favorable rate of exchange) or dollars (with which one could buy almost anything in Poland). Some eight to ten thousand retired Polish Americans were living in Warsaw alone by 1980 and, according to some informants, were driving up the price of apartments—already scarce and expensive—because they could pay for them in dollars. Now that the black market has been effectively abolished, the living standards of Polish American retirees has presumably fallen. Nonetheless, their retirement checks are still likely to be double, triple, or an even greater multiple of the average Polish paycheck. As long as Poland's development policy remains unchanged and its debt to the West remains at its present level, it will be forced to pursue policies that promote inequality in all realms of life.

The Poor in Wola Pławska

A far less desirable alternative to out-migration in the period before World War II was "going out to service." Daughters went to live and work in the households of gospodarzcy or noble families as domestic servants and sons as stablehands or other agricultural laborers in exchange for subsistence and a meager annual wage—part of which was usually sent home to parents. Alternatively, children went to work permanently on a manor. Unless all other options failed, only bedniki, either the smallest landholders or the landless workers, allowed their children to go into service. The Kogut family, for example, was virtually landless in the early decades of this century. When he was young, the head of household migrated on a seasonal basis to work on Junker domains in Germany. In time, he was unable to continue migrating (because only the youngest, strongest single men had a chance of being hired), so he sharecropped a hectare or two with a larger landowner in Wola Pławska and worked seasonally on the manor in Rzędzienowice. Two of his six sons were also seasonal laborers on the same manor and another followed in his footsteps by migrating annually to Germany. The youngest son went into service in a mountain resort town in southern Poland. All four daughters also went into service as domestics, three of them never returning to Wola Pławska. Janina, who suffered a childhood illness that has left her with a pronounced limp, is the fourth daughter and the only surviving child of this generation. She married into another bedniki family in the village and, now widowed, lives there with one of her sons, his wife, and their children. Janina and her husband received about 2.5 hectares of land in 1947 as part of the socialist land redistribution but were without draft animals and other farm equipment. Janina's husband died a few years later, and the farm was never prosperous. Today, the Kogut farm is smaller than average for the village and in the lower third in terms of total income, in part because of the initial lack of draft power and other capital infrastructure and in part, other more fortunate villagers say, because the family members did not have the skill or knowledge of the land and of farming practices that can only be acquired through generations of farming one's own land. "They simply don't know how to manage," said one of the Nowaks about the Koguts. "They are chłopi." Janina is bitter about her family's history and ashamed of having been a servant. It was only after I had known her for most of a year that she told me some of the history of her family.

Janina's reticence about the poverty of her family is unusual, but her story is not. Władysława Mach, one of twenty-two children, was also a servant, married a field hand from Wola Pławska in 1924, and had eight children of her own, all but one of whom have long since left the village. She and her husband also received a few hectares of land from the state after 1947, the first they had ever owned outright. I asked Władysława why her parents had so many children when they were so poor. "In the old days," she told me, "most of her babies died. Fourteen brothers and sisters died . . . of this and that—maybe not enough food. I don't know. Children were always sick. Lots died of cholera and other sickness. So many babies don't die now. Women are smarter now; they don't have so many babies. People don't need so many children."

Like the Koguts and the Nowaks, the Mach family has also reproduced its class standing. The daughter and son-in-law with whom she lives have a marginal farm that barely provides subsistence; her son-in-law is employed by the gmina for the minimum wage, as a "helper" on the truck that delivers coal. Władysława, her daughter, and granddaughter provide the bulk of the labor power for the farm. Her granddaughter is one of the few young people in the village who has not completed elementary school. A single parent, she participates in the family's farm work in the most desultory way and seems to have no other prospects. By village standards, the family is considerably less respectable than even the Koguts.

The Koguts and the family of Władysława were "ruined" peasants before the land reform of the 1940s awarded them small farms. Moreover, none of their family had ever managed to emigrate permanently. Although they are no longer impoverished, they are poor within contemporary standards; their status in the community is very low and their social identity is chłopi, a term that now has unmistakably derogatory connotations. Some of the current generation of Nowaks, who call themselves rolniki, or farmers, are as well-off today compared to other villagers as they were two generations ago. The difference between the Nowaks and the Koguts was the range of options their landholdings and economic and social standing allowed, for example, working as seasonal agricultural workers versus inheriting farmland and a blacksmith business and skills. The possession or lack of capital of all kinds was expressed in contrasting social identities. The economic capital of the Nowaks was transitive; their accumulation of the one kind allowed them to accumulate other forms and thus to exercise power in the village.

A family's place in the social hierarchy has always been inscribed in choices in marriage partners and other maneuvers associated with "institutional rites" such as the choice of godparents and sponsors for other sacral occasions. These, like immigration and other economic gambits, are also an integral part of the system of strategies of reproduction.[10] As long as the landlord remained the legal owner of all land and exerted control over the labor of serfs, there had been a limited sliding mobility. Thus, marriage between relatively affluent owners and farmhands did sometimes occur in some villages in the (Russian) Lublin area until the 1860s but disappeared in the next generation, after emancipation (Kieniewicz 1969:53). Although the parish records for Wola Pławska for the years between 1787 and 1868 suggest that only rarely did people marry outside their stratum, the numbers are small and, because records for the years 1869–1945 were destroyed during World War II, it is impossible to say if there was any change after emancipation.[11] However, Kieniewicz's own analysis of the rapid polarization of peasants in the Prussian sector of partitioned Poland indicates that marriages between gospodarzcy and the ever-poorer małorolni and bezrolni after 1807 must have been infrequent. Literary and ethnographic sources all suggest that status, dowry, and landholdings were still decisive in marriage arrangements in the 1880s; there is no reason to suspect a lack of continuity with earlier or later periods. The ranking of rural society solidified so that in addition to the ranking within villages, field hands on the manor, the parobcy, had little social intercourse with the skilled craftspersons of the same manor. The craftspeople, by the same token, were ignored by the house servants, who were scorned by the officials who managed the estate. The managers, of course, were hardly the equals of the noble family who owned the estate, but none of the manor workers of any rank were acceptable to landowning peasants. The social and economic hierarchy was virtually absolute, so that "humility toward the superior and arrogance toward the inferior appeared quite natural; no moral condemnation of any kind is attached to them" (Thomas and Znaniecki 1984:134–135).

Social cleavages are suggested in surviving aphorisms. "No dainties for dogs, and no honey for hogs," says one adage referring to social and economic distinctions. The difficulty in moving from one stratum to another is encoded in the proverbs "A dog is barefoot everywhere" and "Where'er the poor man goes, the wind against him blows." In the decades between emancipation and the reconstitution of the Polish state (1848–1918), the loss of land because of the inability to pay indemnification or the need to sharecrop—both common occurrences—marked a peasant's demise as a productive member of village society. It destroyed social and personal integrity and implied social isolation. In describing the wedding of a wealthy gospodarze, a character in *The Peasants*, Władysław Reymont's novel about Polish peasants set between

1880 and 1900, observes "None of your one-acre starvelings were there; nor any of the small fry that eke out their existence by working for others" (1924:18). Well-to-do families would not allow a child to marry a field hand or a domestic servant unless there was something physically or mentally amiss with the child and no better prospects could be found. Love matches between nonequals found little sympathy, even among those of the same generation. All members of the extended family had a vested interest in preserving or increasing the fortunes of the family as all would receive a share. Therefore, everyone was expected to maintain the property of the family and turn it over to the next generation in as good or better condition than when it was received (Thomas and Znaniecki 1927). In addition to ownership of the means of production, there was a certain implicit and not always acknowledged status associated with being a member of a particular class segment that reinforced social exclusiveness and helped to perpetuate social boundaries.

It is hardly original to observe that peasants have difficulty in organizing horizontally in their own interests because of individualism and competition for scarce resources—the image of limited good has currency under conditions of absolute scarcity (Foster 1965). When the grain of society is hierarchical, those at the bottom form unequal coalitions with those above, in the case of peasants, for credit, for the loan or rent of draft animals, and for favors, in return for which they give political support, loyalty, and often labor power. Poor and middle peasants compete with their coequals for economic resources controlled by the better-off and politically more powerful, thus debilitating horizontal grassroots structures. Reinforced by Catholic consciousness that emphasizes idiosyncratic salvation through faith and personal effort, both secular and religious strategies for betterment were individually rather than collectively oriented. Replicated even at the family level, sibling rivalry and competition for favors, particularly from parents who controlled the all-important inheritance, were accentuated (see Benet 1951; Thomas and Znaniecki 1927). Although there are far more options open to young people today and not all who may inherit a farm necessarily want it, it is still the case that those who will inherit take care to marry into a "suitable" stratum.

The 1980 marriage of Stanisław Nowak, grandson of Wincenty Nowak, illustrates the small range within which socioeconomic standing is negotiable in forming a new economic unit. The family has enjoyed a relatively high status for at least three generations. Elzbieta, the bride, was the daughter of one of the most affluent farmers in Borowa. Although she has a brother and several younger sisters, she was designated heir. Her family would not have given her permission to marry a man who would not bring assets to the union as valuable as hers. Even though general opinion in Wola Pławska was that it would have been better for Stanisław to have married within the village and for the new couple to have set up residence there, the match met with village approval. Although Stanisław's family has less land than Elzbieta's, his has comparable symbolic and political power, respectability, influence in the commune, and a long history as prosperous farmers that compensated for their relatively small landholding.

In summary, there were three main groups within the peasant population that crystallized between the official end of serfdom and 1945: the few well-to-do peasants who leased or bought the land of their impoverished neighbors, produced for the market as well as for their own subsistence (often using the hired labor power of their neighbors), and often had craft or artisan shops; the middle peasants, who were primarily subsistence farmers, neither buying nor selling full-time labor power; and, finally, the majority, who had tiny landholdings or none at all and were dependent upon the sale of their labor power. Although some forces tended to level differences among villagers in the intervening years, others were neutral or actually increased them. Thus, there may not have been sharp boundaries between groups, but segmentation into fractions that looked very much like Lenin's rural petit bourgeoisie, middle peasants, and the poor and landless was already well under way in Wola Pławska and undoubtedly throughout rural Poland when World War II began.

NOTES

1. The contrast among the bezrolni and the three final małorolni seems odd unless one supposes they are derived from centuries-old jural distinctions having to do with access to land and labor obligations to landlords. In fact, Kieniewicz (1969:53) cautions that the terms had somewhat different meanings in different parts of Poland and a kormorniki, for example, might have a small plot in his possession.

2. *The Polish Peasant in Europe and America* was published in five volumes between 1918 and 1920. Although the book was written in English, Florian Znaniecki was a native Pole, educated and socialized in turn-of-the-century Poland.

3. I make rather much of what would otherwise be an historical and theoretical footnote because the opus of Thomas and Znaniecki was condensed and reissued in 1984, edited and abridged by Eli Zaretsky. Zaretsky's extensive introduction calls attention to the continuing relevance of the insights of Thomas and Znaniecki for sociology in general and for an understanding of Polish peasants in particular.

4. A gmina is an administrative unit roughly comparable to a township; the commune of Borowa, which takes its name from the town, contains twelve villages including Wola Pławska and Orlów but not Rzędzienowice or Czermin, which are part of the neighboring gmina of Mielec.

5. An obszar dworski is officially defined as a property owing more than 200 *korons* (Austrian crowns, now obsolete) per annum in taxes.

6. From the firsthand observations of Jan Michalowski in *Wieś nie ma pracy* (The village is without work) (Warsaw, 1935), p. 49; quoted in Polonsky 1972:351.

7. Bodnar cites for this statement the original research of Franciszek Bujak in "Wychodztwo zarobkoe w Galicyi, Z. Odleglej i blizkiej przeszlosce" (Wage immigration from Galicia in the distant and recent past) *Studja historyczogospodarcze* (Lvov, 1924), pp. 229ff.

8. I interviewed the U.S. members of this family at length in 1980–1981 in New York City and several upstate cities, cross-checked historical data, and recorded reminiscences so as to contextualize the Polish data. All members of the older generation of Nowaks have since died.

9. These figures have changed in the intervening years, of course, but the proportion is more or less the same.

10. Bourdieu characterizes what are usually known in anthropology as rites of passage as institution rites, which are "consciously or unconsciously aimed at establishing or reproducing social relationships that are directly usable in the short or long term, i.e., at transforming contingent relations, such as those of neighborhood, the workplace, or even kinship, into relationships that are at once necessary and elective, implying durable obligations subjectively felt" (1986:249–250).

11. Thanks to the record-keeping propensity of the Austrian empire in the interest of state, the church records for Wola Pławska begin with 1787 and include births, deaths, and marriages. With the exception of a single volume of marriages that was lost during World War II, they are complete and continuous until the present.

5

You Can't Get There from Here

As World War II drew to a close and the Nazi defeat seemed assured, the Communist party, which formed a provisional government under the auspices of the Soviet Union, was faced with internal legacies of underdevelopment, war devastation, and political cleavages that had to be alleviated before any steps toward a socialist political economy for the new people's republic could be taken. It was also the heir of a theory of political and economic development formulated and imposed from the outside. The initial measures the Party took to restructure society and to construct a new set of social identities more appropriate to socialism were a direct result of its dual inheritance. They also set the stage for the contradictions of later decades.

Socialist Transformation: Stage One

Of the three internal legacies that Poland faced, its lack of development was perhaps most trenchant. The country was far behind Western European capitalist countries on the eve of the war. It was also less developed than many of its soon to be socialist neighbors, especially Czechoslovakia, East Germany, and Hungary. Structurally, socially, and economically Poland was what we might today call a Third World country: Three-fourths of the population was rural and more than 60 percent peasants. Large estates owned by former magnates and szlachta and a few well-off peasants were worked by rural proletarians; much of the grain they produced was exported. Villages were poor and large numbers of peasants faced hunger on a regular basis. The working class was constituted by no more than 15 percent of the people and was politically weak; society was dominated by a small elite class drawn largely from the former aristocracy and the upper segments of the intelligentsia (Vaughan 1971:318–319).

When the Nazis invaded in 1939, between 60 and 80 percent of the capital in the small industrial sector was owned by firms based in more developed countries, mostly Germany and France, and the remainder by a bureaucratic state that cooperated closely with the foreign cartels. The bureaucracy was composed of intelligentsia, the upper ranks of which were drawn from the landed classes and which had a vested interest in maintaining the status quo (Davies 1982:196; Benet 1951:32). Because reforms would infringe on their class interests and property rights, they, like bureaucrats in prerevolutionary France and Russia, were often opposed to land reform, the rationalization of taxes, and other measures necessary for an underdeveloped nation to withstand the encroachments of more developed countries and to modernize (Skocpol 1976, 1979). The limited land reform that was passed in the interwar period was partially motivated by fear of a Bolshevik-style revolution of workers emanating from Poland's eastern borders rather than a concern with social justice (Jackson 1966); it was therefore minimally implemented.

The second legacy was war devastation and population losses (see Douglas 1972:22–32). In all, over six million perished, only 600,000 of whom were direct casualties of war. Although a disproportionate share of the dead were urban, including many of the country's intellectuals and bureaucrats and almost all its Jews, the entire population of a number of peasant villages was also killed, especially along the Soviet border. High compulsory levies in kind were imposed on peasants, who were assigned the task of feeding the Reich, further impoverishing an already destitute countryside. With the nearby Wisła (Vistula) River marking the boundary between the Third Reich and the Soviet Union, the situation of the inhabitants of Wola Pławska and other border villages was especially desperate. In villages that were not destroyed altogether, young and able men were inducted into forced labor brigades by German and Russian armies alike, and the largest portion of farm produce and animals was requisitioned. Men who managed to escape to the forest left women, children, and the elderly to face the soldiers. Helena Nowak's husband, for example, joined the underground. She was terrorized repeatedly by Nazis who subjected her to relentless interrogation. Eventually she fled to the relative anonymity of Lublin with her two tiny daughters, only to return at war's end to find that her brother, three nephews, and two brothers-in-law were facing charges of treason by the new Polish government. Because their farms and houses had been confiscated, for several years after the war Helena and her husband supported three families in addition to their own on a farm that had fallen into disrepair in their absence.

In spite of their undoubted tragedies, the Nowaks were fortunate. Some 2.5 million Poles were sent to forced labor camps inside Germany, and many died there. No one knows how many perished in Siberia or elsewhere in the Soviet Union. Stories are only now beginning to surface as the Soviet Union opens to the public records of the Stalinist period. Half a million Polish farms of all sizes were destroyed, drainage systems were disrupted, and fields mined. The number of livestock of all kinds plummeted; 75 percent were killed in some parts of the country, 90 percent in others. By 1945, 7.5 million hectares of farmland were standing idle (Kostrowicki and Szczesny 1972:13). In the latter days of the war, two-thirds of the mining and industrial plants, half of all power installations, 80 percent of all transportation, and innumerable small commercial establishments and workshops were destroyed by the retreating Nazis. Whole cities, notably Warsaw, were leveled; others suffered substantial damage.

Gunther described the situation:

This concentrated tornado of pure useless horror turned Warsaw into Pompeii. . . . After liberation the Polish government took the heroic decision to rebuild. This was a herculean step, and Poles nowadays laugh about it with a peculiar rough tenderness, saying that the reason must have been their "romanticism." . . . The decision to rebuild Warsaw, and keep it the capital no matter at what cost, was, of course wise—and not romantic at all—in that it gave the patriotic focus and an urgent aggressive faith to the workings of the new regime. . . . Much of this furious reconstruction is done by voluntary labor; most, moreover, is done by human hand. Even cabinet ministers go out and work on Sunday. In all of Warsaw there are not more than two or three concrete mixers and three or four electric hoists; in all of Warsaw, not one bulldozer! A gang climb up a wall, fix an iron hook on the end of a rope to the topmost bricks, climb down and pull. Presto!—the wall crashes. Then some distorted bricks go into what is going up. . . . At one end of a small building may be a pile of dust; at the other you will see curtains in the window. (Enzensberger 1990:133–134)

Although the people's spirits were high, they were not enough in the end to compensate for the third part of the legacy—political cleavage. The Communist party was not in undisputed control of the political apparatuses in 1944 when a provisional government, which also included the Peasant party (PSL) and the Socialist party (Polska Partia Socjalistyczna, or PPS), was formed in the eastern zones liberated from the Nazis by the Soviet Union. The weakness of the Communist party was aggravated by the depletion of its ranks during the 1930s, a result of Stalinist purges that had spilled over from the Soviet Union into the parties of adjoining countries. The Communist party never had large numbers of followers in interwar Poland in the first place, especially among peasants (Korbonski 1965:64), most of whom were loyal to one or another of the peasant parties. The prewar elected government, dominated by right-wing parties, was in exile in London, and the Nazis still occupied the western part of the country. Although the Socialist party had the support of the majority of industrial workers, the working class itself was still quite small. The omnibus PSL, which contained leaders with a range of political philosophies from progressive to reactionary, was the only extant political organization in Poland with sufficient backing in 1944 to have opposed Communist party domination. However, the Communist party co-opted PSL and PPS leaders if possible and strong-armed them if not, eventually imposing new leaders who voted for unification with the Communist party. The PSL was later reorganized as the ZSL, part of the loyal opposition.

Finally, the Communist party had to face a heritage of general suspicion and distrust of the Russians. The 1920 border war between Poland and Russia was one of a long series of conflicts between the two countries; imperial Russia had occupied over one-third of the former Polish Republic for 123 years, ruling with an exceptionally heavy hand. The experiences of World War II—the Soviet Pact with Hitler, the subsequent dividing of Poland between the Soviet Union and the Nazis, the internment of tens of thousands of Poles in Soviet prisoner-of-war camps, the execution of several thousand Polish soldiers in Katyn Forest—all these added further grist to the mill of anti-Soviet sentiments. The Soviets were widely recognized as directors of the activities of the Polish Communist party, and resistance to any political or economic program that seemed to suggest Soviet imperialism was widespread. Still, Soviet policy until about 1954 centered on siphoning off vast amounts of Poland's resources, contributing to anti-Soviet attitudes and making the Polish Communist party's tasks more difficult.

The coalition provisional government had to take all these considerations into account in formulating its early policy. The predominantly foreign-controlled urban and industrial capitalist enterprises were nationalized without event, but the introduction of collectivized agriculture was more problematic. All of the interwar opposition political parties had programs for land reform, but none of them had seriously considered the possibility of a new Communist party-dominated state. Consequently, the land reform program of the interwar Party, until it was disbanded on Stalin's orders, was not different in any major way from that of the Peasant or the Socialist parties (Korbonski 1965:66). By late 1944, when allied victory seemed assured, it was clear to new Communist party leaders that given the war devastation and anti-Communist sentiments in the countryside the Party was not in a position to force the issue of the nationalization of farmland; it simply could not afford the social and material costs. A first step toward the long-term plan to collectivize was meaningful land reform, demanded by peasants for decades. The major question became not *what* land reform was going to entail but *which party* was going to get credit for implementing it and presumably win the political support of peasants, still the majority of the population. Although the reform finally executed by the Communist party had both political and economic aspects, political concerns were primary. In brief, the Party-dominated state had to constitute itself from whatever materials were available.

Public discussion of land reform and the "agrarian problem" at the highest levels of the Party focused on the necessity of a uniquely "Polish road to socialism," not patterned on the Soviet experience. Commentators emphasized differences between the "feudal" conditions of Russian and Polish peasants and the "higher development" of Polish peasant production compared to that of prerevolutionary Russia (Korbonski 1965:93–94). Party leaders repeatedly and publicly repudiated any suggestion that the Party intended to recapitulate the Soviet forced collectivization and denied both the necessity and the expediency of a "dictatorship of the proletariat" in Poland (Korbonski 1965:91–92, 139–140). They finally took the decision that all estates belonging to ethnic Germans and all of over 50 hectares, or 100 in areas where the quality of the land was poor, would be appropriated. The confiscation of land owned by German speakers and their deportation from areas in which they were in many cases the majority provided "Poles" with jobs, promotions, land, equipment, even houses and furniture. The ethnic chauvinism of these measures was a matter of embarrassment and shame to a woman from Wola Pławska, who showed me the deserted and desecrated German Protestant cemetery in Czermin and enumerated to me which "Polish" families had acquired land and houses from former, German-speaking neighbors. Polish speakers with farms of up to 50 or 100 hectares were not affected by the initial measures of land reform because the Party wanted to prevent them from allying themselves with the rich. Even though these farmers were probably sympathetic to owners whose lands were appropriated, they would also expect to fill any gaps left in political and economic power and prestige. Party theorists initially viewed the support of middle and large peasants as essential to the final "stage" of the bourgeois-democratic revolution they regarded as necessary before a socialist transformation of agriculture could be achieved (Korbonski 1965:91).

The land reform that was finally instituted beginning in 1946 was not radical; all the considerable lands of the Catholic church were left untouched, for example, and the state paid expropriated landlords compensation at a fixed rate. Two-thirds of the 14 million hectares confiscated were redistributed to smallholders and the rural landless, with the remainder used to create state farms and a few collectives, mostly in the western and northern provinces acquired from Germany as part of the war settlement. As explained in Chapter 3, the infrastructure for large, capital-intensive farms was already in place there, and most of the dwellers were already rural proletarians, working on large estates (cf. Romanowski 1977:98). The average size of farms throughout the country was supposed to be increased to 5 hectares as a result of the reform, and an upper limit of 5 hectares was set for all newly created farms. Rural overpopulation was so severe in some parts of the country, however, particularly in Galicia, where Wola Pławska is located, that there was insufficient land available to raise all farms to that size. The reform was not expected to increase agricultural production for the market in the short run and, in fact, Communist party leaders recognized that overall production might even decline unless they could provide the new farms with economic aid in the form of implements, loans, and credits—which they could not always do. Even though the government, in an official reply to a United Nations survey, stated that the prime purpose of the reform was to create the largest possible number of economically viable medium-sized farms (Korbonski 1965:94), this goal was almost surely recognized as unattainable in the short run. The land reform did have purely economic aspects. Farmers with middle-sized holdings and rural bourgeoisie had larger surpluses than small farmers, and their marketed surplus product was necessary to prevent food shortages in the critical months at the end of and immediately after the war and to begin to rebuild the war-torn country.

Only a few restrictions were initially placed on peasants; for example, farms could not be sold, divided, or rented without authorization, and the compulsory food deliveries the Nazis instituted during the war continued. In keeping with Lenin's ideal of a worker–small peasant alliance, small- and medium holders were assisted via government-sponsored organizations that excluded the relatively wealthy from participation. Class struggle, however, was given minimal emphasis, and the land reform was a success in terms of neutralizing potential peasant opposition to the Communist party (Korbonski 1965:67–68). Although the land reform supported individual private ownership, Party theorists considered it but a resting place in a projected progression leading to a fully socialized economy.

Even though rural living conditions were still harsh, they had been improving until 1948. The land reform had increased the holdings of the smallest farms and together with rapid industrialization had eliminated the rural landless altogether. Roads were paved and schools built and made accessible to everyone for the first time in Polish history. Rural electrification was begun, gas lines were laid, and indoor plumbing made its first appearance. Many people took jobs in the greatly expanded local industries, especially as inexpensive and regular public transportation facilities were constructed. Others left farming altogether to take advantage of new urban and industrial opportunities. It would be an exaggeration to say that rural Poles prospered, but semistarvation for many and seasonal hunger (*przednowek*) for others was rapidly becoming a memory. Thus, though rural hierarchies shifted because of the land reform and the vagaries of the war, there remained decided continuities with the past.

In spite of Lenin's early dictum about the probable fragmentation of farm commodity producers (1956), Polish Party leaders insisted that the state provide financial aid and equipment, that is, tractors, fertilizers, and other capital inputs, to all farmers regardless of the size of their holdings. In addition, all rural cultivators would have to be convinced of the superiority of collective farming and gradually weaned from their "individualistic" ways (Korbonski 1965:145–149). In other words, early Party leaders argued that socialist consciousness could not be developed until or unless the forces of production were first built. They gave no target date for collectivization but recognized that it would take a long time.

The implicit theory informing the Communist party's early agrarian policy owed more to classic Marxism than to Marxism-Leninism. Classic Marxism implies the separation of politics from economic structures and social processes and hypothesizes inexorable laws that, once set into motion, give a social formation a life of its own. In this view, all levels of social reality, including human agency, will, motives, and consciousness are located in the superstructure and are, therefore, determined "in the last instance" by the society's economic mode of production. Any and every change in the social system, including changes in ideology and consciousness, are said to be caused or at least preceded by change in the economic system. Politics, in other words, do not affect economics. Therefore, if capitalism, for example, because of its structural contradictions, will collapse of its own weight and give way to socialism, political action such as people's organizing around specific issues is *relatively* insignificant to the final outcome. Anti- or nonpolitical action theory has taken different forms among Marxists, from the gradualism of Nikolay Bukharin and the reformism of Eduard Bernstein to the scientific materialism of Karl Kautsky, Louis Althusser, and others.[1] Until 1948 the faction of the Polish Communist party representing a nationalistic version of classic Marxism managed to hold off the Leninists and Stalinists both within its own Party and from the Soviet Union. It eschewed the necessity or desirability of a dictatorship of the proletariat in Poland and emphasized exclusively the rebuilding of the country's productive forces as the first and most important task of the Party.

An alternative view of socialist development, of course, locates politics and particularly political consciousness and action outside of and affected but not directly determined by economic structures. The split between Mensheviks and Bolsheviks in the early days of the Soviet Revolution revolved around this very point, with Lenin and the Bolsheviks arguing that it was not necessary to await the development of the productive forces. Lenin argued that Russia presented two special conditions not covered by theorists of the Second International. One was that Russia was not economically developed to the point where the social conditions of production could inform revolutionary consciousness. Second, the Russian bourgeoisie, weakly developed and ensnared by foreign capital, was incapable of fulfilling its "historic role" of winning a bourgeois revolution that would then permit the capitalist development necessary to set the stage for a proletarian revolution. According to Lenin, however, a long period of bourgeois democracy was unnecessary to develop the productive base as a precondition for a proletarian revolution *if* a vanguard party of revolutionaries was in place and was capable, through its political action, of directing the progressive socialist revolution. By political action, Lenin meant political cadres made up of an elite, that is, the vanguard that was to lead the dictatorship of the proletariat. Lenin's dictatorship assumes control of state power in the name of and to the benefit of the working class, commanding and guiding the revolutionary process. In this socialist stage, class divisions remain, but conscious, active efforts are made to break them down.

Contradictions in Leninist theory and methods of socialist transformation have contributed to the ideological and practical failure of the Bolshevik project throughout Eastern Europe. The mechanical base/ superstructure model and the mystification not to mention the elitism of the dictatorship engendered the domination of society by what eventually became a tiny aristocracy with many of the trappings and functions of a ruling class. The new elite insisted that popular ideology and consciousness (as opposed to the ideology and consciousness of the vanguard) could only be entirely transformed to mesh with altered material conditions and communism after the economic order of society was reconstructed along socialist lines. In other words, ideology, located in the superstructural part of society, is determined by the class position of its holder and antagonistic classes have perforce very different ideologies. However, because ideologues were unwilling to await that reconstruction, they mandated new class locations, by force when necessary. The inconsistencies in Leninist theory between economic determinism versus political action and class struggle allowed Polish theorists on both sides of the issue to quote exegesis from Lenin to bolster their political positions.

By 1948 economic recovery in Poland was under way, the worst of the postwar hardships had been alleviated, the Communist and Socialist parties had merged, and the opposition of the PSL had been neutralized, thus stabilizing the internal economic and political situation and giving the Communist party the dominance it sought.[2] New discussions within the Party hierarchy about the necessity of transforming rural social and economic structures and class consciousness began, motivated, no doubt, by the need to continue to expand industrial production to meet ambitious five-year plans.[3] One way to increase production is to dramatically increase the total number of workers. Only one source for large numbers of new workers existed—the countryside. Coupled with international events, the collectivization campaign in Poland became inevitable as the faction with the closest ideological affinities to Stalin gained the upper hand. Also by 1948, the United States and Great Britain were taking an increasingly aggressive stance toward the Soviet Union; the cold war had begun. At the same time Yugoslavia was beginning to exert its independence from the Eastern bloc. In an effort to draw Poland and the other Eastern European countries closer to Moscow and prevent further defections, the Soviets gave increasing support to the faction of the Polish Party with the closest ties to the Soviet Union—and hence with Stalinist views on the most efficacious way to transform society. That way, of course, was to implement economic and class changes through political action, by force if necessary but preferably through consensus, in other words, through the operation of hegemony.

The Leninism/Stalinism model, some theorists point out, required "displacement" of responsibility for revolutionary action (Laclau and Mouffe 1985; Mouffe 1990) and was, consequently, inadequate to the task of forming and maintaining a hegemonic state with constitutive power that was taken for granted. Western European Marxists recognized that revolutionary activities had to be displaced from the economic to the political after the failure of the Left throughout Europe in 1848. This shift in responsibility, however, did not alter its class location. In Russia, though, because there was no bourgeoisie to build the productive forces, that task fell to a different class. In other words, in addition to being moved from the economic to the political level, revolutionary action was also assigned to another class. Because there was no progressive proletariat, a vanguard Party had to take responsibility for the political, cultural, *and* economic development of the Soviet Union. The Polish case is comparable in that the Polish Communist party had to assume political responsibilities for which the economic ground had not been prepared. But a third kind of displacement was also effected within Poland, that of the task of "development" from Poland and the Polish people to the Soviet Union (Laclau and Mouffe 1985:49). Thus the difficulty of a deliberate transformation in political economy in Poland was further compounded by a displacement of "revolutionary responsibility" from one nation to another. Enacted mainly in the realm of culture and ideology, such development was hampered to the degree that Polish nationalism was historically constituted by anti-Russian sentiments, which were reinforced by the actions of the Soviet Union. The Polish "revolutionary" state and the Polish Communist party faced a challenge they could never meet.

Socialist Transformation: Stage Two

Part of the Stalinist prototype was agricultural collectivization, voluntary or otherwise. Notwithstanding promises to the contrary, collectivization began in July of 1948. The Polish road was abandoned as its leading proponent, then Party chair Władysław Gomułka, was placed under house arrest. In addition to collectivization, strict production schedules, and the priority of heavy industry, the new plan emphasized class struggle through political activism, the revolutionary nature of the "vanguard," the value of work for its own sake, and political and ethical rather than material incentives. The state extended social benefits to workers in the socialized sector but not in private enterprises and especially not to peasants, as agriculture was the main source of accumulation. Income leveling was instituted, and manual workers were favored especially over the bourgeoisie but also over nonmanual workers in the allocation of food rationing and available housing. The educational system was changed to provide privileged access to the children of workers and small (but not medium or large) peasants. Restrictions were placed on the movement of church officials, particularly on Cardinal Stefan Wyszyński; church estates were nationalized on the grounds that they were being used as centers of anti-Party activities and that priests were encouraging peasants to avoid fulfilling compulsory deliveries and to resist the attempts of the state to persuade them to join collectives or give up their land to state farms (Korbonski 1965:204–207).

For the first time in the people's democracy, rural class became a primary issue as Party activists claimed that peasants with larger holdings were contributing to grain shortages by hoarding it for later speculation, buying inexpensively from smallholders in the fall and selling dear in the spring, and failing to pay their share of taxes. They also accused them of monopolizing government credits, buying up scarce industrial goods intended for all peasants, and contributing to inflation by hoarding cash (Korbonski 1965:143). In spite of the plausibility of these allegations (people of Wola Pławska old enough to remember verify them, some approvingly, others not), no one could decide just who the "kulaks" (rural bourgeoisie) were. This was a result of theoretical ambiguity and inconsistency at the highest level of the Communist party about exactly what constitutes capitalist agriculture, socialist agriculture, or even a transition from one to the other. Some defined kulaks only as those who hired labor power; others insisted that it was impossible to define them in such a straightforward way, that the most basic form of capitalist exploitation in the countryside was the hiring out of implements and draft animals. Yet others cited nothing more than the size of landholdings.[4] The ambiguity was never to be resolved.

Equivocation was recast as confusion at the level of local Party bureaucrats who, though politically unsophisticated, were charged with translating theory into practice. Because theory changed rapidly as factions within the national Party apparatus alternately charged one another with "left adventurism" or "right deviations," the task of local activists became impossible to implement. Kulaks were defined and redefined but never with sufficient clarity to suggest a principled course of action. Ultimately any farmer who ran an efficient farm was liable to be called a kulak (Korbonski 1965:185–186). Quotas were given to all households; those who met them had them raised. Farmers with medium holdings made no effort to increase their production for fear of being branded kulaks and suffering the consequences of being denied credit, membership in cooperatives, and access to capital inputs, or, worse yet, being run out of farming altogether, often by brutal means (though the recalcitrant were neither killed nor deported as had been the case in the Soviet Union). Larger farmers divested themselves of legal ownership in any way possible and retrenched their production or concealed it. The more farmers resisted, the more theory fluctuated, and the cruder and more brutal practice became—all in the name of class struggle. Ultimately only 6 percent of all farms were collectivized. Nonetheless, even in areas like that around Wola Pławska where only a few collectives and no state farms were organized, farmers who had originally adopted a neutral attitude became disaffected and anti-Party, antisocialist feeling grew. Agricultural production fell almost immediately after collectivization began and continued to drop during the early 1950s—the first manifestation of the resistance that was to later become endemic and synonymous with a general failure of the socialist state's hegemonic project.

The other guiding principle of the Stalinist period was the maximum increase in the production of heavy industry at what was intended to be the temporary expense of consumption and equal compensation for all. Between 1949 and 1953 industrial production rose dramatically. The early rapid pace was spurred by the exodus of underemployed rural residents streaming into urban areas seeking work. When that source was exhausted, it was given further impetus by the collectivization campaign that forced a million peasants from the land. Industry, however, had not been operating at or even near full capacity until 1953. By then, shortfalls of raw materials, fuel, labor, and capital began to appear (Harman 1974:94–97). The already greatly expanded industrial plant could no longer be supported by what had already been an underdeveloped and undercapitalized agriculture. Moreover, private farmers had cut back or concealed production in resistance to collectivization, and the production levels of collectives and state farms were an embarrassment. Collectives had an output of 83 and state farms 63 percent per hectare of that of private farms (Harman 1974:95). Under a regime guided by Stalinist practices of repression, open dissent was not possible, but passive resistance grew. When the necessary resources for the growth of heavy industry became unavailable domestically, planners, in order to maintain the emphasis on heavy industry, compensated for shortages by further cutting back production of consumer goods and putting the "saved" resources into importing raw materials. Standards of living dropped precipitously, by up to 10 percent according to some estimates (Zauberman 1964:94–97), as supplies of food and other necessities became precarious. Private agriculture, as it had been constituted in the late 1940s, might have provided the raw materials necessary to industrial expansion had not village political leaders, generally the most prosperous farmers (as we saw earlier), been estranged from the Party by the brutality of the Stalinist version of the "class struggle" (Fejto 1971). Peasants resisted the expropriation of their surplus by the Party, just as their ancestors had resisted the requirements of magnates and szlachta overlords. The ranks of the rural population closed around well-to-do farmers and the church as the defenders of private property, individualism, and the ideology of agrarian populism. By redistributing land rather than immediately socializing it, the Party won the short-term allegiance of farmers but in the long run strengthened a stratum of highly individualistic cultivators without a vested interest in socialized agriculture. The measures it did take to raise rural consciousness were sure to alienate the majority, not just the bourgeoisie.

One indication of the alienation of ordinary people was the shift in membership in the Communist party. Although the proportion of Party members who were workers dropped from 62 to 45 percent from 1945 to 1955, and that of farmers from 28 to 13 percent, intelligentsia and bureaucratic membership grew by even larger proportions, from 10 to 41 percent during the same ten-year period (Harman 1974:96).

The revived prestige of the Catholic church is ironic. During the interwar period anticlericalism (as opposed to antireligion) was common, even among peasants, because of the huge landholdings of the church, its support of the rural status quo (it opposed land reform), and the juridical identification of church and state. Regardless of the religious affiliation or lack thereof of citizens, all marriages had to be ratified by the church, for example, and school grades included marks in religion. All but the right wing of the interwar Peasant party regarded the church as a curb on rural social progress and recommended appropriation of church lands and curtailment of the privileges of the clergy as part of a progressive reform. The silence with which the church hierarchy treated the shooting of striking miners by soldiers in 1931 and of striking farmers in 1937 and the passivity with which the Vatican treated the Nazi occupation of Poland exacerbated anticlerical attitudes on the part of most Poles (Deutscher 1981:71; Korbonski 1965:207). Certain postwar reforms such as the secularization of education and civil ceremonies and the land reform had neutralized popular resentment of the church, but the antipathy toward the socialist state, communism, and the Soviet Union, accentuated by events of the Stalinist period, caused former critics of the clerical hierarchy to renew their support of the church because of *its* antistate, anti-Communist stance. The church hierarchy has since repeatedly reiterated its support of individual private property, thus keeping the political backing of farmers. It would be inaccurate to attribute all or even most manifestations of religiousness to these causes; the church did, however, become a vehicle through which many demonstrated their opposition to the state, the Communist party, and the Soviet Union, just as it had in the nineteenth century.

The Polish Road Revisited

Throughout Stalinist Eastern Europe and the Soviet Union, not only were living standards uniformly dismal and work discipline severe but social harmony was falsely maintained through massive and relentless oppression. Stalin's death allowed some of the long-standing but subterranean divisions to come more or less into the open in the Soviet Union. During the ensuing struggle within the Communist Party of the Soviet Union (CPSU), Nikita Khrushchev eventually emerged as leader. At the same time, general unrest was threatening to percolate up from just beneath the surface; it was necessary to take some immediate steps to moderate the rigors of Stalin's regime lest outright rebellion threaten all. Food prices were consequently cut, large groups of prisoners were released, and the hated and feared Lavrenti Beria, head of the secret police, and others were scapegoated and soon executed as "antisocialist spies." Similar divisions and power struggles began to surface in the Eastern European parties before Stalin was in the ground, but citizens of these states did not initially enjoy the same (limited) social reforms, largely because the winners and losers there took longer to sort themselves out. In fact, an uprising by East German workers just after Stalin died in 1953 was put down by the East German army with the help of some 25,000 Soviet troops and tanks.

It was not until after Khrushchev's famous denunciation at the Twentieth Party Congress in 1956 that serious and widespread criticism of Stalin resulted in concrete changes in Eastern Europe. In Poland leaders associated with Stalin and his practices were swept from office as worker riots erupted in several cities. Workers were protesting low wages, high prices, the unavailability of consumer goods, and unbridled repression of civil liberties. Faced with an almost simultaneous uprising in Hungary, the Soviets withdrew their support of the Stalinist wing of the PZPR. Gomułka, with the backing of the working class, farmers, clergy, and a sizable segment of the intellectual establishment, was ushered back into power as Party chair. Restraints on the church were reduced, and Cardinal Wyszyánski was released from house arrest. State censorship was suspended and economic and political reforms were openly discussed and, to a certain degree, implemented—at least initially.

The Polish road to socialism, reembarked upon in earnest, incorporated some of the ideas of market socialism, derived from the writings of the well-known Polish economist Oskar Lange. Concepts of profit, price based on cost and supply, marginal analysis, and scarcity of nonlabor resources were revived. Enterprise autonomy with workers' councils was established. The PZPR reversed its stand on independent village cooperatives and allowed the formation of machinery partnerships. Villagewide agricultural circles that had been disbanded as strongholds of kulaks and agrarian capitalism were revived, and the construction of small and medium tractors suitable for use on private farms was planned. Gomułka promised to end the hated compulsory delivery system, to decollectivize farms, and to allow farmers to expand production at will (Celt 1972:335). At the village level, farmers who had as a group lost the most because of former policies, supported Gomułka wholeheartedly. This support was bolstered by clergy, who were grateful for the lifting of restraints on the church. Some priests actually exhorted their parishioners to vote for Gomułka. There are stories, perhaps apocryphal, of village priests leading their entire congregations to the voting places and threatening to use religious sanctions against those who opposed Gomułka (Korbonski 1965:207).

When decollectivization had run its course in 1957, 82 percent of the land was being farmed by three million landowning households, a number that increased to almost four million by 1968 as farms were further fragmented by inheritance customs (Lane and Kolankiewicz 1973:47). Although collectivization remained the long-term stated goal, the Party henceforth supported "productive" farms, without considering the class nature of their proprietors and, since the 1970s, without considering the size of their holdings. The ideological commitment to an alliance between small farmers and workers ended with the October 1956 plenum of the PZPR. Thereafter, plenums devoted to agriculture concerned themselves almost entirely with issues of productivity and economic performance in general and not at all with class (Korbonski 1965:239). Obstructions to production on large farms were removed, their scale of taxation reduced, and a market in land (albeit with some restrictions) was once more permitted (Lane and Kolankiewicz 1973:44). In short, a Polish version of the Soviet New Economic Policy (NEP) of 1925–1929 was instituted.[5]

The ostensible goals of new agricultural policies were threefold: to reduce rural inequalities, now said to be the result not of class differences but of a combination of "old-fashioned peasant attitudes," outdated technology, and, consequently, the low productivity of small farms (see, for example, Gałeski 1972; Klank 1978); to increase overall production; and, finally, to convert subsistence peasants into surplus-producing farmers who, besides alleviating agricultural shortages, also would help fuel the internal growth of the country by absorbing more commercial and industrial output. Increased productivity would allow greater surplus accumulation to finance industrial development and increased exports, also essential to industrial expansion. Moreover, increased production that would satisfy the consumption demands of the urban working class would also presumably promote the rural consciousness necessary for the elusive socialist agriculture. In short, theorists adopted a gradualist approach to the transformation of farming reminiscent of Bukharin, the early Soviet agricultural theorist who was purged and killed during the 1930s (Cohen 1971).

On the national level the democratic political changes involving the broad base of society were short-lived. The entrenched bureaucracy, unsurprisingly, did not voluntarily relinquish its prerogatives or un-mediated control of the state. Gomułka forged a new power base composed of technocrats, clerics, bureaucracy, and better-off farmers. Workers were gradually excluded from the coalition as concessions to the trade unions and workers' councils were neutralized or eliminated altogether. Once more the vision of a liberating socialism came up against a bureaucratic Party that was able to protect its interests by invoking its imputed esoteric knowledge. Workers and students revolted in 1958, protesting the curtailment of newly won workers' councils with genuine input into enterprise management. But by 1959 many of the old planners had been called back and open dissent was repressed. Dissident intellectuals were isolated and poor farmers and workers had nowhere to turn. Effective power, underwritten by portions of the intelligentsia, was back in the hands of a highly centralized bureaucratic party (Celt 1972:335; Fejto 1971:250–251).

The logical corollary of the Polish emphasis on advanced technology in order to increase production, that is, "modernization," was its recapitulation of the Soviet reliance on highly educated experts incorporated into the bureaucracy, experts who were part of the ideological foundation of the state. Bourdieu would refer to them as the dominated section of the dominating class. They accounted for an ever increasing share of PZPR membership, so that by 1975, 44 percent were bureaucrats whereas only 36.6 percent were workers. In the meantime farmer membership had shrunk to 9.5 percent in 1975 (Shoup 1981:93), dropping to 8.7 percent by 1980 (*Rocznik Statystyczny* 1982:25).

Although the political status quo was restored and industrial reforms nullified by 1959, decollectivization was not abrogated; the regime could not have controlled the workers if civil liberties, political influence, *and* food were in short supply. That, it was assumed, would be the outcome if the collectivization campaign were resumed. Compulsory food deliveries continued, however, and increased farm productivity became the slogan.

There are at least two senses in which increased productivity can be understood: productivity of labor or productivity of land. The former can be increased by lengthening the workday, of course, but also more efficiently by augmenting capital inputs, the latter either by intensifying the application of labor or through the use of fertilizer and certain kinds of technology. Historically, rural overpopulation allowed the intensive application of labor to maintain or increase the agricultural production levels. Now, the exodus to urban jobs and an aging rural population made that strategy problematic. Although technology was to be the answer, the agricultural sector still claimed only 18 percent of the country's capital inputs from 1966 to 1970, and most of that went to state farms. Tractors promised to private farmers were not forthcoming in sufficient numbers. Domestic food supplies were further limited by the continued export of processed agricultural products (including meats), which in the 1960s amounted to 60 percent of the national earnings in hard currency (Fejto 1971:120–121). Agricultural production on privately owned farms *did* rise by about 30 percent between 1956 and 1965, but the increase fell short of the desires of consumers and the needs of the expanding livestock industry. Poland consequently imported 2.7 million metric tons of animal feed annually between 1956 and 1965. Imports remained stable over this period and grew only slightly during the next five years (Korbonski 1965).

Gomułka attempted to keep wages down to the level of food supplies, and living standards of workers began to fall, especially after retail prices were raised in 1968. The economy was on the verge of collapse; real wages for some workers had dropped between 1966 and 1970, and overall Poland had the lowest rate of increase of all the COMECON countries (Green 1977). The centralized planning system, staffed by entrenched bureaucrats, had produced economic chaos in the industrial sector, and the limitations placed on capital inputs available to private agriculture and the compulsory deliveries continued to antagonize farmers. Those that could take steps to mitigate the control of the state did so. Despite legal restrictions on the private sale or transfer of farmland, private land transactions were widespread. According to Lane and Kolankiewicz (1973:75), 39 percent of a sample of such deals between 1957 and 1967 were unrecorded and presumably extralegal.

The number of "peasant-worker" households, the majority of whom have minuscule farms of between 0.1 and 2 hectares, rose sharply during the decade of the 1960s, reaching 14.4 percent of all farms by 1970 (Shoup 1981:269). The maintenance of a farm in conjunction with wage work can represent either a family strategy for survival (i.e., ensuring a food supply) or increasing impoverishment. "Peasant-worker" is not, in other words, a homogeneous category. Farmers who were producing for both the legal state and the illegal private market and some of those who had access to wage labor were able to purchase the limited consumer goods that were available. As the 1960s drew to a close, the standard of living for some fractions of the farming class improved. The net income of farmers as a group increased by about 12 percent, compared to 6 percent nationwide between 1956 and 1965 (Fejto 1971:260). Although their average net income had increased at double the rate of the country as a whole, farmers with the smallest holdings and limited access to draft power had started from a much lower base. Rural improvements were thus far from equally distributed. In general, however, farmers and "peasant-workers" felt the economic crunch of the late 1960s somewhat less sharply than urban workers because a portion of their food supply was home-produced. Knowledge of the plight of urban workers underscored their relatively more advantageous position and, if anything, made farmers even less inclined to acquiesce to any plan for eventual collectivization.

The bureaucracy announced another increase in retail food prices and a rescheduling of wages in December 1970, prompting another rebellion of industrial workers. In many of its essential details, 1956 was replayed. Gomułka was swept from power on the crest of battles in which hundreds of workers were killed by government security forces. He and his followers were replaced by a new set of bureaucrats, this time headed by Edward Gierek. For the second time since the advent of the socialist state in Poland, worker discontent forced a change in the national leadership and consequently a shift in the policies of the government.

The major aim of Party Chair Gierek's policies was to improve the economic well-being of workers and to defuse their discontent and hence threats to the power of the bureaucracy. Gierek therefore immediately rescinded the announced price increases, restructured the highest echelons of the PZPR and state, and promised workers, among many other things, increased standards of living. The policies of the Party and state henceforth represented additional corrections to the three levels of displacement from the classic model referred to above. In other words, the Gierek state undertook to an even greater degree than before the restoration of the primacy of the economic over the political, ordinary people over an elite vanguard, and domestic rather than Soviet direction. That the Soviet model of the Stakhanovite was already counted a failure is symbolized by the immense popularity of the Andrzej Wajda film *Man of Marble*. Set in 1970, it shows how a Polish Stakhanovite hero of the earlier and more hopeful day of the October 1956 revolution is dethroned, his marble statue taken down and stored away in a basement. In early 1990, crowds tore down those other emblems of failed tasks: Statues of Lenin and of Russian soldiers/saviors came tumbling down throughout the country.

Agricultural Policy, Then and Now

But we are getting ahead of the story. In 1970 everyone in the new government formed by Gierek agreed that something had to be done about agriculture. "Our law does not and will not protect private ownership from interference based on progress and social interest," said an Agricultural Ministry official, J. Tejchma in the early 1970s (Romanowski 1977:98). The problem was that "progress and social interest" were poorly defined and often seemed to contradict one another. This is exemplified by a number of contrary policies implemented during the 1970s and 1980s.

By the early 1970s, fully one-third of private farm-owners were over sixty years of age and another 35 percent were peasant-workers. According to agricultural economists, the prime responsibility for farming in peasant-worker households is assumed by women and children, and only crops that meet the household's consumption needs and require minimal labor inputs are cultivated (Ratajczak 1978). As a result, experts say, peasant-worker households and the elderly rarely, if ever, participate in commercial agriculture (Kostrowicki and Szczesny 1972:27). We will empirically examine this observation in Chapter 7 and will see it as problematic, at least in Wola Pławska. The same economists found that even on holdings employing young or middle-age farmers on a full-time basis, the productivity of the land was meager in relation to the outlay of labor (Kostrowicki and Szczesny 1972).[6] In order to raise labor productivity, the bureaucracy attempted to stress capital intensification, preferably in the socialized sectors, first of all by increasing the size and number of state farms. Given the social realities, however, they were forced, sporadically and reluctantly, to try to enhance technology on private holdings as well. Foremost, this meant enlarging them. It translated into unsuccessful efforts to eliminate the tiny, labor-intensive holdings of peasant-workers and attempts to increase the average size and technical efficiency of the remainder by, among other strategies, providing special supports for larger farms at the expense of smaller.

The issue of equipment and who has access to it highlights a shortcoming of this tactic as it has been put into practice in Third World countries. It has been demonstrably the case that the ways in which technology, provided for underdeveloped countries by capitalist agencies and promoted by the governments of those countries, is packaged, financed, or otherwise made available favors already affluent farmers, exacerbating rural differentiation and creating misery for the majority (see, for example, Lappé, Collins, and Kinley 1981). The green revolution as implemented in parts of Asia and Latin America is but the most notorious. The actual technology of the green revolution, designed for peasant agriculture and involving high-yield seed varieties, massive application of chemical fertilizers, intensive irrigation, deep plowing, monocropping, and the use of the latest machinery, may be neutral, and its application does result in overall increases in production in many cases. However, the *social* failures have been spectacular, especially when recipient states systematically distort the availability of fertilizer, credit, and farm machinery such that the larger farmers are able to usurp the benefits, contributing to already existing economic stratification. In some regions where rural inequalities already exist, the transfer of technology for poor peasants has led to an increase in landlessness and poverty. Commercial production for export displaces production for domestic consumption, and rural social relations are increasingly monetized. Among those who earn too little to buy the food they once grew, nutrition suffers. Even those who do not actively participate find themselves with less land to cultivate, leading to overexploitation of the land they retain, ecological degradation, and sharply increased prices for urban commodities (Hewitt de Alcántara 1978; Griffin 1974).

That mechanized equipment was only available to the more affluent Polish farmers and thus accentuated social inequalities was acknowledged by at least some officials (Lane and Kolankiewicz 1973:54), but they were generally ignored. Beginning in the early 1970s, 20 hectares was defined as the absolute minimum desirable farm (Romanowski 1977:112), in contrast to the past, when policymakers sought to curtail the size of individual holdings on political grounds. In spite of potential adverse social costs but in keeping with the effort to eliminate small subsistence and peasant-worker farms, the ceiling on the maximum size of private farms was doubled to 100 (or 200) hectares and "qualified" farmers could obtain credit to purchase land from the once sacrosanct State Land Fund. Only farmers who already had at least 5 hectares of land and had graduated from agricultural extension schools were eligible for credits and loans. These provisions together eliminated at least 70 percent of all farmers. The requirement of agricultural school, entirely reasonable on the surface, defines farming as a skill that can only be learned in an academic (and controlled) environment and transforms the cultural capital appropriate to farming into an exclusive attribute.

Additional policies also offered the larger farmers subsidized credit with terms especially attractive for the construction of farm buildings and the expansion of livestock production and cash crops. In addition to short-term production incentives, higher profits allowed them to purchase chemical fertilizer, construction materials, and machinery. Specialized farms, for example, those that concentrated on dairy, animal production, and plantation crops, were given priority access to supplies of lime, fertilizers, pesticides, animal feed, and coal; price discounts were made available to those who contracted to sell all or most of their produce to the state. Production was thus tied to the official marketing system. By 1979, however, bureaucrats had become worried about the dependence of livestock producers on expensive imported feed grain, some 36.3 million metric tons of which was being imported by then from the United States, all of it to be paid for in increasingly scarce and expensive hard currency. Prices of commercial feed were consequently raised sharply to encourage at least a partial return to domestic animal feed, favoring farmers with the largest holdings but penalizing others.

At the same time, successive five-year plans still anticipated insufficient production of machinery suitable for the use of family farmers. Even though the number of tractors produced doubled between 1970 and 1977, fewer than one-third of them were owned by family farmers (*Rocznik Statystyczny* 1978:236), in part because most tractors produced by the state were too big to be used on any but the largest private

TABLE 5.1   Percentage of Private-Farm Ownership in Poland (in hectares)

	0.5–2	2–5	5–7	7–10	10–15	> 15
1970	26.9	32.0	14.4	14.1	9.8	2.8
1978	30.5	30.2	12.9	12.7	9.2	4.5
1980	30.0	29.5	12.8	13.0	9.7	5.0
1982	29.8	28.9	12.6	12.9	10.1	5.7
1984	30.1	28.3	12.5	12.8	10.3	6.0
Net change	−3.2	−3.7	−1.9	−1.3	+0.5	+3.2

Source: *Rocznik Statystyczny* (Warsaw: Główny Urząd Statystyczny, 1973, 1980, 1984).

holdings. The competition for the few available small tractors was consequently fierce and the price high. Thus tractors remained the exception on private farms. In Wola Pławska sixty-six of the village's seventy-five farms (88 percent) relied on horses or were without draft power altogether in 1978–1979, and nationwide only 8 percent of the private farms had tractors (Central Statistical Office 1978:44–45). Although there has been some increase in mechanized farm equipment in Wola Pławska between 1979 and 1990, it is still relatively scarce. Some farmers use fertilizers and have obtained loans for new buildings, local Party bureaucrats taking delight in exercising informal and officially unsanctioned political power over exactly which farmers received access to loans and scarce technological inputs (Korbonski 1984). By and large, however, only the most prosperous and politically powerful of the family farmers were successful in obtaining machinery and other capital inputs, which further marginalized weaker ones, making them more dependent upon neighbors and kin or driving them out of farming all together. The latter result is not necessarily a negative outcome at a national level if there is sufficient urban employment to absorb the dispossessed; this, however, is not the case in Poland.

All during the 1970s and 1980s, the growth of larger farms proceeded, as can be seen in the statistics that appear in annual censuses (see Table 5.1). Farms larger than 10 hectares grew from 12.6 percent in 1970 to 16.3 percent in 1984. After 1976, statistical sources divided the category into farms of from 10 to 15 hectares and those larger than 15. In spite of intensive efforts to consolidate medium-sized holdings and eliminate small ones, the latter category simply grew from 4.4 percent to 6.0 percent between 1976 and 1984.

Official statistics in Poland, however, present some awkward dilemmas because they are inconsistent in reporting private ownership of land. For example, *Rocznik Statystyczny* reports that in 1970 33.6 percent of privately held arable land was in farms larger than 10 hectares. By 1973 that figure had risen slightly to 34.5 percent, but 1973 is the last year

TABLE 5.2 Percentage of Land in Farms of Specified Size (in percentage of total)

	0.1–0.5	0.5–2	2–10	> 10
1970	0.6	6.3	59.5	33.6
1973	0.7	6.3	58.5	34.5
Mid-1970s	na	6.3	55.4	38.3

Source: Central Statistical Office, Poland 1978: Statistical Data (Warsaw: Polish Scientific Publishers, 1978), 45; Karl-Eugen Wädekin, Agrarian Policies in Communist Europe: A Critical Introduction (Totowa, N.J.: Allanheld Osmun, 1982), 99.

data was reported in that form. Henceforth, statistical sources only show the percentage of total *farms* in a given category, but not the total area in that category. Nor are average sizes within categories indicated. However, occasionally these figures appear elsewhere. For example, Augustyn Woś and Zdzisław Grochowski list the following figures for "the mid 70s": Farms over 10 hectares accounted for 38.3 percent of the arable land, whereas those between 2 and 10 hectares accounted for 55.4 percent and those between 0.5 and 2 hectares only 6.3 percent (Woś and Grochowski 1979, quoted in Wädekin 1982:99). These are the figures used in Table 5.2. It would appear that a minimum of between 4 and 5 percent of the arable land was shifted out of the 2-to-10-hectare range and into the larger-than-10-hectare group; the number of farms larger than 10 hectares grew by 3.7 percent from 1970 to 1984.

Using available figures, I have tried to calculate the average size of farms larger than 15 hectares, wondering *how* much larger they are. The figures are not consistent from one source to the next, however, and official censuses are impenetrable, apparently deliberately so. That the maximum allowable size of private farms was increased from 50 to 100 or 200 hectares in the 1970s but that the largest category in contemporary censuses is still 15 hectares is suggestive. People from Wola Pławska told me of very large private farms of more than 100 hectares in the north and western part of the country. I never personally saw such a large farm, but an agricultural economist attested to their existence in a private conversation in 1979, noting that they were not always officially acknowledged. In the northeastern provinces of Olysztyn and Suwalski, where the land is not particularly fertile, almost 24 and 26 percent, respectively, of the farms have more than 15 hectares, compared to less than 6 percent nationwide and a mere 0.2 percent in Rzeszów, where Wola Pławska is located (Table 5.3). In fertile northwestern provinces, however, between 12 and 16 percent were larger than 15 hectares in 1978. Nonetheless, there probably still are not many farms over 100 hectares nationwide. The point is, however, first, that the average size at the upper end of the scale was increasing and,

TABLE 5.3   Farm Size in Selected Provinces (1981)

	0.5–2	2–5	5–7	7–10	10–15	> 15
Poland	30.0	29.3	12.7	12.9	9.8	5.3
Rzeszów (SE)	39.8	45.9	9.4	3.8	0.9	0.2
Pila (NW)	33.3	17.0	5.3	11.0	18.1	15.3
Olysztyn (NE)	29.1	13.1	3.8	9.7	20.8	23.5
Suwalski	19.3	12.1	5.8	12.0	24.9	25.9

Source: Rocznik Statystyczny (Warsaw: Główny Urząd Statystyczny, 1982), 235.

second, that official sources are ideologically designed to obfuscate rather than illuminate this trend. The Central Statistical Office simply does not gather the pertinent data or present it in a form that could falsify the official claim that "capitalist farms are but an archaic survival of the capitalist era and are declining in both absolute numbers and in influence" (Gałeski 1972:133). This is material evidence to add to my earlier contention that the bureaucracy as representative of the state was either convinced it could ignore evidence of potential class difference based on ownership, did not want to know about it, or even wished to conceal it. Units of analysis define and reify categories and, by collectively representing them, remind us of the ideological underpinnings of the state and of who the subjects of analysis are. In Chapter 6, we will examine the circumstances under which class was replaced as a sociological unit of analysis by strata based on occupational differences and cultural and educational levels. Recondite units of analysis can also be collective misrepresentations.

The Affair with International Capitalism

Between 1970 and 1975, workers' real wages rose by 40 percent, twice the rate of increase during the preceding decade (Green 1977); although real wages continued to climb precipitously throughout the remainder of the decade and into the 1980s, there was an insufficient supply of durable consumer goods on which to spend new discretionary income. Instead, Polish workers spent a larger proportion of their income on food (38 percent in 1978), particularly on high-quality meats. The average consumption of meat soared 12 kilograms per capita to 72.8 kilograms between 1970 and 1978, an increase of 68 percent since 1960.[7] This is considerably more than average consumption in the United States (65 kilograms in 1983, 52.1 in 1989).[8] Polish farmers, however, consumed 1.6 kilograms less than urbanites in the early 1970s, and "peasant-workers" ate 8.1 kilograms less a year than city people (Romanowski

1977:110). Meat consumption became a status symbol having little to do with nutritional requirements. The substantial overall increase was made possible by sharply increasing U.S. imports of feed grain, oilseed, and other concentrated protein necessary to increase livestock herds.

The fuel driving the unprecedented rate of wage hikes and increased consumption was the policy of intensifying industrialization by obtaining large and, in the beginning, low-interest loans and credits from Western bankers (mostly from Germany and the United States) to support the import of both animal feed and advanced industrial technology. Imports from capitalist countries jumped from 26 percent of the total in 1970 to 51 percent in 1974 (National Foreign Assessment Center 1980:95). The idea was to produce for export to the West in order to pay for imports, at the same time raising the living standards of the country as a whole and defusing worker discontent. The leadership was attempting to buy off the workers with material gains and in this way forestall political dissatisfaction. The strategy, however, was predicated on the salability of Polish industrial products on the world market and the continued expansion of Western economies (as well as on the acquiescence of workers); the economic crisis in capitalist countries was not anticipated. With the recession and slump in the mid-1970s and again in the late 1970s and early 1980s, Poland's industrial market, never as large or as prosperous as expected because of the generally poor quality of its products, dried up. Moreover, inflation in the West caused the cost of the already contracted-for imports to soar. Successive plans called for steadily increased exports in an effort to raise the hard currency needed to pay the mounting foreign debt. Rising interest rates on new loans to service the already existing foreign debt made the situation even more critical. Although Western imports were cut back after 1974, declining to 37 percent of the total by 1979 (National Foreign Assessment Center 1980:95), the hard-currency debt almost doubled from $11.5 billion to $21.1 billion between 1976 and 1979 as interest accrued and imports already contracted for had to be paid for at inflated prices (National Foreign Assessment Center 1980:39). The debt further increased to $27 billion by 1981, to $30 billion in 1985 under the new leadership of General Jaruzelski, and to more than $40 billion in 1989. Increases after 1981 came about not because of new imports but because unpaid interest was added on. Economic and political dissatisfactions were not alleviated.

This is the context in which the underground movement flourished and finally emerged publicly in 1980 as Solidarity, ostensibly a workers' union but one that was promptly joined by ten million people from all walks of life. Less well known was Rural Solidarity, the farmers' union formed in 1981. As a group, farmers were silent during the worker uprisings of 1956 and 1970 that brought down two successive governments, and they did not participate in the unrest of 1976 that caused the PZPR bureaucracy to rescind proposed retail price increases. The events of 1980–1981, however, produced a marked change in rural activism. Hitherto, rural resistance had been primarily an individual affair—cutbacks in production, for example, to protest lowered prices, and so forth. 1981 marked the first occasion in which farmers saw themselves and acted as a class in opposition to the bureaucratic PZPR that had been managing the state and that they accurately perceived as having attempted to curtail their independence. Among other things, Rural Solidarity called on the state to endorse the permanence of private farming; to provide private farmers with equal access to all means of production, including a free market in land; and to allow the formation of rural self-government associations. In contrast to demands of workers, many of which were rejected out of hand or canceled when martial law was declared in December 1981, not only were most of the farmers' demands met but none was later repealed. For example, PZPR officials removed existing barriers to the purchase of land from the State Land Fund and promised to channel any increases in fertilizer, pesticide, or small tractor production to family farmers. According to a November 1985 interview with the head of the agricultural department of a regional committee of the PZPR:

> After the crisis of 1980–82, Poland created more favorable conditions for young farmers. It was a turning point. It made private farming profitable. That is one of the main reasons why these farmers do not join the cooperatives. The policy worked out by the Extraordinary Ninth Congress of our party provides equal aid to all segments of agriculture. There is only one condition: produce as much food as possible. . . . The state guarantees the lasting character of the productive family farm (Tadeusz Cygan, quoted in Davidow 1985a:19).

Few of these promises were ever actually realized, not because of ideological opposition but partially because of the notorious inefficiencies in central planning, production, and distribution, and partially because of the dire economic straits of the country, including the need to service the foreign debt. Food shortages in 1982, 1983, 1984, and 1985 were more severe than they had been in recent history. Sugar, meat, butter, flour, and other commodities were actually rationed. The black market flourished. Nonetheless, the commitment to private farming was made— testimony to the state's failure to create socialist farmers as a subject category, the incoherent agricultural policy, the success of farmers in influencing state policy, and dramatic and public indication of their *apparent* social cohesion. Thus, the formation of first Rural Solidarity in 1980 and then the continued activism of at least some farmers all during the 1980s established the precedent for the reemergence of the Polish Peasant party in 1989 and the increasing importance of privately producing farmers as political actors and subjects on the national scene.

NOTES

1. Marx, of course, much admired the productive accomplishments of capitalism. He said that the social relations of capitalism, organized by the very mechanisms of capitalist production, would prove to be its undoing. As consciousness of its dilemma grows as a result of its social organization as a work force, the working class will recognize its unjust deprivation of ownership and organize itself on its own behalf to overthrow capitalism. The revolution was expected to occur first in the most developed countries. Underdeveloped nation-states required a "bourgeois-democratic" revolution to overthrow the remnants of the feudal order and release the energies of the bourgeoisie. Explicit in classic Marxism, developed by the theorists of the Second International, was the assumption that after the bourgeois-democratic revolutions, the national bourgeoisie would develop their societies. Only then could a working-class consciousness develop the potential for a socialist revolution. This mechanistic model of base and superstructure in which the economic base is the motor driving the superstructure required that priority be given to the development of the productive base.

2. The PSL was reformulated as the ZSL in the late 1940s and for the most part was made up of the remaining larger landowners. It ordinarily acted at the behest of the Communist party, at least until it defected in 1989, paving the way for Mazowiecki's election.

3. See Lampland (1987) on the "teleology of the plan."

4. The discussion in Poland recapitulated that in the Soviet Union a generation earlier. There, too, the ambiguity was never resolved. The results in the Soviet Union, however, were ultimately far more tragic than in Poland. The loss of life during the forced collectivization of peasants in the Russian countryside was stupendous. See Lewin 1968 for a comprehensive assessment of the relations between Russian peasants and equivocation on the part of Soviet theoreticians.

5. The Soviet NEP was a period of so-called market communism with a mixed economy of socialist industry, private farming, and small business. Peasants were encouraged to "enrich" themselves in order to alleviate food and raw materials shortages; both private farmers and urban merchants prospered. The NEP ended in the Soviet Union with the beginning of the collectivization campaign in 1929 and increasing curbs on private enterprise.

6. The private sector is still considerably more efficient than the state in the use of labor (Korbonski 1984:82).

7. See Central Statistical Office 1978:64 and U.S. Department of Agriculture 1981:17. Meat consumption declined during the 1980s in the face of overall economic difficulties, and it was in fact rationed for a time.

8. See *World Almanac and Book of Facts* 1985:213 and *World Almanac and Book of Facts* 1990:121. Meat consumption is probably declining in the United States because of concerns about health.

6

Peasants and Farmers in Wola Pławska

THE ERSTWHILE SOCIALIST STATE faced a major set of problems right from the beginning: The need to place a floor beneath which people could not fall and a ceiling above which they could not rise, yet allow supply and demand to influence production and at the same time prevent the emergence of exploitative classes. Party planners, of course, were long aware that policies that increased land concentration and made private farming more attractive might lead to a surge of "non-socialist elements" in the countryside (Gałeski 1963a). That independent, prosperous farmers might develop "bourgeois consciousness," however, was officially rejected at the highest levels of the Party. Augustyn Woś, director of the Institute of Political Economy and Planning and an agricultural economist, for example, denied any possible contradiction between commitment to principles of equality and the retention of farms privately owned and operated for profit. "The younger generation of farmers rely on their *work* rather than *ownership* as a form of material security" (quoted in Goodman and Redclift 1982:22, emphasis added). Private entrepreneurs are neither impediments to socialist planning nor are they, according to one acerbic interpretation of Woś's position, "repositories of individualistic and reactionary values which threaten the successful dissemination of Marxist principles," as Party planners might have expected (Goodman and Redclift 1982:22). Although Marian Orzechowski, former minister of foreign affairs and rector of the Academy of Social Sciences and now the leader of the PZPR minority faction in the Sejm, deplored "the life style . . . and concern with self-interest as opposed to the interests of society of urban small commodity producers," he asserted at the same time that the ongoing consolidation of farms into larger, profit-seeking units was not producing consciousness or practice inimical to socialism (Orzechowski, quoted in Davidow 1985b:15).

121

With statements like this to guide their thinking but also confronted with undisputed inequality, academics have had to search for stratification criteria more acceptable than ownership and control over capital. Tamas Kolosi and Edmund Wnuk-Lipiński, Hungarian and Polish sociologists, respectively, are explicit about the absence of class in Poland and Hungary and its consequent absence in their analyses. "The concept of social status is based on the socio-economic structure since we accept the premise that, in the socialist type of society, traditional class structure has been replaced largely by occupational strata" (1983:6). Kolosi, Wnuk-Lipiński, and other scholars proceed from the premise that class is an individual or at best a family attribute that can be encapsulated by occupation. They then use quantitative methods to isolate the "variables" (age, education, parents' occupation) that account for or retard social mobility, which is, they say, nothing more or less than movement from one occupational status to another or to a different occupational status from one's parents (see, for example, Kolosi and Wnuk-Lipiński 1983; Wesołowski et al. 1978; Szczepański 1973:186–188).

Functionalism, Sociology-of-Development Theories, and Other Dinosaurs

When these analyses are used to examine inequality in the countryside, "the problem" becomes one of contrasts between those who have and those who have not made the transition from farming as a way of life to farming as an occupation (Gałeski 1972:132ff.). With respect to class consciousness and its relation to practice, we have statements like, "the evolution of the class structure in socialist societies involves the gradual standardization of the attitude of various groups towards production and simultaneously a gradual reduction of the part this attitude plays in determining other features of social position and the content of social consciousness" (Wesołowski, quoted in Kolosi and Wnuk-Lipiński 1983:39). In other words, the terms of the debate have been found in, of all places, structural functionalism, with its emphasis on stability, order, and the integrity of the whole or, failing that, on social pathology.[1] The failure of people to adjust appropriately becomes a critique of the disorganized rather than an analysis of the system, and inequality is tautologically reduced to the result of itself.

The parallel between the assertions of Polish scholars that the obsolete lifestyle of peasants is a major impediment to the development of agriculture and the dualistic stage theory of the sociology of development current in Western academic and development agency circles in the 1950s and 1960s is unmistakable. The sociology of development, based on functional theories, has been devastatingly attacked (Frank 1966; Amin 1974; Clammer 1978; Oxaal et al. 1975; Roxborough 1979; Taylor 1979), and few current analysts of development would attribute underdevelopment to behavioral characteristics. Structural functionalism also has been widely criticized as ideological justification for the status quo, albeit with the possibility of a limited internal analysis of change, minor tinkering or adjustment, as it were. This is a task that falls to bureaucrats (see, for example, Giddens 1979; Taylor 1979; Gouldner 1970).[2] Polish scholars within this tradition, like their counterparts in the West, neglect to specify the social and historical conditions under which social structure, class, and class power will either be reproduced or transformed. They fail, in other words, to recognize the social foundations of their own practice (see, for example, Kolosi and Wnuk-Lipiński 1983; Majkowski 1985; Starski 1982). The tendency to take for granted one's own background is in itself an aspect of the habitus specific to the wielders of symbolic power.

If the peasant economy is really an aspect of an archaic lifestyle that needs to be converted to an occupation, the conservative, present-oriented, tradition-bound, subsistence-motivated, nonprofit emphasis of poorly educated and ignorant "peasants" that impedes development of the forces of production and the formation of socialist ideology (see, for example, Klank 1978; Ratajczak 1978) must be changed.[3] The mission to correct "maladjusted" peasants and to instill (I use the term advisedly) in them modern, urban values; the desire for modern farming techniques; and presumably socialist ideology was to be achieved (besides by means of agricultural policy) through schools, media, and cultural activities. This suggests another parallel with structural functionalism, namely, with the sociology of education theorists who regard socioeconomic status as dependent primarily on level of education rather than the level and content of education as part of class identity.[4] Critical alternatives that view educational systems as one of the means by which the structure of society is reproduced and children socialized into occupying a given class position have no visible currency in Poland.

That Polish social scientists have sustained a paradigm that is, first of all, long outdated and superseded in the West and, second, was especially characteristic of the most politically conservative of Western theorists, coincides with their prolonged embrace of the sociology of development and is evidence that unanalyzed continuities persisted during the putative "socialist period" between the conservative social relations of the presocialist past and those of the socialist period itself.[5] It is not especially useful to characterize blind adherence to the dictates of dogma—the mechanical equations, the unthinking application of inappropriate developmental models, even the structural functional world view—as simply politically inspired myopia. The normative vision or Communist ideal is a free and equal society in which there are no dominant and subordinate classes. Critical social science attempts to determine the conditions that sustain asymmetrical relations of power with the intention of providing the knowledge that can assist the realization of the ideal. Polish (and Soviet) leaders long assumed, however, that they already led "advanced socialist countries," as they began to call themselves during the Brezhnev era, countries in which class antagonisms had been overcome. They viewed their own societies as ones in which the elements constituting class in a capitalist system could not logically pertain, as an avowedly socialist political economy was already in place. Therefore, the leaders repudiated the necessity of class struggle and turned away from an internal critical analysis. The predominance of the neopopulist world view; of sociology-of-development theories, with their emphasis on modern versus old-fashioned; and of functionalism, with its emphasis on equilibrium, is explicable only if we understand that many scholars long assumed there would be no more basic structural change. The revolution, such as it was, was over. Problems of residual stratification and inequality had to be individually constituted and solvable as technology and science advanced and industrialization and new economic opportunities arose. Indeed, it was expected that sufficient industrial production to eliminate material scarcity would cause the disappearance of alienation. That is why industry was preferred over agriculture since the beginning of the socialist period in Poland (and elsewhere in the Eastern European countries). But the emphasis on industrialization at the expense of agriculture entailed a paradox. Gouldner notes that a form of mechanical, deterministic Marxism "emerges when the contradictions inherent in a commitment to increasing productivity intensify; that is, when an increasing division of labor is seen as both the source of a hateful alienation and, at the same time, of an increased productivity that is prized precisely because it will supposedly remedy that very alienation" (1980:187).

These contradictions in Poland were also driven by the state's need to accumulate substantial wealth from its own agriculture rather than that of, for example, (nonexistent) colonies. As long as Polish scholars were able to view their society as one in which the destination of socialism had been more or less reached, then private enterprise and even the apparent contradiction of increasing differentiation among farmers could be ignored or read as insignificant and in no way impeding progress toward greater industrialization and rationalization of their economy—and hence of the goal of socialism and eventually communism. A more cynical interpretation is that functionalism and the sociology of development served and continues to serve a conservative political/ideological agenda and has helped to perpetuate existing social differences.

In addition to structural functionalism, there are also undercurrents of unresolved, purely political (rather than economic) Leninist practice to be found in agricultural policies that have been implicit since the failure of the collectivization campaign. The observation of Włodzimierz Wesołowski and K. Słomczyński that "in socialist countries, economic decisions derive from political decisions, and therefore, transformations of the class structure are also largely due to political decisions" (1977:4) can be read as it was intended, as an explanation for initial placing of former workers or peasants in managerial positions. But it can also be taken as justification for the use of bureaucratic measures to obviate the saliency of private ownership and production for profit as a basis (albeit partial) of class consciousness and practice without overtly perverting Marxist theory and practice. "The economic policy of a socialist state has effective instruments to prevent the development of non-socialist characteristics among its farmers" (Tomczak and Niemczyk 1977:unnumbered). These "instruments" were government agencies directed from the top that, by interfering with and exerting control over the production and distribution decisions of private farmers, were to prevent the emergence of the consciousness and especially the exploitative practices associated with agrarian capitalism. In other words, nonsocialist proclivities among farmers were avoidable if their livelihood could be made contingent upon decisions of policymakers rather than their own individual incentives. According to this formulation, *control* is the prime shaper of production relations.

Control as a Class Marker

The theory of state control begins with the farming household itself. In the domestic mode of production, the head of the household was said to need a diverse set of skills that could be acquired only with formal training. Because the very nature of domestic economy and the lack of occupational expertise contributed to low production, it followed that various experts, employed by the state, should make major decisions and advise farmers, thereby providing a social division of labor according to occupational specialty and contributing to the continued socialist transformation of agriculture. It was expected that under the guidance of the experts, who were now in control of farming expertise and knowledge, capital investment would increase, cultivators would seek more agricultural training to better fulfill their role as general managers, there would be more farm specialization, and greater production would ensue. The specialization and greater production would in turn ensure that farming as a domestic economy would become less feasible, as more of the former functions of the peasant household were taken over by the societywide division of labor that was institutionally mediated by the state (Gałeski 1972:134–150). The landowning peasant became a farmer, a cog in the wheel of the agricultural production process—a sort of proletarian with land, a farmer by occupation under the enlightened control of the state. Because the socialist state asserted that it had control over private production and agricultural knowledge, the status of farmer depended upon an occupational definition; ownership of land was no longer regarded as a primary criterion of class. If there were no class, there could be no class conflict, nor could the rural population become fragmented into antagonistic segments.

This ingenious (perhaps disingenuous) argument encouraged family farmers with the largest holdings to augment them, in the name of Marxism, at the expense of those with smallholdings. Further, it gave institutionalized privileged status to farmers who sold to the state. As this process unfolded, the new farmers, who acquired the land of their former neighbors, produced a surplus for the use of the entire society (see also Brzóska 1977; Hunek and Rajtar 1977; Tomczak and Niemczyk 1977; Klank 1978). Theorists of the 1980s approvingly note "indicators" (such as participation in cultural activities outside the village) that the professionalization of farm work had begun and that farming was rapidly assuming the features of a trade rather than a way of life (Kolosi and Wnuk-Lipiński 1983:44).

John Berger, in his poignant description of a French peasant beleaguered by his state's efforts to thrust "modern" technology upon him, captures the essence of a process that seems almost universally to penalize the poor:

On top of the hay, he again explained the machines to himself. They make sure we know the machines exist. From then onwards working without one is harder. Not having the machine makes the father look old-fashioned to the son, makes the husband look mean to his wife, makes one neighbor look poor to the next. After he has lived a while with not having the machines, they offer him a loan to buy a tractor. A good cow gives 2,500 litres of milk a year. Ten cows give 25,000 litres a year. The price he receives for all that milk during the whole year is the price of a tractor. This is why he needs a loan. When he has bought the tractor, they say: Now to use the tractor you need the machines to go with it, we can lend you the money to buy the machines, and you can pay us back month by month. Without these machines, you are not making proper use of your tractor! And so he buys a machine, and then another, and he falls deeper and deeper in debt. Eventually he is forced to sell out.

Which is what they planned in Paris (he pronounced the name of the capital with contempt and recognition—in that order) from the very beginning! Everywhere in the world men go hungry, yet a peasant who works without a tractor is unworthy of his country's agriculture! (Berger 1979:81–82).

It is both ironic and prophetic that the new capitalist-oriented government has similar agricultural and social goals for farmers. Rather than creating socialist consciousness, however, the state hopes to free up the rural entrepreneurs who have been hiding beneath the surface of the conservative and old-fashioned "peasants." To paraphrase the rhetoric of the present leadership, it wishes to enable the most forward-thinking, the most hardworking, and the most enterprising among them to produce enough to feed the nation (and support an aggressive export policy). In short, there is no room for backward peasants who are tied to their land and their outdated technology but only for modern farmers dedicated to the principle of free enterprise and individual achievement. The agricultural and social policies of the new government are, as far as one can tell, intended to realize many of the same goals of the socialist government in precisely the same way the previous government set about achieving them.

A sketch of Wola Pławska between 1978 and 1990 with some of its material conditions and attitudes of its inhabitants will allow us to assess, in a preliminary way, the claim that only residual conservative, "old-fashioned" ideas and practices impede productive farming and the furtherance of socialism or, alternatively, productive farming and the furtherance of capitalism. Thus sketched, the drawing can be compared for its fit to the picture provided by officially sanctioned sources and idealized by much of the rest of society, including farmers themselves. The efficacy of state control over farming decisions will be taken up in Chapter 7.

Are We All Equal Here?

As I walked along the main road through Wola Pławska in the autumn of 1978, an old man driving a farm wagon pulled by two horses stopped when he came abreast. He beckoned. "Are you the American, the one who wants to know how we live here? Do you know about Katyn Forest? Do you know what *they* did to us there? They are not our friends (*przyjaciele*) and we don't want them or their kind here, not [then Party Secretary Edward] Gierek, not the Party. We are gospodarzcy. We are all gospodarzcy." *They* are the Soviets and Katyn Forest is the location of the massacre of several thousand Polish military officers in the waning years of World War II. The Soviets blamed the Nazis. No Polish history book refers to Katyn Forest, and official acknowledgment of the Soviet role only came after the change in the government in 1989 and as the result of the persistent demands of the Polish opposition. Nonetheless any Pole could have recounted the story prior to 1989; there was long an unofficial memorial in a Warsaw cemetery on which fresh flowers were anonymously placed every day for years; each day they were as religiously removed, presumably by state functionaries. Most Poles always believed that the Soviets killed the officers because they were loyal to the anti-Communist Polish government in exile in London and would have hindered the establishment of the alternative Soviet-backed government that was in fact eventually declared on 22 July 1944 in Lublin. Few, however, would publicly discuss their convictions in 1978, especially with a relatively unknown foreigner such as myself, making the old man's comments to me particularly noteworthy. In spring 1990 the Soviet government itself finally admitted publicly and officially that Soviet troops had indeed been responsible for the death of the soldiers.

By invoking the Katyn massacre in his first encounter with me and telling me that everyone in the village was a gospodarze, the old man encapsulated several themes that dominated village relations with the state until 1989. First, villagers are pervasively anti-Soviet, a characteristic shared by most Poles, if popular accounts are to be believed. The farmer's use of the term *przyjaciel*, literally, "friend," was significant. Between 1948 and 1956 especially, the Soviet presence in the internal affairs of Poland was palpable. The dignitaries of the Polish Communist party took to referring publicly to the Soviets as *nasze przyjaciele*, "our friends," in ways that Poles understandably found offensive. Since then the word has had a somewhat pejorative meaning and may be used either to refer ironically to the Soviet Union or to suggest that someone is a bogus friend. Many now prefer the term for "colleague," *kolega*, to denote a friend. Second, the old man was implicitly asserting that the people of Wola Pławska are not ignorant peasants who take the official version of history at face value. Third, he was the first of what were subsequently many Wola Pławskans to tell me that "we are not Communists here, we are farmers." That the two are mutually exclusive was usually explicit, always implicit. Finally, he asserted the essential unity and equality of all village residents with his use of *gospodarzcy* to describe them. Of course, we have already seen that historically few of the residents of Wola Pławska were independent, landowning, draft-animal-employing farmers, as gospodarzcy are defined. However, an alternative version of history and social location, born of opposition to the Party, the socialist state, and the Soviets, has emerged in the village as well as in the imagination of new government leaders. This is an invented tradition of independence and self-sufficiency. The "facts" thus present a theoretical and a methodological issue as we attempt to document and account for the lack of resonance between the ideology of the state, past and present, and its spokespersons with respect to the nature of village farming and rural development and that of actual local ideology and class relations.

The inhabitants of Wola Pławska claim a shared world view, regardless of the size, wealth, or success of their farms. Much like the populism that dominated nineteenth- and twentieth-century rural philosophy and politics and that is explicitly anti-Communist, this essentially neopopulist view assumes the symbolic and practical unity and equality of all farmers on the one hand and their fundamental antipathy to socialism on the other. The ideal is the autonomous household that controls its own resources, including its land and its labor power. Symbolic linkages notwithstanding, that status is one most seek, many claim, but few attain. Let us examine the distribution of land and other resources, material and symbolic, in Wola Pławska.

There are seventy-eight houses containing eighty households. Households consist of those individuals (invariably family members) who live in the same dwelling, cook and eat together, and contribute farm labor, wages, or both to the group. In contrast to two and three generations ago, the majority of households in Wola Pławska, like those in other contemporary Polish villages (Bloch 1973; Skreija 1973), are composed of nuclear families. Forty-two (52.5 percent) contain only parents and offspring, whereas another nineteen (23.8 percent) include a widowed grandparent of either sex. Eighteen (22.5 percent) are three-generation stem families, more common now than in nineteenth-century European communities (Anderson 1972), presumably because people now live longer. Three of the stem families also include a divorced son or daughter and in one case the child of an unmarried woman. Only one household could be characterized as that of an extended family, but this is a situation of temporary expediency in which two of the married children and their spouses are awaiting housing in Mielec, where they work. Another young couple alternates between this same household and that of the woman's parents.

Kinship is bilateral. According to early sociological sources, relatives to the fourth degree of collaterality are regarded as "family" and deserve loyalty and material and immaterial help at all times (Thomas and Znaniecki 1918, 1:87). Now, however, the household is an autonomous unit of production and consumption. If a tendency toward patrilocality can be discerned, it is because even though historically both sons and daughters inherit land in this part of Poland, there is a strong bias toward bequeathing land to sons and household goods and livestock to daughters (Thomas and Znaniecki 1918, 1:87). Villagers say they are even more likely to confer land on males after its partitioning was prohibited by law in 1967 in order to prevent further parcelization of already highly fragmented land. Male inheritance, though, is far from universal; I know of several recent cases in which women have inherited all their parents' land. As discussed in Chapter 3, historic reasons for maintaining family solidarity, that is, as a way of resisting labor demands from landlords, have not been relevant for over a century, and most farms are already too small to be further split. Consequently, few children are likely to acquire them, and the economic rationale for village endogamy, once the ideal and usual practice, has largely disappeared. The ideology informing inheritance is, however, continuous with the past: All are expected to marry at the same or higher socioeconomic status of their own household and bring goods and productive means of more or less equal value to the partnership.

All but five of the households in Wola Pławska now own their own land, many of them as a result of the land reform that began in 1946, and all but these five cultivate crops to a greater or lesser extent. The five that do not farm include the three elementary school teachers, two of whom (the principal and vice-principal) live with their families in apartments above the school. The third teacher and her husband, a bus driver, occupy a separate house, as do a retired couple who turned their land over to the State Land Fund in exchange for a pension because they were without heirs. A woman who separated from her husband also lives alone in a house. As nonfarmers, these families are peripheral in varying degrees to the social and economic life of the village.

Many of the landowning households contain members that combine wage labor with farming. Of the 202 economically active members of the community, defined here as able-bodied men and women between eighteen and sixty-five, ninety work for wages, mostly though not exclusively in the socialized sector of the economy.[6] Villagers who farm in addition to having wage employment are called "peasant-workers" in the Polish sociological literature and are among the farmers both the former socialist and the present state would, because of their reputed low productivity, like to eliminate by incorporating their land into that of the larger farmers. We will have more to say about them presently.

Some observers have commented on a surge in prosperity in rural areas since the late 1960s. James Morrison, for example, asserts that "the peasants have become the wealthiest group in Poland" (1968:114); similarly, Tamara Deutscher claims that "the Polish state has allowed the peasant standard of living to increase more than any other layer of

TABLE 6.1   Distribution of Private Landownership (in percentage of total hectares)

	0.5–2	2–5	5–7	7–10	10–15	> 15
Wola Pławska[a]	26.6	52.0	18.4	14.0	0	0
Poland	30.0	30.5	13.1	12.8	9.2	4.4
Rzeszów	39.8	45.9	9.4	3.9	0.9	0.2

[a]N = 75.

Source: 1979 village census; Rocznik Statystyczny (Warsaw: Główny Urząd Statystyczny, 1978), 23.

society. . . . TV aerials adorn rural roofs while peasant children go to the universities and technical schools, abandoning the villages for good" (1981:70).

These observations, however, must be placed in perspective, for such rural prosperity is far from universal. The farms of Wola Pławska are still predominantly small or medium in size; the largest is just under 10 hectares, the smallest 1 hectare, and the average 3.4 hectares. Although it contains fewer very small farms of between .5 and 2 hectares than the national average and no larger farms of more than 10 hectares, Wola Pławska is probably not atypical for a Polish village in this part of the country (see Table 6.1). Like many parts of Poland, land fragmentation continues to be a problem. The 200-odd hectares of arable land within the confines of the village and another 100 hectares located in adjoining villages but owned by Wola Pławskans are divided into some 400 separate plots ranging in size from .01 to 5.67 hectares. The individually owned and cultivated fields are separated by very narrow grassy strips (some as narrow as 20 to 30 cm) called miedzi. It is easy to give credence to informal estimates that 15 percent of Poland's arable land is made up of miedzi. Every bit of land is fully utilized; little girls, for example, who for generations have been responsible for tending cows as their first farm chore, graze their charges on the miedzi.

Primary crops are sugar beets, potatoes, mangold (a type of beet fed to livestock), and other roots, as well as wheat, rye, barley, corn, oats, and hay. Some farmers devote part of their acreage to "specialties" such as cucumbers, poppy seeds, and broad beans, and all households maintain a garden in which they grow cabbage, tomatoes, cucumbers, radishes, onions, and garlic for home use. A few have tiny apple or cherry orchards, but the total land given over to tree crops is less than 1 hectare. Fruit not used by the household is sold to other villagers or at the jarmark in Mielec. Virtually every household has at least one cow and a pig and raises poultry for domestic consumption, for the jarmark, or for both. A number of households raise swine or dairy cows commercially and most sell milk. The range of ownership of livestock

TABLE 6.2   Livestock Ownership and Sales in Wola Pławska, 1978

	Minimum	Maximum	Mean	Standard Deviation (% of Mean)
Swine	0	35	6.5	69
Cattle	0	28	4.9	98
Poultry	0	80	24.0	70
Sales per hectare	0	90,430	23,334	70
Total sales	0	97,100	83,070	96

Source: 1979 village census.

and sales to the state is surprisingly large in a village with such a small range of landholdings (see Table 6.2). Compulsory farm sales were eliminated in 1972, but in 1979 there were still incentives, such as the coal allotment, to induce farmers to market to the state.

Although the coal allotment has since been abolished, the way in which it operated is illustrative. A metric ton of coal is far below the bare minimum for the most frugal household to heat and cook for a year. In order to be eligible to purchase more than a tonne of coal at a state-subsidized price, farmers had to sell a certain amount of their produce to the state. A year-old pig, for example, fulfilled the prerequisite. Those who could not or chose not to sell to the state had to pay a higher price for their fuel. Farmers considered the rationing of coal not only ludicrous—Poland is the world's second largest producer of soft coal—but a particularly galling example of what they regarded as the state's arbitrary exercise of power over their lives and, because much of Poland's coal production was (and still is) exported to the Soviet Union, one of the many ways in which that country exploits Poland.[7] In spite of their resentment of the state apparatus in general, most of the seventy-five farming households in Wola Pławska marketed a portion of their produce to the state procurement agency in Borowa in the late 1970s, some on a substantial scale.

One need not be in Wola Pławska very long as a participant observer to note that, in spite of undoubted material advances since 1945, there are dramatic differences in living standards among households and individuals in terms of lifestyle, ownership of consumer goods, and consumption patterns. Men and women attired in some version of the latest European fashion can be seen on the village road or waiting for the bus alongside others in the ubiquitous *chusta* (kerchief) and flowered shawl or in worn and faded work clothes and boots dirtied with manure. (In contrast to rural people in the southern mountain regions of the Podhale, however, nobody in this village or this area wears a "traditional" costume, even for festive occasions.)

Variations in housing were also obvious to the most casual observer in 1979 and have not changed in the ensuing decades. Seven of the farmhouses (less than 10 percent) are new, two-story brick structures with indoor plumbing and central heating. They generally contain the modern electrical appliances: a refrigerator, washing machine, possibly even a stereo with a tape deck. One of the few cars owned by villagers, not a new or a large one, but a car nonetheless, may be parked outside. A guest may be seated at a table set with fine linen, china, and crystal and be served costly refreshments, including meat and the best vodka. At the other extreme are a handful of old (well over 100 years), two-room cottages built of hand-hewn timbers; the last dwelling with a thatched roof—unoccupied for some years—collapsed during the winter of 1979, but a few similarly roofed barns are still in use. Only one-third of the houses have running water; the sanitary facilities for the remainder are located "behind the barn," water must be hauled from the well and laundry hand-scrubbed in the yard. Although all houses have electricity, few have refrigerators or other appliances, and the coal cooking stove in the kitchen and another in the second room provide the only heat. Perishables are lowered into the well in warm weather.

Turning to production techniques, one notices immediately that many farmers in Wola Pławska rely on the equivalent of late nineteenth-century U.S. farming technology. Nonetheless, the most cursory look also reveals variation among households. Arriving in the village for the first time during the summer harvest season, I saw men cutting grain with scythes and women following, gleaning with sickles, while not 200 meters away a harvester combine was in use. A few old farmers still thresh wheat with a flail (two poles joined by a leather throng) whereas others have the use of gas-powered threshers. Some were taking their harvest to Borowa in tractor-drawn wagons, others had only a horse and cart, and a few were without draft power altogether. In short, the initial impression of Wola Pławska is one of glaring material inequalities. Visits to nearby and distant villages reveal the same differences.

A point that must be kept in mind as we proceed with our description of Wola Pławska is the size of landholdings in this village. Given the relatively small size and narrow range (1–10 hectares), we might expect less of a tendency toward inequality here than in Polish villages in general. The degree of disparity in terms of ownership, access to and use of means of production, and capital inputs is, therefore, surprising. Thus, if we find that land and other means of production are an important element not just of socioeconomic differences but of growing class fractionation in Wola Pławska, they are likely to be even more significant in other parts of rural Poland where there are concentrations of larger farms and historically more disparity among landowners.

Some of the poorest farms in Wola Pławska are owned and operated by the elderly or by the few unmarried household heads. Overall, however, there is no correlation between age and landownership, livestock, house construction, tractor ownership, or the education of household members over eighteen. Nor is there a simple relationship between age or education and farm sales, taken as a proxy for the material success of the farm, or between full- or part-time farming and productivity. Thus, the younger or better-educated full-time farmers (those theorists would identify as "farmers by occupation") are not necessarily the more successful—a notable finding because age, education, and occupation are often seen by Polish social scientists to account for differences in productivity (Gałeski 1972; Gałaj 1965). In short, the small, poorly equipped households and farms are not necessarily the loci of old-fashioned, "traditional" means of farming, nor are they owned and operated solely by the elderly or by part-time farmers.

All but eight of the farming households, including all of those containing part-time farmers, marketed a portion of their produce in 1978 via the official market; a few of the largest producers sold products worth Zł .5 million whereas others yielded only Zł 3,000 to 4,000. Larger farms generally increased their official sales from 1977 to 1978, some of them substantially, while the sales of smaller ones remained stable or fell. Further, the data suggest that farm size is directly related to ownership of other means of production and to differences in productive practices. The correlations between landholding size and tractor ownership, and landholding size and number of cattle owned are .58 and .64, respectively, with smaller but significant correlations between landholding size and sales per hectare, the number of swine, available labor power in the household, and the use of capital inputs such as chemical fertilizers (nitrogen-phosphorus-potassium, or NPK) and lime needed to correct the soil's pH balance (see Table 6.3).

It is not surprising that landownership is a major factor in accounting for other means of production. There is, however, no relationship between landholdings and the elaborateness of houses or consumption patterns. For one thing, the owners of larger farms tend to accumulate capital and invest in their farms rather than purchase consumer goods. But landholding does appear to correlate with influence in the public domain. Even though some of the smaller farms have high living standards and are thriving enterprises as measured by sales per hectare to the state, it is those with large farms who wield the greatest share of both economic and political power in village and regional affairs. The variable glossed as political influence, defined as the ability to procure a necessary agricultural input in a time of national scarcity, approaches but is just short of significance ($r = 0.23$), indicating that the larger the farm, the

TABLE 6.3   Correlations of Important Variables[a] (N = 63)

	Sales (per hectare)	Land
Tractor	.43	.58
Cattle	.27	.64
NPK per hectare	.34	.36
Lime per hectare	.47	.38
Sales per hectare	1.00	.27
Swine	.44	.36
Labor power	.09	.34
Political influence	.41	.23

[a].25 is significant at .05 level.
Source: 1979 village census.

greater the influence, but that other considerations, such as sales to the state (r = 0.41), come into play. Public influence and economic viability facilitate access to the scarce capital inputs, for example, tractors, chemical fertilizer, and fodder for livestock production, that in turn pave the way for entry into the lucrative black market, especially but not exclusively the market in meat. Note the large and apparently anomalous contrast between the correlation of cattle and sales to the state (r = 0.27) and cattle ownership and land (r = 0.64). The figures for sales per hectare do not reflect milk sales, accounting for what appears to be an aberrance, but the figures also reflect only sales to the state, not unofficial sales. The issue of black marketing will be taken up in Chapter 7; for the moment it is sufficient to note that official sales to the state account for only a portion of many farmers' production.

It is difficult to see clear-cut patterns of economic differentiation based on land ownership alone. Although land is important and there are significant differences in production because of it, it is an insufficient criterion of class and economic power. Furthermore, if we take the formal hiring and selling of labor power as a crucial diagnostic of class relations, there is no apparent class structure in place. Nobody in the village claims to receive any part of his or her income from farm labor, nor did any farmers say they hired labor. Yet if villagers generally say "we're all equal here; we all face the same worries, the same problems; we all work hard," they are also aware of political and economic differences based on both ownership of productive means and the power that is associated with it. They are equally aware, as we shall see, that a cause and consequence of this disparity is that small farmers who lack adequate draft power or machinery of their own must depend upon unequal labor exchange with larger farmers or must rent equipment from them.

This sensibility is encoded in the honorifics Pan (Sir) and Pani (Lady), the use of which was once the prerogative of the szlachta but now extends to everyone. *Pan* and *Pani* are generally used in the village as terms of address to those who are neither kin nor close friends or neighbors. However, they are applied as terms of reference for only a handful of village residents: the director of the school and her spouse, the other teachers, and the farmers who wield or are perceived as wielding power. The few farmers who are regularly referred to as Pan or Pani are the largest landowners who also own most of the village's few tractors, forklifts, and other modern farm equipment. All other farmers are usually referred to by given or surname only (unless sarcasm is intended, but this is no different in Poland than in many other places).

Since dividing the farmland was proscribed, noninheriting children have had to seek their fortunes outside the village (although there are many cases in which villagers circumvent the inheritance law). Seventy-seven percent of men and women in the village between the ages of twenty and thirty-five are employed for wages outside of it. Wola Pławska had but one or two university graduates in 1990 and none in 1978. They as well as many of the high school graduates *have* left the village, as Deutscher charges (see above). The majority of the village's employed have found little more than semiskilled work; the children of farmers do not enjoy the same advantages as those of intelligentsia, bureaucrats, or even workers. According to a professor of education at the Polish Academy of Sciences with whom I talked in 1979, "a Marxist-Leninist state is dedicated to redressing generations of class disparity. Children of farmers (and workers) are supposed to have privileged access to educational facilities." Nonetheless, the professor observed that rural youth are particularly underrepresented in secondary schools, technical institutes, and especially in higher education. Moreover, village schools throughout the country are inferior to urban schools, and those in working-class neighborhoods inferior to schools attended by the children of upper-level bureaucrats and Party members. It is noteworthy, in this respect, that none of the teachers in the Wola Pławska elementary school has more than a middle school education.

Although another cornerstone of Marxist-Leninist theory is the superior value of the productive worker, everyone is aware that "mental" work is more highly rewarded financially and is more prestigious than either farming or the unskilled and semiskilled jobs that most working villagers have, partly as a result of the historic role of the intelligentsia in defining social value. Recall that the category of "intellectual worker" first appeared in the interwar censuses. Villagers are embittered by the juxtaposition of institutional devaluing of their productive work and official eulogies to production and by the privilege, status, and material reward that bureaucrats, the quintessential nonproducers of value, enjoy. As J. Fiszman points out "Education is indeed a mark of status [in Poland], along with

TABLE 6.4   Educational Levels of Rural Children (in percentages)

	Poland 1970	Wola Pławska 1978
None	7.2	4.8
< 7 years	45.2	40.1
8 years	42.0	37.5
Trade	3.1	14.7
Secondary	1.9	2.9
Higher	0	0
Unknown	0.6	0
Total	100.0	100.0

Source: Paul Shoup, *The East European and Soviet Data Handbook* (New York: Columbia University Press, 1981), 253; 1979 village census.

family background and socio-economic position as it affects one's ability to pursue the 'good life.' The educational structure itself is highly differentiated, with lines of demarcation between status and prestige" (quoted in Dziewanowski 1977:289).

This relationship has not changed in the almost twenty years that have intervened since Fiszman's observation. Władysław Majkowski notes that farmers have moved as high as they can on the prestige scale without further dramatic advances in their educational level. "In Poland, no other advantage can guarantee more prestige than education" (1985:128). Moreover, in spite of the prevalence of the works of Marx and Lenin in higher education, few well-educated people admit to being Marxists in any theoretical (or practical) sense. Of course, with the change in government in 1989, anything and everything associated with Marxist thought of any kind has fallen into disrepute. The works of Marx and Lenin have been removed from the curriculum of public school and university courses. Just as significantly, other critical scholars may also fall into disrepute.

Returning to the issue of educational levels and comparing the figures for Wola Pławskans with the national figures (see Table 6.4), we find that the people of Wola Pławska seem to be slightly better educated than "peasants" as a whole, especially with respect to trade schools.[8] No Wola Pławskans who have reached school age since 1945 are totally without schooling; in fact, almost everyone born prior to 1939 has at least completed elementary school. However, surprisingly few who still live in the village have more than the obligatory eight years (raised to ten in 1980); those who do are either the teachers, their children, or are from the handful of families that have been the village elite for generations. Poland, like most societies, has some degree of intergenerational mobility, thereby reducing social perceptions of class differences.

Nonetheless, in Wola Pławska as throughout Poland, the educational apparatus contributes to the reproduction of class and social location as well as cultural and social capital, not unlike school systems elsewhere in the world.

Moreover, the content of school curriculum in history, for example, though critical of the power and influence of prewar landed classes, pays no attention to the dynamics of contemporary class stratification in villages, nor to the ways in which the ideas and ideals of elite classes permeated the practice of the state throughout history—and certainly not to the way they continue to do so today. Nationalism is a recurrent theme except when Polish-Soviet relations are under discussion. Yet the works of Marx, Lenin, and Stalin were ubiquitous until 1989. The version of Marxism taught, in other words, was the most rigid, the most deterministic, and the most orthodox. Contemporary critical and neo-Marxist historiography was (and, I think, remains) rare or nonexistent not only in village schools, which is to be expected, but also apparently in university curricula.

The relatively larger number of Wola Pławskans than in the general rural population with a trade school background is remarkable. First of all, the rubric *trade school* includes institutions teaching such technical specialties as electronics as well as more mundane skills; a trade learned by a village resident is more likely to be upholstering than computer technology. The most likely explanation for the large number of trade school graduates is the proximity of WSK, the transport factory in Mielec that is the area's largest employer. It originally drew its employees mainly from Mielec. Until 1947 only one villager from Wola Pławska worked there, and he boasts of poling across the river in a flat-bottomed barge and then riding a bicycle 10 kilometers to the far side of town where WSK is located. In conjunction with the expansion of the factory after World War II, several vocational schools were commissioned to provide training for prospective employees. Area villagers were able to commute, first to the schools and then to the factory. Almost all the forty-seven residents of Wola Pławska who worked at WSK in 1979 were semiskilled employees earning between Zł 4,000–4,500 a month, close to or less than the 1978 national average of Zł 4,500. Villagers typically still hold jobs as upholsterers, joiners, or stitchers. The other wageworkers in the community also have primarily semiskilled or unskilled jobs such as those of retail clerk, baker, tailor, laborer, truck driver, or bus driver. Thus, even though most wageworkers from Wola Pławska appear to have few highly valued skills, in fact they have relatively more than "peasants" in more remote districts.[9]

There is some variation in how wage earners define themselves occupationally. Mired in the lower echelons of the working class with virtually no opportunity of joining the privileged ranks of management and bureaucracy, some regard their present employment as but a stopping place before they assume total responsibility for a farm now headed by their parents. In the interim, their jobs provide income funneled mostly into the farm, and contacts acquired in the industrial sector facilitate access to scarce inputs. Others, whose households lack sufficient land and other necessary means of production and potential access to them, do not expect to farm on a full-time basis but keep their land as a hedge against food shortages and as a means of asserting autonomy from the state. Many identify primarily with farming rather than the fully proletarianized working class because landownership is one of the few available means by which they can at least partially maintain autonomy.

The model for most villagers, the norm from which all others depart, whether they work for wages or are full-time farmers, is the successful, independent cultivators of the village—the entrepreneurs who produce enough both for the family needs and for either the state market or what became the increasingly significant and lucrative black market. By virtue of their success, these farmers demonstrate dominance over life circumstances. This ideal, or "peasant essentialism" as constructed by would-be and never-to-be "peasants," is antithetical to the "socialist person" who works unstintingly for fellow citizens and for society. It is consequently symptomatic of (but does not define) the failure of the hegemonic penetration of socialist identity. Indeed, the ideal of the fully autonomous rural producer is emblematic of a counterhegemony that is taken by villagers as an unanalyzed given of human nature.

The Church and Other Ways of Asserting Autonomy

Far from showing almost mindless attachment to land for its own sake, a characteristic with which "traditional peasants" are often charged, villagers see land as the means through which an encompassing value is expressed, namely, control over labor power, time, one's very existence. Control is a means of expressing individual autonomy, in the past from the landlord and in the contemporary context from state and employer and even from "the family," broadly defined. One's personal integrity and social integration into the village is measured by the ability to successfully manipulate the social and physical environment. Someone is thus not fully a member of the community, regardless of age or other status, until or unless that individual heads a farm.

The ineffable emphasis on independence and autonomy resonates with features of village life that might otherwise be inexplicable or reducible to hard-headed conservatism. Not the least of these features is Catholicism, identification with which symbolizes incorporation into a collective self in opposition to the collective other—in this case a vague other that encompasses "the state," "the bureaucracy," and "the Party" but is not exactly coterminous with any of them. In fine, "others" are all those who seek to curtail the autonomy of "the farmer," especially his or her control over labor power, land, and surplus.

Thus, the symbols of Catholicism—not outwardly diminished by decades of Communist condemnation, and possibly reenforced by it— remain part of the social fabric of Wola Pławska, as indeed they do throughout Poland. Village boundaries are marked with roadside shrines; crucifixes, portraits of Mary, the "bleeding heart of Jesus," and votive candles adorn almost every house. It is not uncommon to be greeted, especially by the elderly, with *Niech Będzie Pochwalony Jezus Chrystus* (Praise be to Jesus Christ), to which one responds *Na Wieki Wieków* (World without end). Each day is the feast of a particular saint, specified on the religious calendar that hangs in every kitchen. Virtually all Poles, urban as well as rural, are named after saints—many of whom have long since been dropped from the ecclesiastical panoply; name days rather than birthdays are always celebrated. Weddings, baptisms, first communions, and confirmations are marked by elaborate rites and festivities. The first communion, taken at age seven when children are said to have reached the age of reason and can distinguish right from wrong, and confirmation, a rite in which baptismal vows taken on behalf of infants by their sponsors or godparents are affirmed by the children themselves in about their thirteenth year, are the most important rites of passage for children, far overshadowing graduation from school, for example, or other secular events. For the first communion, children are dressed all in white, miniature versions of wedding attire, complete with veil and flowers for the girls. For a full year preceding the event itself, the children receive religious instruction from the priest. Following the ceremony, the families of the celebrants provide a feast for kin and neighbors who bring gifts to the child. It is not uncommon for domestic preparations to begin months in advance and even include painting the house and other renovations in honor of the occasion. Weddings are always solemnized by the priest in a church ceremony and similar but even more elaborate parties—usually lasting two days—are given. Contrasts between the weddings and first communion parties of the long-established well-to-do and the poor (or nouveau riche) are textbook examples of class markers.

Actual piety and depth of religious sentiment are difficult to gauge, but until 1989 it was apparent that for at least some villagers, participation in such ceremonies was a self-conscious manifestation of resistance to attempts by the socialist state to exert control over peoples' lives by limiting their autonomy. As such, Catholicism exerted a counterhegemonic force, rivaling institutional ideology (a paradoxical shift in the historic relations between church and state in Poland). Apart from religious significance, therefore, having one's child baptized or receive first communion was also a palpably political act symbolizing intransigence and self-assertion to Party and non-Party members alike. For those few for whom overt religious activity was politically suspect—village officials and the few members of the Communist party who are also farmers—religious celebration was conspicuously and sometimes hilariously surreptitious. Marrying or having one's child baptized or receive first communion in a distant church was, for a Party member living in a village of farmers who prided themselves on noncompliance with state directives and programs, a way of affirming village solidarity in spite of Party affiliation. Such clandestine religiosity was an open secret in Wola Pławska in which everyone colluded to some degree. ·

Ubiquitous Catholicism—nominal and actual—takes additional and more straightforward forms. Even though weekly fasts have not been mandated by the Vatican since the early 1960s, virtually all rural Catholics (that is to say, almost everyone) continue to abstain from meat on Fridays as well as observing the still obligatory fasts during Lent. Traditional meat- and fat-free Lenten dishes, a broth of soured rye grain and water, for example, are ceremoniously prepared and consumed. Holy Week, Good Friday, Holy Saturday, and Easter Sunday, in particular, are fervently observed with special food, flowers, rituals, and numerous and lengthy church services. However, all religious feasts receive prominent notice, in rather striking contrast to such national socialist holidays as May Day and Polish Independence Day, which were studiously ignored in the village itself other than in the elementary school.

Schools, consciously organized as part of the "ideological apparatus" of the state, heavy-handedly promoted socialist events and attempted to "instill" socialist consciousness and practice as part of mandated curriculum. That this aspect of the curriculum coexisted with a glorification of Polish history and nationalism is just one more of the many contradictions. During 1990 there was considerable discussion in the newspapers about ways in which "traditional values," said to be lost to society over the past four decades because of the Communist educational system, can be restored. As a first step in this direction, religion—removed from the public school curricula in the 1940s in what has been branded a leftist act—has been restored in the classroom. The religion to be taught is Catholicism, of course. Throughout the decades of socialism, middle and high school students marched with their classes in May Day and Independence Day parades in Mielec, as did contingents of workers in socialized industry, especially those few with supervisory jobs who were prevailed upon to set an example for others. The religious celebration of the Virgin Mary in the village, however, conspicuously competed with May Day celebrations.

The commemoration of International Women's Day (8 March)—an overtly socialist occasion—was long ago transformed through popular participation into a combination of Mother's Day, National Secretary's Day, and Valentine's Day. All women are given flowers, candy, greeting cards, and small gifts by husbands, bosses, sons, lovers, and coworkers in a celebration of womanhood. The emphasis on womens' contributions to society that was originally intended seems to be totally absent.

The "old priest," as the villagers called him, a man in his mid-eighties in 1979, had been the pastor of the church shared by Wola Pławska and Rzędzienowice from its construction in 1927 until his death in 1983. A live-in couple looked after the pastor's personal needs and, with the help of four nuns who lived in a small convent in Wola Pławska, maintained the church and the rectory. Of peasant background, the old priest could often be found puttering in the garden or tending his bees. The "young priest" (actually between forty and forty-five) rented rooms in the house of a farmer in Rzędzienowice. The two shared ecclesiastical duties, the younger giving weekly religious lessons to the adolescents preparing for confirmation and the old priest and the nuns instructing those awaiting first communion. Except in his official chores, the young priest seemed to interact with villagers on a less regular basis and was less popular than the old priest. Coming from an urban area, he was regarded as more of an "outsider." The influence of the clergy in village affairs seemed as pervasive in 1990 as it was in the presocialist countryside. The old priest, in particular, was privy to almost everything that happened in the village for two and a half generations. Arbitrator of morals, family life, sexual practice, child rearing, and village conflict; dispenser of justice; and giver of advice, both formally from the pulpit and informally in daily interaction, his opinion was sought or offered on every conceivable topic, not excluding the national political system.

After the death of the "old priest," a replacement arrived, and the "young priest" was subsequently transferred to another parish. As vehemently anti-Communist and committed to the rights and prerogatives of the individual over the collectivity, the sanctity of private property, and the necessity of bowing to the will of God in the distribution of material resources (presumably as they were allocated prior to 1944), the new priest, like his two predecessors, contributes substantially to the disregard with which the basic assumptions of socialism in general and the PZPR in particular are held. The election in 1978 of Karol Wojtyła, cardinal and bishop of Kraków, to the position he now enjoys as Pope John Paul II, enhanced the power and prestige of the Polish church, especially after Wojtyła paid his first visit as pope in June 1979. Hundreds of thousands turned out to pay homage, and villagers articulated what was a general sentiment in Poland, namely, that the new Polish pope was going "to show" the Party. Theirs was a demonstration of the power and prestige of the Catholic political world view that had been publicly expressed for the most part in ostensibly religious terms since the 1950s. Indeed, the adulation with which the pope was received gave massive voice to hitherto stifled opposition to the political and social dominance of the Party.

Thus, in spite of the material progress of the period between 1945 and 1990, much of which is attributable to the social revolution instituted and maintained by the socialist state (progress that no one denies), the social ethos of an earlier era has been largely reproduced. This ethos embodies the values and rhetoric of independence and individualism and is echoed by church doctrine assigning more or less personal responsibility for salvation (though not to the same degree as Protestantism). The claim that one could only get "proper" care from a private physician or could buy the best clothes or the best meat, building materials, fertilizer, and so forth and receive the best service from employees and proprietors in private stores and the assertion that private farm production for profit is superior to socialized agriculture became part of a routine condemnation of all aspects of socialism, at least as it was put into practice in Poland.

Private also equalled prestige, and anything imported from the West has long been the most prestigious of all. To buy privately, especially for dollars, denoted yet another level of autonomy because it signified that one had not been "coerced into buying what bureaucrats, in their wisdom, chose to produce," as one Wola Pławskan put it. The conflation of private with prestige and prestige with the West allowed those who could afford it to exercise the power and convertibility of symbolic and economic capital at the same time they resisted Party and state.

Many generalized their invective against state socialism to include anything vaguely associated with socialism or communism anywhere in the world. These attitudes had a certain poignancy in late 1990 as the system of socialized medicine was being dismantled. Even with its not inconsiderable warts, the system tried to address the basic needs of all citizens. People now say that they cannot afford to be ill; one woman speculated about a return to home-delivered babies,[10] and young people say that they are postponing marriage because they cannot afford to furnish a house or have children.

To be sure, hospitals were overcrowded and supplies and drugs, particularly imported ones, were in short supply in the late 1970s (a situation that became critical after 1980, when the balance of payments made most imports prohibitive). People often bemoaned the slow service and the cavalier manner of medical personnel and lamented the paucity of private physicians, complaints symptomatic of pervasive sentiments regarding the efficacy and superiority of individual over socialized enterprise. With the institutionalization of a system of small bribes to ensure good treatment, however, poor service and poor attitudes became self-fulfilling prophecies.

Consumer benefits were notoriously unequally distributed in socialist Poland. During the Stalinist period of "accumulation," most people lived at subsistence levels while only the top members of the Party could frequent the special stores in which desirable but scarce goods were distributed. These stores were behind closed doors, and though ordinary people suspected their existence, few had any firsthand knowledge of them. That changed in post-Stalinist years of limited decentralization and "market socialism."[11] Although a market-driven distribution system was not implemented to the same degree in socialist Poland as in Hungary or Yugoslavia, after 1970 the Polish state did attempt to quell worker discontent by, for example, stepping up imports from the West. Income differentials, gradually increasing supplies of consumer goods in ordinary stores, and the proliferation of private enterprises with usually more expensive goods intensified both the perception and the reality of economic inequality.

In order to siphon off excess purchasing power in the late 1970s, the state opened "commissaries," meat shops with high-quality cuts available in almost unlimited supplies at twice the price of meat sold in ordinary stores. Many consumer goods, including those only purchasable with foreign currency in the PEWEX stores, were priced out of the reach of ordinary workers and farmers. Only highly paid middle- and upper-level Party bureaucrats, technicians, and, ironically, farmers and workers with family members in the United States or farmers who produced for the black market could afford certain items.

There was never a socialist "culture" in Wola Pławska in the sense of a shared vision of a classless future. Farmers (and here I mean all farming households) identified themselves in terms of their opposition to the bureaucracy—surrogates for the socialist state—creating a we-them dichotomy that, because of a common antithesis to forces that threatened their autonomy, subsumed potential or real differences among the farmers themselves. The claim of the theorists of the socialist state that rural consciousness was "really" socialist because farmers derived their satisfaction from their work rather than ownership of land turns out to be illusory. Land continued to be the most celebrated value in Wola Pławska because it implied control over labor and surplus, independence, and autonomy from the state. The additional official claim that the farms of the elderly and so-called peasant-workers were producing less food and other agricultural products than the needs of the nation demanded had a certain validity. Nonetheless, this generalization glosses over notable differences among farmers that were not based on either age or occupation. Charges of conservatism seemed to be just another way of asserting that farmers were resistant to the inroads of socialist consciousness and practice. Further, at least in Wola Pławska, where antisocialist, anti-Communist sentiments were widespread and freely expressed, any assertion of a fundamental ideological difference between "socialist" and capitalist farmers cannot be substantiated.

NOTES

1. Because of my status as visiting scholar in Poland, I often had occasion to attend lectures in sociology at the Jagiellonian University in Kraków. I was surprised to find Znaniecki and Thomas, Malinowski, Radcliffe-Brown, and other functionalists regularly referred to as leading contemporary theoreticians. Gouldner (1980) discusses the prevalence of functionalism as a theoretical paradigm in other Eastern European countries and the Soviet Union.

2. Bell (1962), for example, attempted to demonstrate that prostitution, crime, and gambling in the United States only *appear* to be social pathology; in fact, he suggests, they conform to ordinary, acceptable U.S. business practice and consequently have the "latent function" of furthering free enterprise.

3. Some theorists also describe "peasant agriculture" and "peasant economy" as perhaps internally consistent but an anachronism in the modern world (see, for example, Majkowski 1985; Hann 1985); critics and dissidents blame farmers' relative lack of productivity on state policies of regulation and control over pricing and capital inputs as well as sometimes deliberate obstructionist practices of local Party bureaucrats (Korbonski 1984).

4. See Giroux 1983 for a critical review of recent work on the sociology of education, as well as Willis 1977 and all the work of Bourdieu.

5. Worsley (1984) discusses the structural functional underpinnings of Eastern European scholarship at length.

6. Historical accounts of household economics in Poland assume members under age fifteen and over fifty-nine are not productive (Kochanowicz 1983:155). I have used boundaries of eighteen and sixty-five because in contemporary Poland most children are in school until eighteen and those under sixty-five are generally economically active.

7. A joke current in Poland in 1979 had Soviet Union Party Secretary Leonid Brezhnev meeting with newly installed Chinese Premier Deng Xiaoping to discuss peace and new cooperation between the two countries. "What can the Soviet people offer to our Chinese comrades to demonstrate our sincerity?" asks Brezhnev. Deng thinks a moment and then asks for a bushel of wheat for every man, woman, and child in China. Without hesitating

Brezhnev agrees and asks what more he can do for his Chinese brothers and sisters. "A tractor for every state farm would be helpful," answers Deng. "It is yours, good friend, and is there anything else?" Brezhnev asks. "Yes," Deng concedes, "I would like a bushel of rice for every man, woman, and child in China." "Absolutely impossible," snaps Brezhnev, without hesitation. "I don't understand, Comrade," says Deng. "You are willing to give wheat and tractors to the Chinese people in the name of peace. Why not rice?" "Ah, Comrade Deng," replies Secretary Brezhnev, "you have forgotten that rice does not grow in Poland."

8. All "peasants" are included in the national sample whereas those for Wola Pławska include only those living in the village at the present time.

9. The concept of "skill" is ideologically loaded, defined as it is in industrial societies as something that people must sell. If it is not salable in the current marketplace (like the social knowledge required to know when to cultivate, plant, and harvest, or the knowledge women need to run a complicated household), then it is not a "skill."

10. Universal hospital births attended by a doctor would not necessarily represent progress in many Western circles (Martin 1987). In Poland, however, home birth with a midwife would be regarded as old-fashioned.

11. See Rakovski's (1978) penetrating analysis of the class effects of economic reform and market socialism.

7

Class Stratification in Wola Pławska

A KEY OBJECTIVE OF THIS STUDY is to demonstrate, first, that class has never ceased to be relevant to people's daily lives in Polish villages and, second, that a process of class fragmentation was under way during the "socialist era." The latter resulted and was manifest in a discernible rural hierarchy of class fragments with opposing interests. In other words, relations among different kinds of households in Wola Pławska are now part of a system of differentiation that is not predicated upon personal characteristics such as "modern" and "old-fashioned," as many Polish scholars would have it, or even upon landownership alone, though both are germane. The ownership of draft power and other means of production is also salient to class location but inadequate to distinguish households with sufficient draft power from those with insufficient means of production given other factors, such as available labor power, age, degree of land fragmentation, and access to fertilizers and other inputs that require both a cash flow and a farm of minimal size. Thus, it is clear that no single attribute is an adequate criterion of proto–class membership. It is equally clear that there are alternative ways in which social and economic relations among households and relations to the land and wage labor are expressed and that must be taken into account.

Demographic Differentiation or Class Fractions

The differentiation of farming households into "rural bourgeoisie" who enter the market economy using the labor power of others in addition to family labor, "middle peasants" for whom commodity production is not highly developed and who neither buy nor sell labor power, and

147

"poor peasants" who hire out their labor power locally to the rural bourgeoisie or are seasonal migrant workers was part of what Lenin called the American road to agrarian capitalism (Lenin 1956; Rochester 1942). In the American form of agrarian development, small farmer households become capitalist producers if abundant cheap land and suitable technology are available to replace scarce labor. There is not yet a completely free market in land or adequate technology in Poland for a fully capitalist American farming system to develop. The *process* Lenin theorized, however, may be applicable to contemporary Poland, but, because of the absence of plentiful inexpensive land and the presence of ample labor, it may unfold in a retrograde form.

Using household surveys and descriptive statistics, I have separated the eighty households of Wola Pławska into five groups, four of which farm, depending on land ownership, availability of labor power, and the other attributes listed in Table A.1 in the Appendix. The groups have dissimilar ideologies with respect to farming and their role in it, national politics, and a number of other elements of daily life. Formed in the family, in the village, in places of employment, and in class-mediated rural culture, ideology also has a material existence seen in the routines, rituals, and social practices that structure and mediate day-to-day activities and interaction within the village and with state institutions. The material aspects of ideology are also embodied in farming practices, the use of space, building materials, and choice of where to put scarce resources. The four farming groups are hierarchically ordered for some but not all purposes. The major question to be asked of the data is how completely power relations among groups have caused them to crystallize into unambiguous strata. Of the eighty households in the village, seventy-five own land and farm to a greater or lesser degree.[1] The five landless, nonfarming households are discussed in the context of village social organization but are excluded from the statistics described because most of the analysis pertains to economic relations among farmers.[2]

The groups are named, rank-ordered, and defined as follows. *Subsistence farmers* (Group 1) own land, receive little or no cash income from sales to the state, and have no cash income from wages. *Worker-farmers* (Group 2) are households in which the male head of household has full-time, nonfarm wage employment whereas other "workers" (able-bodied household members between eighteen and sixty-five) take primary responsibility for farm work. *Farmer-worker* households (Group 3) are those in which the male head of household is a full-time farmer, but others also have income from full-time, nonfarm employment that they contribute to the household. *Commercial farmers* (Group 4) are households in which

TABLE 7.1   Stratified Groups-Analysis of Variance[a] (N = 63)

	Gp 1 (N = 6)	Gp 2 (N = 19)	Gp 3 (N = 20)	Gp 4 (N = 18)	Probability Value	Total Mean
Farm size[b]	1.7	2.2	4.3	5.3	.00	3.70
Average plot size	0.5	0.4	0.5	0.7	.01	0.53
Lime per hectare	28.0	104.0	125.0	147.0	.01	115.00
Tractor	0.0	0.0	0.1	0.4	.00	0.14
Cattle	2.5	3.2	5.5	7.6	.01	5.10
Sales per hectare[c]	6.4	17.6	21.5	24.6	.01	19.86

Note: Gp 1 = subsistence farmers; Gp 2 = worker-farmers; Gp 3 = farmer-workers; Gp 4 = commercial farmers.

[a]Average plot size of the subsistence households is skewed on the high side because the number of subsistence households is small and one has its entire farm of just over 1 hectare in a single plot.

[b]Mean number of hectares.

[c]In thousands of złoty.

Source: 1979 village census.

all workers are employed exclusively on the farm and the household has a significant income from farm sales.

A note of explanation with respect to the two groups I call worker-farmers and farmer-workers is necessary. Conventional wisdom about what Eastern European sociologists (and sociologists and anthropologists of Eastern Europe) refer to as peasant-workers (Hann 1980; Kolankiewicz 1980; Halpern 1969) is that they are neither good farmers nor good workers. The number of peasant-workers in Poland has grown steadily since 1950. Notorious as "malingerers" on the job and for taking time off to plant or harvest, to tend a sick animal, and a dozen other farm-related tasks, they are said to bring less energy and commitment to farming as a profession than full-time farmers and to produce only for the family's consumption. These allegations and the accelerating numbers of peasant-workers were the justification for the socialist's state's effort to eliminate them from the farming population in order to free their land for use by commercially oriented farmers. The 1990 agricultural program of the nonsocialist state similarly sought to eradicate part-time farmers. My findings, however, suggest that the characterization of peasant-workers as inefficient obscures essential differences between *worker-farmers* and *farmer-workers* and thus calls into question state efforts to unilaterally dispossess them.

A definite pattern among the farming groups named and described above can be seen when the data in Table 7.1 are compared. Full-time commercial farmers (Group 4) have the largest average farms and the largest individual plots, own the most cattle, have the most mechanized equipment and the largest sales per hectare, and use the most lime per

TABLE 7.2   Stratified Groups–Analysis of Variance[a] (N = 63)

	Gp 1 (N = 6)	Gp 2 (N = 19)	Gp 3 (N = 20)	Gp 4 (N = 18)	Probability Value	Total Mean
Land[b]	1.7	2.2	4.3	5.3	0	3.7
Age	59.0	43.0	59.0	53.0	0.0001	53.0
Household size	1.6	5.2	5.2	4.0	0.00004	4.5
Workers[c]	1.0	2.7	3.5	2.0	0.0001	2.6
Education	1.7	2.3	2.4	2.1	0.001	2.2

Note: Gp 1 = subsistence farmers; Gp 2 = worker-farmers; Gp 3 = farmer-workers; Gp 4 = commercial farmers.
   [a]Incomplete data set for an eighty-year-old widow omitted. Because of small number of households, average age skewed to low side.
   [b]Mean size in hectares.
   [c]Between ages eighteen and sixty-five.
Source: 1979 village census.

hectare. They are the "professional" farmers of the village, in contrast to the subsistence farmers (Group 1), who have the least of these means of production. The worker-farmers (Group 2) and farmer-workers (Group 3) fall between the two extremes. Note that there are significant differences among the means of the groups on each of the variables; the proposed division of households into four distinct, hierarchically organized and stratified groups appears reasonable.

When we compare the four groups with respect to the age of the head of household, the size of households, the number of workers, and the amount of land owned (see Table 7.2), a different pattern emerges, one that suggests that demographic differentiation may account for what I call stratified groups. In other words, if we sort the four farming groups by the age of the head of household and size of landholdings such that the order is Group 2, Group 4, Group 3, Group 1, each group looks as though it may represent a stage in a demographic cycle. Such a cycle would work as follows. Because a young couple has probably only inherited a small parcel of land that would not require the labor power of both adult members of the household, the man may work in the industrial sector for wages while the woman does most of the farm work—creating the worker-farmer household of Group 2.[3] As the family increases in size with the birth of children, the couple might purchase more land and the head of household might give up wage labor in favor of full-time commercial farming—Group 4. When the children reach maturity, however, all the available labor power cannot be utilized on the farm; the adult children take wage jobs, making the household farmer-workers (Group 3). After the parents retire and land has been given to the children, the parents' farm reverts back to its original size or smaller—the subsistence household of Group 1. We need to examine

TABLE 7.3   Comparison of Subsistence and Worker Farmers (Groups 1 and 2)

| | Group 1 | | Group 2 | |
	Mean	Standard Deviation	Mean	Standard Deviation
Age	58.8	8.6	43.6	8.9
Land	1.7	0.8	2.3	1.1
Household size	1.6	0.8	5.2	1.1
No. of workers	1.0	0.6	2.8	0.1

the premises of the family-cycle demographic differentiation model and determine whether it indeed fits the data in Wola Pławska.

The Demographic Differentiation Model

The name of A. V. Chayanov, the early Soviet neopopulist, is particularly associated with the family-cycle model of demographic differentiation; the model itself and the theory of peasant economy that informs it have become increasingly popular with Western neopopulists since Chayanov's work was translated into English and published in 1966.[4] Chayanov's theory is a permutation of the sociology of development and is often incorporated into that model, though Polish sociologists do not generally mention him by name for reasons that will shortly become apparent.

Let us look at the empirical data first. If the demographic differentiation model pertained, the worker-farmers should have the youngest heads of household, the smallest families, and the fewest workers as well as the smallest farms. The age of the head of household in worker-farmer and subsistence households should be at the polar ends of a continuum, but their farm size, family size, and number of workers in the family should be more or less equal. The figures in Table 7.3 compare subsistence farmers and worker-peasants on these dimensions. The criterion of different age is met, but even though there is some overlap on the average land size, the family size and number of workers is not equal. In fact, though worker-farmers are the youngest heads of household with a mean age of forty-three and (except for subsistence farmers) have the least amount of land, they have considerably more workers than subsistence farmers and even more than commercial farmers (see Tables 7.2 and 7.3). As for the size of the family, worker-farmers have an average of 5.2 members, compared to 1.7 for the subsistence farmers and 4.0 for commercial households.

We would also expect, if the demographic differentiation model applied, that the elderly and retired persons would all be subsistence farmers whereas their sons and daughters would be in various stages of progression throughout the cycle. In fact, though many of the elderly are indeed to be found in the subsistence category, not all members of this group are retired and not one has children active in farming in the village. Finally, equations that attempt to predict which group a household will be in by the number of workers or age of the head of household do not account for any of the variance, even when comparisons are limited to those with roughly equal amounts of land (see the Appendix, Table A.4, Equations 1, 2, and 3). Nonetheless, the simple correlation between age of the head of the household and amount of land farmed ($r = -.03$) is consistent with the U-shaped relationship predicted by Chayanovians. If nonlinear equations had been run, they might have indicated such a U-shaped relationship between age of the household head and amount of land owned. Thus, although the evidence is not conclusive, it would appear that demographic differentiation does not unambiguously account for the intergroup variation in this village.

The criticisms of the Chayanovian model of peasant economy on theoretical grounds are more compelling than the empirical shortcomings. Michael Harrison comments that neopopulist theory is based on a coherent ideological construct that tells us more about "the process of ideological formation within which [Chayanov] developed his work than about the peasantry as such" (1977:324). The ideological construct under discussion is the dispute between early Soviet Marxists and neopopulists—a debate that has been implicitly recapitulated by Polish rural sociologists and economists, telling us something about the prevailing ideology in Poland in recent decades.

In contrast to Marxists, neopopulists assume there is no inherent tendency of family farms to segment into class fragments but that they essentially reproduce themselves unchanged over time. Both this and a related assumption that asserts the economic superiority of family farms over capitalist enterprises are predicated on Chayanov's observation that the economic rationality governing the operation of family farms differs from that of capitalism, with family farms operating on a survival rather than a profit-making principle (Thorner, Kerblay, and Smith 1966). The concepts of cost-price ratios and profits, for example, are said to be foreign to the family farm, which will overexploit family labor power whereas the capitalist enterprise must rely on calculations of wages, profits, rents, and interest. Capitalist farms usually have access to market factors denied the family farm, for instance, credit and technology, which permit them to increase the productivity of labor. The family farm, on the other hand, can increase the productivity of land by the more intensive application of labor, an option denied to the capitalist enterprise. The theoretical debate about the relative efficiency and productivity of one type of enterprise over the other is generally posed in positivistic rather than normative terms. That is, the question is not whether family farming *should* be dominant in a specific setting in spite of the super-exploitation of family labor power (including that of children) but whether, in fact, it economically outperforms capitalist farming in that setting (de Janvry 1980:157). Neopopulists ordinarily use the family farm on which no labor is hired as the basic unit of analysis rather than the structure of agriculture and its relations with the overall society.

Chayanov introduces other notions, such as utility maximization and a trade-off between total factor income and leisure, from neoclassic economics. The key concept is that "the degree of self-exploitation is determined by a peculiar equilibrium between family demand satisfaction and the drudgery of labor" (Thorner, Kerblay, and Smith 1966:6). ". . . All other conclusions and constructions follow *in strict logic* from this basic premise" (Thorner, Kerblay, and Smith 1966:42). Thus, "the satisfaction of family demands (determined by the habitual demand level) is constrained *only* by the drudgery of labor" (Thorner, Kerblay, and Smith 1966:13) because the marginal utility of increased labor does not bring proportionate rewards. The basic contention is that peasants only produce the social product necessary to continue to work at a given intensity and to reproduce themselves; peasants do not produce surplus value.

According to the theory, observed inequalities among farms have nothing to do with capitalist relations of production or class differentiation but are the result of the natural history of the peasant family, or demographic differentiation. As the family size changes throughout its life cycle, the size of agricultural holdings changes in proportion. Thus, young families with few dependents and few farm workers will have small farms. As the family grows, it acquires additional land to provide for the next generation. This is possible because the labor to work the land is now available within the family. The peak period of ownership will be just before the oldest child marries and claims his or her inheritance. By the time all the children have left the natal household, the farm will have reverted to its original size. In other words, the balance between consumer satisfaction and the degree of drudgery is affected by the size of the family and the ratio of working to nonworking members of the family. What is observed at time x is simply a snapshot of a cyclical process. Peasant communities are, therefore, homogeneous entities existing and persisting in harmony with no apparent tendency to create groups of rich or poor or landless with an unstable middle group, as Lenin had suggested. Because of family histories that have led to continuity of relative status through generations, this scenario has already been shown to have limited applicability to Wola Pławska.

There is a certain plausibility to this internal model, however, just as theories of the firm are credible but if and only if the peasant household (or the firm) is taken as *the* unit of analysis, abstracted from regional, national, and international contexts. The ceteris paribus assumption is implied and the model presupposes a free market in land at a price the peasants can invariably afford and both the production of surplus value and surplus the family can save. Therefore neopopulist theory is inapplicable to feudal society because, by definition, serfs do not have free access to land. It has been remarked in many places that peasants subsisting close to the margin of existence, as do most peasants in most places, must frequently hire out their labor power or even borrow at usurious rates to make it through the year. It will be recalled from Chapter 3, for example, that some nineteenth-century peasants in Galicia had to borrow money at interest rates of from 50 to 100 percent per annum just to meet their daily living expenses (Kieniewicz 1969:105). Constantly strapped for cash in order to pay rents and other cash expenditures, poor peasants must often sell their harvest at peak season when supply is high and prices low and then buy it back later when supplies are scarce and prices correspondingly high. It defies reason to assume that most peasants are able to save money in order to purchase land as the demands of a large and growing family require. Chayanov himself recognizes the limitations of his internal accumulation model and suggests that poor peasants, faced with the necessity of expanding their base to meet the needs of a growing family, simply work harder or develop "greater energy" (Thorner, Kerblay, and Smith 1966:218).

The Chayanovian theory is fundamentally a behavioral model. The most significant behavior under consideration is the imputed non-profit-seeking, self-exploitative nature of the family farmers. Small family farms receive low returns on their investment of capital and labor power and, if calculated, a low wage and profit rate because of the unequal relations of power and capital that require small farmers to surrender most of what little surplus they realize through unfavorable relations to the market (de Janvry 1980:159). There is a sound basis for assuming that well-managed larger farms realize economies of scale in land, technology, and labor for many crops, enabling their owners to retain more of their surplus for reinvestment and accumulation. If we further assume that the low surplus retention of small family farms is not primarily the result of a behavioral "calculus of pain and pleasure," but that the observed behavior is the outcome of a struggle over capital and its control, then differentiation, as economic capital in the countryside is commodified, becomes more comprehensible.

The only circumstances under which family farmers might reproduce themselves more or less unchanged rather than segmenting into class fractions is when land, labor, and other means of production have not been commodified and are hence inalienable, preventing farmers from using their surplus to enlarge their farms, hire labor as necessary, and take advantage of suitable technology. This set of circumstances does not pertain to the structural conditions of capitalism (de Janvry 1980:159), did not completely apply in Poland even when peasants were enserfed, and did not apply to the conditions of state socialism where there was already a market in land, technology, and food, albeit restricted. What is more, this market is now almost completely commodified as the reforms of 1990 proceed. To characterize family farms as fundamentally different from capitalist enterprises because farmers do not calculate wages and profits is a mystification of relations of dominance and subordination.

Neopopulists share the romantic view of peasants that often coincides with Chayanovian populism. They find the "traditional rural values" of balanced reciprocity and mutual assistance to family among the basics to which they would have society in general return. Implicitly, they assume that "peasants" still regard all blood and law relations to the fourth degree as family. As Thomas and Znaniecki put it seventy years ago, "all attitudes of social pride are primarily familial and only secondarily individual. . . . the social standing of the family is influenced by the social standing of its members, and no individual can rise or fall without drawing to some extent the group with him" (1984:73). However, in small ancient villages with a norm of endogamy such as Wola Pławska—Wola Pławska is typical in this respect—it is difficult to find anyone who falls totally outside the bond of family so broadly defined. In a contemporary world that emphasizes liberal individualism, the boundaries of four degrees of family create contradictory social relations, the multiple bonds of which demand reduction and social management by the parties to them.[5] Rather than uniting people into a web of a ubiquitous family writ large, the very principle of such imputed family solidarity ensures that the individual household or marriage group is the basic unit of production, reproduction, and consumption, and that loyalty and sacrifice to the broadly defined family can be honored only in the breach. Generally speaking, primary emphasis is placed on a tightly bounded group as the effective pool of kindred. In the contemporary sociocultural order the nuclear family is the primary unit of economic and political relations. Individuals and, by extension, households, not an extended familial unit, take the initiative in forming or declining to form economic and other kinds of relations and alliances. The evidence presented in Chapters 3 and 4 suggests that this is a long-standing pattern rather than one of the mid- to late twentieth century.

Wola Pławska Divided

Returning to the stratified groups in Wola Pławska, I predict that a household's location in one or another of the four groups will be associated with ownership and use of certain agricultural means of production. The figures in Table 7.4 substantiate this predication and lend further support to the proposed hierarchy. The position of a group in the hierarchy, in other words, more or less corresponds to the amount of land owned by each household in the group, the average size of individual plots of land, the use of both chemical fertilizer (NPK) and lime used for each hectare of land, the number of cattle and swine owned, and whether or not the household has a tractor. Stratified groups also differ in gross sales per hectare to the state, indicating that those with the most resources tend to put all household labor power into farming rather than allocating a portion of it to wage work and produce more for the commodity market. The amount of land owned is a markedly better predictor of stratified group than sales per hectare, though land and gross sales together appear to act differently among the groups. By holding land constant, for example, land and sales together predict 41 percent of the variance (see Table A.4, Equation 6), verifying that economies of scale pertain even to such small landholdings as are found in Wola Pławska. Land alone accounts for 36 percent of the variance whereas amount of sales alone predicts 15 percent (see Table A.4, Equations 4 and 5).

Having substantiated the credibility of the established groups in Wola Pławska, let us now turn to a discussion of the most important economic and social characteristics of each and specify its relations to the others.

Subsistence Farmers (Group 1)

Subsistence farmers are defined as households that have minimal farm income from sales to the state.[6] There are eight such households in Wola Pławska, and I have complete data for six. The village poor are, on the average, the oldest and least educated, have the smallest resident families and number of economically active workers, live in the poorest houses, own the smallest farms, use the least amount of fertilizer, have the fewest farm animals, use no mechanized farm machinery, and have the least political or economic influence. Seven of these households are headed by single persons, six of whom have never been married or are widows or widowers. In one case in which both partners are living, the household is headed by a woman whose husband is a hospitalized

TABLE 7.4   Correlation of Stratified Groups and Means of Production[a] (N = 63)

Means of Production	Stratified Group
Land	.61
Average plot size	.34
NPK per hectare	.28
Lime per hectare	.37
Cattle	.43
Swine	.28
Tractor	.42
Gross sales per hectare	.43

[a].25 is significant at .05 level.
Source: 1979 village census.

invalid. The eighth head of household is working in the United States and sending dollar remittances to his wife, who, with the aid of her elderly father, has taken temporary responsibility for the farm work.

Villagers pity the unmarried, divorced, or widowed because it is so difficult to farm adequately without a mate and children. It is no accident that the households headed by single persons are economically marginal. Church proscriptions against divorce are probably more closely adhered to in villages for the same reason. Households without active males are in particularly burdensome straits, given the level of technology and the strenuousness of farm labor. Although the socialist state provided free medical care and other minimum social services, such households are economically precarious. Many of these, of course, have since been eliminated or drastically curtailed. Private health insurance is planned. "Pray God," an elderly widow said to me in July 1990, "Pray God that I do not get sick this year. I can no longer afford to be sick."

Two households in the subsistence category are made up of lone, elderly widows and another two of elderly widows and their middle-age unmarried daughters. The fifth is that of a single, middle-age woman who lives next to her married brother and his family. This woman, although she owns a tiny plot of her own, also helps on her brother's land, takes care of his children, and assists in other ways in his household. The sixth household is that of a single man, age sixty-five. The village eccentric, he is something of a recluse. All six have less than 2 hectares of land each and have minuscule gross farm sales.

The seventh household is one in which the male head of household has been hospitalized several times in recent years for acute psychosis apparently brought on or at least contributed to by chronic alcoholism. As he has been in a sanitarium for most of 1979, both his wife, Maria, and his widowed mother-in-law, Zosia (who is part of the household), said that he would probably not return this time. Although this household has a 4-hectare farm, slightly larger than average for the village, it is one of the shabbiest of its size. Completely lacking mechanized equipment, it also has an acute labor shortage. Zosia is in her late sixties and her three grandchildren are all under eleven. Labor and equipment shortages have led Zosia's family to "sell" their labor power to the commercial farming household of Helena Nowak and her daughter and son-in-law, Katarzyna and Adam. In exchange for the use of draft power from the Nowaks at crucial times of the years, that is, planting and harvesting, Zosia and Maria work on the Nowak land. Thus, Adam may spend a day plowing Maria and Zosia's 4 hectares with his tractor and plow, and they would devote five days each to helping him plant and harvest his 9 hectares. Adam mows their hay for a morning, and they are in his fields for two days. That Maria and Helena Nowak are second cousins (their grandmothers were sisters) and that Maria and Zosia are grateful and would find it impossible or much more difficult to cultivate their land without help does not change the unequal nature of the relationship. Even if there is no exchange of money involved, Maria and Zosia are the equivalent of seasonal laborers on the Nowak land, and their labor input allows that family to increase its surplus product, which it then reinvests in the farm. From the Nowaks' point of view, they are simply helping a needy member of the family. As Maria and Zosia cannot increase the surplus product of their own farm proportionately, the relative economic distance between their farm and the Nowak's widens. Maria, Zosia, and the three grandchildren are well on their way to becoming rural proletarians.

The eighth household in the subsistence category is that of the Kossaks. Marek Kossak was in the United States working for most of 1978 and all of 1979. The effect of his absence on farm receipts was dramatic: They dropped by two-thirds between 1977 and 1978. The Kossak household owns almost 3.5 hectares, just about the average for the village, and a two-story brick farmhouse was under construction in 1978 and, of course, long completed by 1990. The house was paid for with the dollar remittances sent from the United States. A trip to the United States with the resulting acquisition of dollars, which long smoothed the way for almost any enterprise in Poland, is associated with residence in a more modern house (Pearsons's $r = 0.33$). Building materials are more easily available if paid for in hard currency and, until recently, might only be afforded if that currency is traded on the black market.

The households that have managed to send temporary migrants to North America or receive money from American relatives are evenly distributed across all farming groups. However, ties to American relatives, regardless of how the connection manifests itself (as actual migration or simply the receipt of gifts), are related to improved living and farming standards in general, not just improved housing. For example, the association of the receipt of dollars with ownership of a car, with the number of swine the household raises, and with ownership of a tractor is 0.56, 0.38, and 0.33, respectively. When Kossak returned to Poland in 1979, he bought a tractor, consolidated his landholdings, and began to raise flowers commercially. Later, he bought additional land, increasing his farm from 4 hectares to 12.[7] Not only was the Kossaks' categorization as subsistence farmers a temporary one, their success in "managing things" is a standard by which others measure themselves.

Worker-Farmers (Group 2)

Nineteen of the farming households are headed by those who work full time in nonfarming occupations, leaving the farm work to women, children, and the elderly. (Others in the household may also work for wages.) In terms of land size, worker-farmers have the second smallest farms; 68 percent have smaller than average landholdings for the village with a mean of 2.2 hectares. In contrast to subsistence farmers, who have the oldest mean age, worker-farmers are the youngest heads of household. They have already inherited all the land they can (none has parents farming independently), and their chances of purchasing more land, even if they wanted it, are limited by availability. In general, worker-farmers have too little land to support a family, regardless of the amount of labor or capital they invest in it. They have, therefore, turned primarily to wage labor as a means of earning a living.

A handful of worker-farmers, those with the slightly larger individual plots, rent portions of their land to farmer-workers and commercial farmers who, after putting in a crop, market the proceeds, keeping a portion of the return for themselves and giving the remainder to the owner as rent. This sharecrop arrangement allows the commercial farmer with an underutilized tractor and other mechanized equipment to put them to greater use and ensures the worker-farmer a return on the land the family cannot work. As in most sharecrop arrangements, it is the owner who has the primary advantage, in this case because the farmer who markets crops grown on a worker-farmer's land does so in the owner's name. Thus, although the owner's share of the proceeds is the smaller, his credit with the state is maintained and he or she can always reclaim the land for family use. The few worker-farmers with larger farms intend to do exactly that as their children grow older and can help with the farm work. In effect, the commercial farmer is holding the worker-farmer's land in trust until the owner has sufficient labor power to work it within the confines of the family. For the most part, however, worker-farmers have neither the land nor the means of acquiring it to enter farming on a commercial basis.

Worker-farmer households receive annual gross wages that are slightly lower than those of farmer-workers, but because their families are younger, there are also fewer people of working age. As farmers, they sell less per hectare to the state than farmer-workers or commercial farmers, a reflection of economies of scale and the fact that, although worker-farmers have even more workers in the household than commercial farms, much of that labor power is necessarily invested in wage work.

The members of worker-farmers' families are better rather than less educated than either subsistence or commercial farmers, a finding that contrasts with earlier studies (Gałaj 1965), which indicate that "peasant-workers" have significantly less education than full-time farmers. The members of worker-farmer households in Wola Pławska have about the same number of years in school as farmer-workers. Education, however, does not predict membership in this or any other stratified group (see Table A.4, Equation 7). The young and well-educated are not necessarily opting for either farming as a profession (in accordance with the expressed desires of the agricultural bureaucrats) or even for wage work, but are choosing instead to become worker-farmers. Many worker-farmers perceive themselves and are perceived by urban workers as better-off than their urban counterparts, for whom regular supplies of many desired agricultural commodities, especially meat, have become increasingly unreliable in recent years.

The social identity of worker-farmers is primarily that of worker. They consider hired labor a permanent condition and an end in itself. Worker-farmer households have slightly more consumer goods and material comforts, as measured by the houses they live in, than any other group, but the variance among means is not statistically significant. Based on qualitative data not reflected in the statistical data set, however, worker-farmers in general spend discretionary income on improving houses and on consumer goods. In contrast, commercial farmers invest first in their farms and only secondarily in improved housing. Thus, the most well-to-do of the commercial farmers have fully equipped farms *and* fine houses whereas the other groups have sufficient resources to invest only in one or the other.

Aspirations of worker-farmers are to advance at the workplace, get promotions, and acquire schooling for their children. Education is valued as a way to move out of the peasant class economically and socially. Wages, as the major means of support of the household, are unlikely to be willingly shared with members of the extended family in times other than those of dire need. In other words, they feel no obligation to ensure, by their contributions, that other members of the family do not fall below the family's historical standing in the village, nor do they have the sense that their own position in the family entitles them to special consideration. The fact of the matter is that households in the worker-farmer stratum do not have large extended families in the village or even in nearby villages. They tend, by and large, to be descendants of seasonal farm workers or manor hands rather than of long-established landowning families. Thus, links to other members of the family, when an extended kin group exists, are more likely to be based on personal relations than status or hierarchy. This is not to say they refuse to help parents or siblings, but generally altruism does not extend beyond the immediate natal group of either partner in a marriage. When it does it may be partly from generosity and partly from the desire to manifest personal importance. Social relations are more likely to be with workplace acquaintances or selected members of the family.

With social ties to the workplace, worker-farmers often receive Sunday afternoon visits from urban friends. Conversation frequently centers on how fortunate worker-farmers are to live in the country, to raise chickens and pigs, and to have a regular supply of fresh milk, eggs, and other farm products. Worker-farmers, however, suffer some economic disadvantages that they and their urban friends do not articulate. For example, they pay a larger proportion of their income in property taxes on their privately owned houses than workers who live in state-subsidized housing pay in rent (Szelenyi 1977). And, if we take the undifferentiated category of peasant-workers as a whole, they appear to be less well-off than the typical worker with respect to, for example, meat consumption (as we saw in Chapter 6).

Peasant-workers are not a homogeneous group; those in Wola Pławska who do enjoy material comforts have better-paying semiskilled jobs, enabling them to maintain living standards higher than those of their urban counterparts. By cultivating a few hectares and raising a few cows, hogs, chickens, and ducks, they assure themselves of milk, butter, eggs, poultry, and occasional ham and bacon. Peasant-worker adults and adolescents spend more time (and money) in Mielec than any other group, well-dressed young people from that stratum frequenting cafes, discos, films, concerts, and sporting and cultural events. Their small farms, which yield relatively low sales to the state, are a form of insurance against the fluctuations of the national economy and the availability of the necessities. These farmers are the prototype of the peasant-workers the state seeks to eliminate. Even though the socialist state wanted to incorporate them into the socialized sector, worker-farmers refused to give up their land and rural houses and move to the cities, even if they could get housing there. (Urban housing is overcrowded and in short supply, and there are long waiting lists.) Under the national economic conditions of the late 1970s, the best-off among them thought that to do so would mean their living standards would fall. In the face of massive layoffs in 1990, even the tiniest piece of farmland is a hedge against potential hunger.

The Małek family is typical of this kind of household. Jan is a city bus driver and Amelia, his wife, does the bulk of the farm work. Their oldest daughter attends university in the provincial capital of Rzeszów. The second child, a high school student in 1978–1979, later also attended university. The Małek's farm, with about 3 hectares of land, did not provide a sufficiently large surplus for capital accumulation. The major part of the household's income is from Jan's wages, with farm receipts regarded as supplemental. Jan and Amelia ensure that their children have access to whatever cultural events Mielec has to offer, often at the expense of their own comforts or farm improvements.

In spite of basic similarities reflected in statistics already discussed, the category of worker-farmer varies widely within this range. In contrast to households that can afford to purchase consumer goods, some worker-farmers are unskilled and have few prospects of moving up in the working world. Their salaries are barely at or slightly below the average for the country, meaning that they could not afford to buy meat in the (now defunct) commissaries at twice the state price to guarantee themselves a regular supply, nor can they afford to enjoy urban pleasures. The Koguts and the family of Władysława Mach, discussed in Chapter 4, fall into this category. Władysława's son-in-law, it will be recalled, is the driver's helper on a coal truck and earns the minimum wage. Janina's son, with whom Janina lives, also has a poorly paid job. In other parts of the world, their meager income would allow worker-farmers only a shantytown existence.

With two exceptions, none of the worker-farmer families is politically active or belong to a political party. In general, energies are put into work, play, and manipulating the system. Most of their children have no plans to be farmers. The children expect to finish secondary school and a few want a higher education, either university training or technical school—a manifestation of the perceived importance of education for social mobility. Realistically, however, only a handful are likely to go beyond middle school. Although some of the adolescents expect to live in the village and farm after marrying because, they say, it is unlikely economic conditions will improve in the near future, most will probably end up as urban workers or worker-farmers like their parents. Neighbors say that worker-farmers have no more than rudimentary knowledge of the routines of farm work, but it is difficult to assess the accuracy of this observation. Their fields appear less well tended, but this could be a result of labor-power shortages.

Except for the teachers, the only others in Wola Pławska who were said to be members of the Communist party are two worker-farmers with supervisory jobs in their places of employment. Most residents of Wola Pławska are contemptuous of the Party and its members—a cynicism that is widely shared by Polish citizens (Jones et al. 1984:151), and members are often referred to as the "red aristocracy." Privileged access to consumer goods was only one of the many perquisites they once enjoyed, and their conspicuous consumption was a scandal. Moreover, people commonly believed that anything was possible for a Party member and that membership implied privileged access to institutions of higher learning. Fiszman (quoted in Dziewanowski 1977:289) maintains that educational opportunities are unequally distributed in Poland, a perception verified by a professor of education with whom I spoke in Warsaw in 1979.

Although none of the reputed Party members in Wola Pławska talked to me about their membership and its political, economic, or cultural implications, a worker-farmer from Rzędzienowice, one of the few rural or urban residents who admitted to me he was a member or even a socialist, said that most of his colleagues belonged to the Party because of their jobs. "We are not truly Communists," he said and told me of Party members who take their children to distant towns to be baptized so they won't be identified as practicing Catholics in their home districts. Ordinary people are incredulous in the face of those who profess Marxism. The worker-farmer referred to above had a brother-in-law who was a Party member and an avowed Marxist; he thought his brother-in-law a fool, a sycophant, or both. We will return to the implications of such antisocialist sentiments and the reasons for them when we discuss how farmers subverted restrictions on the market in land, technology, and food distribution.

Farmer-Workers (Group 3)

Thirty percent of the households (n = 22) are farmer-workers. There are wage earners in the household, but the male head of household is a farmer. The average age of the head of household is second oldest, only after the subsistence farmers. Farm size is smaller than that of commercial farmers but larger than the village average; the same is true for sales to the state, the number of cows and hogs, and other agricultural variables. The farmer-worker families are the best educated of those who have remained in the village. Some of the farmer-worker households represent the transitional stage of a progression to larger-scale, more sophisticated commercial farming. Others are in a cycle of household formation and decomposition in which an older generation, not yet retired, heads the farm but will at some future time turn it over to the younger generation (cf. Goody 1976). In due course, some of the households will consequently become worker-farmers. In this sense of household cycles, the Chayanovian model has validity.

Farmer-workers have the largest number of workers, averaging 3.5 per household. With a large surplus labor population available in the household, the members of the younger generation take urban jobs. Because the wageworkers in this group are, on the average, younger than those in the worker-farmer group, their jobs tend to be more rather than less skilled, a function of the progressively better overall education available. For many of the younger generation of village-dwelling urban workers, however, wage work is but a resting place and an opportunity to acquire some savings until they can be farmers on a full-time basis. Several of the children of farmer-worker households have attended agricultural school and, although working at industrial jobs, bring their expertise to the farm. Some of their wage income goes toward the farm—toward a tractor, additional livestock (particularly swine), the inputs necessary for raising the livestock, and modern farm buildings. With their larger landholdings and plot sizes farmer-worker families are, like the commercial farmers, able to realize economies of scale. The size of the farm, for example, predicts 32 percent of the variance in tractor ownership (see Table A.4, Equation 8). Farmer-workers with larger landholdings, then, are also better able to use tractors and other mechanized means of production, increasing the productivity of labor, freeing young people to take urban jobs, and increasing the cash flow of the household. As land became sporadically available from the State Land Fund during the early and mid-1980s, those farmer-worker families who had graduates of the agricultural school in the family and already had at least 5 hectares were able to purchase additional land, enabling some of those who were wageworkers in 1979 to leave their jobs in favor of full-time farming.

For farmer-workers, a job is nothing more than an opportunity to earn money for the purpose of purchasing productive means. They are reluctant to spend money on anything that does not enhance productivity, such as clothing, appliances, or education (other than agricultural school for the young). The possibility of mobility is viewed as being within the farmer class itself, that is, one might become a "rich" farmer. In terms of society at large, mobility is primarily economic rather than social. Within the village hierarchy, however, such movement has both economic and social aspects.

For farmer-workers, the family's social standing is critical and must be maintained if not advanced. There is little interest in jobs except as means of acquiring money. Conversation rarely touches on work, and personal ties to fellow workers are minimal or nonexistent in favor of upholding solidarity within the village. Whether familial solidarity is maintained depends on the degree of success the family has thus far achieved. Those who have not expanded farm operations, for whatever reason, tend to invoke the familial connection more frequently, especially when in need of financial help or the loan or rent of farm machinery. The prosperous, however, may regard the familial connection as a brake on further accumulation, for unless there is a labor exchange involved, the better-off always bear the material burden of familial crisis. Consequently, they seek connections with those of this or other villages who are their financial equals, whether kin or not. This horizontal integration of the emerging proto-bourgeoisie is oft remarked upon, especially by those who perceive a loosening of "traditional" ties that provided some material benefit to them. It is therefore common for the less well-off to condemn the affluent for not adhering to "old ways."

The Paluch family exemplifies the thriving farmer-worker household. Kazimierz is a widower of fifty. An unmarried son who has completed three years at the agricultural school farms with his father, and a married son and daughter-in-law with a young son are also resident but work in Mielec. The Paluchs thus have four workers to farm 7 hectares of land. Some of the most modern farming equipment, including a tractor and the only motorized forklift in the village, helps husband fifteen dairy cows, three times the village average and almost double the mean number owned by commercial farmers.[8]

Two able-bodied men, the father and unmarried son, are able to do the routine farm work with the part-time input of two helpers. The other son and his wife are able to accumulate cash through their off-farm employment; the family has used some of this money to modernize the farm and some to raise their living standard. At times of the year when intensive labor is necessary on the farm, the use of the family's farm machinery is traded for the labor power of less affluent neighbors, and son Edek and his wife take time off from their wage employment to participate. The Paluchs, like so many other farmers, were likely to circumvent the socialist state's law against splitting the farm and eventually to transfer a portion of the father's land to each son rather than turning the entire farm over to one or the other (see Lane and Kolankiewicz 1973:15). Because the transfer could not have been legally registered, the sons farmed for a number of years as a cooperative unit. Their father's larger farm and established credit gave them access to the inputs they needed. The brothers later bought additional land from a retiring farmer and from the State Land Fund. Now that restrictions on land purchases have been lifted, they are likely to expand their operations even more.

Part of the reason the Paluchs have such a prosperous enterprise even in the face of the early limitations is because of their abundant labor power. There are several explanations why many farmer-workers (and commercial farmers) have larger than average families, some less plausible than others and none adequate in and of itself. An unlikely explanation, for example, is that farmers with fewer urban contacts have not absorbed "modern" urban cultural values that militate against large families. Equally unlikely is that the Catholic proscription of birth control affects farmer-workers and full-time farmers differently than it does other strata. Lenin's (1956) observation that the wealthier farm families in prerevolutionary Russia were larger because they could afford to be also seems wrong, unless we specify that more children in a wealthy family are likely to survive. It is more reasonable to assume that larger families are richer because they are larger, just as larger families were a source of surplus accumulation under the conditions of serfdom—a means of resistance, as it were.

Many farmer-workers have a basically populist ideology. They are oriented toward improving their living standards and status in the village while maintaining the independence of private farming. The older generation were members of the Peasant party (ZSL) in 1979 if they had any political affiliation at all. They tend to be especially concerned with production and profit enhancement. Some have gone into swine production on the same or even larger scale than commercial farmers.[9] Young workers from these households are more like the stereotype of the peasant-worker with respect to their minimal loyalty to the workplace; primary identification is with the farm. During peak agricultural periods, many take time off to work not only on the family farm but also on larger landholdings that undergo seasonal labor shortages. This phenomenon contributes to the oft-remarked high absentee rate in Polish factories and the infamous shoddiness of industrial products. Only rarely are workers paid in cash for their labor on farms belonging to someone outside family; they ordinarily trade their labor power for the hire of a mower or thresher from a commercial farmer or a more affluent farmer-worker or for access to capital inputs denied them by the state because of the small size of their farms.

There are dramatically different work ethics for farm and factory work. The farmer works as long and as hard as necessary at an essential task. If the harvest requires fifteen-hour days, then the farmers work fifteen-hour days without complaint or slacking off. Factory work, however, reflects class awareness. The Stakhanovite is condemned as a danger to the piecework scale, but the same person working hard and long at a steady pace in the fields is the object of admiration. The work ethic of the village and the group in which everyone works at a task together until it is finished is replaced by a contrasting workplace ethic that implicitly mandates that fellow workers are not made to look bad.

Farmer-workers are roughly analogous to the middle peasants in Lenin's model. Although they aspire to the status of wealthy bourgeoisie, only a few will actually attain it. Others may be forced out of farming altogether. The outcome for each household is affected by the amount of land the household already has, the equipment and labor power it can barter, and the degree to which it can manipulate intangibles such as influence or cultural capital into relative advantage.

Commercial Farmers (Group 4)

Twenty-five percent of the farming families are commercial farmers, the unmarked and most highly valued status in the village. Looking at within-category averages, commercial farmers have the largest land-holdings, with a mean of 5.3 hectares—a full standard deviation above the village average. They also have a monopoly on the few village political offices, the most mechanized farms as measured by the number of tractors they own, and the highest sales per hectare. We might expect that the full-time farmers would use the most chemical fertilizer, being the professional farmers; we find, in fact, that they use less than either the worker-farmers or farmer-workers. This seeming anomaly can be explained by the larger number of cows commercial farmers have, manure being a partial replacement for chemical fertilizer (or vice versa). The living standards of commercial farmers, as measured by house construction and ownership of cars, are lower than those of the other groups except the subsistence farmers. Full-time commodity-producing farmers tend to accumulate capital by reinvesting in the farm rather than consumer goods. With already larger farms and more farm equipment, they put returns into a new barn, for example, rather than a new house, a tractor rather than a car. Dominating the ownership of farm equipment, commercial farmers are the beneficiaries of their neighbor's lack of draft power, renting their equipment in exchange for their labor-power shortfalls and, because they have the largest farms, also dominating the cooperative work parties. The manner in which the Nowaks appropriate labor power from less fortunate neighbors and family, as discussed above, is but one example of the myriad ways commercial farmers are able to pyramid relative advantage.

The values and attitudes of individual effort, hard work, and frugal living and resentment of bureaucrats, intellectuals, and "Communists" are most pronounced here. Farmer-workers and commercial farmers together realize the populist ideal of independence and wealth more readily than the first two groups. An ideology of individualism and utilitarianism is celebrated here in terms that invoke a moral order to explain success and failure. The prosperous disparage those who are not, dismissing them as old-fashioned, saying "they don't know any better" or that they are "dumb or lazy." They refer to their neighbors as chłopi (peasants) rather than rolniki (farmers), which is what they are proud to call themselves. In general, *chłop*, once a positive equivalent to *gospodarze*, has been transformed into a disparaging epithet to describe today's farmers, and it rarely appears in print any more. All recent academic and popular articles seem to use *rolniki* exclusively. The ideology of utilitarianism has been fortified rather than combated by agricultural institutions and organizations, and contemporary farm journals and television programming directed toward farmers emphasize the efficacy of individual effort, hard work, and competition at the level of the individual farm. The values and rhetoric of utilitarianism particularly characterize commercial farmers but have also penetrated deeply into the farmer-worker stratum. Members of the latter seek not merely to survive as farmers but to realize the standards set by the commercial farmers. This is not to suggest that utilitarianism provides the only motivation but that successful farming—and successful equals profitable in this lexicon—is the means by which social validation is both sought and achieved.

Even though the ZSL was long a tightly controlled adjunct of the PZPR until its well-publicized break from the latter in 1989, several of the full-time commercial farmers were members because, they said, there were certain advantages, namely, enhanced contacts with the local agricultural bureaucracy, that helped them obtain what they needed (e.g., credit, fertilizer, machine rental) to farm successfully. These contacts were especially useful when inputs were scarce, as they often were. For example, the amount of lime purchased in 1978 can be seen as a measure of a farmer's ability to procure a needed capital input in a time of shortage. In 1977 the amount of lime purchased for each hectare of land, necessary to all farmers in this area because of the acidity of the soil, was associated with the total amount of land owned (Pearsons's r = 0.38), with the number of cattle owned (r = 0.39), and even more strongly with sales per hectare to the state (r = 0.47). In 1978 there were national shortages of lime, and not everyone could purchase all he or she wanted. The simple association of lime purchase with total land ownership dropped to 0.23 but that with sales only dipped slightly to 0.41. The total amount of land owned did not account for any variance in amount of lime purchased in 1978 (see Table A.4, Equation 11), but sales and the number of cows accounted for 15 percent and 13 percent, respectively (Table A.4, Equations 12 and 13). In fact, sales to the state, number of cows, and total wages received by the household from nonfarm employment accounted for the most variance in lime purchased in 1978—almost 32 percent (see Table A.4, Equation 14). Having a cash income from wages helped in procuring lime, but one would have thought the largest farms, favored by state policy, would have privileged access. In fact, policy was amended in 1978 so that the larger the sales to the state, the lower the cost of inputs (Duymovic 1980:187–191). It seems that state support of larger farms was not unambiguous; those who sold the most to the state, regardless of the amount of land they owned, received access to lime, suggesting another way the socialist state extracted surplus from private farmers.

Even though some Wola Pławskans were members of the ZSL in 1979, none held office or was in a position of power in the gmina itself. Sołtys, or village mayor, however, is a position to which one or another of two commercial farmers have been elected for more than twenty years because, people say, they are so competent that no one wants to oppose them or, alternatively, no one else wants the job. Although the position carries prestige and power in the village, the sołtys has little individual voice in gmina affairs, being only one on a council of a dozen village administrators that is subordinate to gmina officials and that has only advisory capacity.

Like most rural people, commercial farmers and their families are practicing Catholics, not only attending church on at least a weekly basis but also often uttering prayers before beginning and after finishing an agricultural task and invoking the intervention of various saints on any number of occasions. Religious sentiments are undoubtedly genuine, yet there is a certain element of nose-thumbing involved in the almost defiant public rehearsal of religious symbolism. Relations with the authorities in gmina offices in Borowa, where day-to-day business of buying and selling agricultural goods and services occurs, are strained. Status differences are marked; farmers are usually ingratiating and bureaucrats patronizing in face-to-face contacts. In private the farmers are galled by the treatment they are forced to endure at the hands of those higher in the status structure. I have seen farmers with a bottle of vodka tucked under one arm cross themselves as they enter the office of some bureaucrat—the gesture as sure to irritate as the vodka is to soothe.

A community of shared experience and similarity of attitudes separates the successful commercial farmer from the family writ large. The most efficient believe that the family can be a burden rather than a help. The ideology of family solidarity has undergone a subtle shift from obligatory social and economic interdependence as cousins and in-laws from other strata are called upon to help with labor-intensive farm work in exchange for the use of the farm equipment that tends to be concentrated in the hands of the full-time farmers. On the surface, this relationship is still couched in terms of reciprocity, but the poorer family members are well aware of the appropriation of their labor power. For their part, the commercial farmers make individualistic, utilitarian calculations of relative advantage and self-interest; such calculation is integral to their social identity and to the ethos of successful farming.

Commercial farmers and their immediate kin group spend little time or money on social activities outside the village, rarely going to Mielec except to shop for necessities unobtainable in much smaller Borowa. Sunday afternoons are spent calling on neighbors and kin; rarely do commercial farmers visit or are they visited by urban workers. Main topics of conversation during the growing and harvest seasons are production and distribution problems, difficulties with the bureaucracy, successes and failures in circumventing bureaucratically imposed restrictions, or gossip about how others have managed to acquire sufficient fertilizer, insecticides, or building materials. Much time is also spent arranging cooperative work parties or negotiating informal labor exchanges, both of which will be further described in Chapter 8.

Commercial farmers are, by and large, the rural bourgeoisie of the village, dominating economic activities and appropriating the labor power of others, including family members, to their own advantage. They are especially skilled in manipulating the control the state has sought to extend over their production and its distribution, as we shall see.

The Landless

The final group is the nonfarming households, not part of the statistical data set. There are five landless households in Wola Pławska; the members of three are marginal to the community. These are the households of the teachers in the elementary school. Two of them, the director and her assistant, live with their families in apartments above the school itself. The husband of the director, also a teacher and an administrator, is the principal of a secondary school in Mielec and commutes by car to town. The third teacher, a native of Wola Pławska, lives with her husband and children in a new, well-constructed house. Her husband, a bus driver with the Mielec-Kraków route, has one of the better-paid jobs held by village residents but is away much of the time.

The three teachers and their families are for specific purposes only an elite in Wola Pławska but in most ways are outside the social structure of the village. There are social barriers between the teachers, especially between the director and assistant director, and most of the other villagers, in part because the teachers are not farmers, but more importantly because of their higher level of education, urban manners, and relatively greater sophistication. Socially and professionally oriented toward Mielec and to a lesser degree toward Rzeszów rather than Wola Pławska, the teachers consciously impede social intercourse between themselves and the rest of the village. The only village social event in which the teachers participated during the entire year in which I was resident, for example, was a party for the parents of all elementary school children, hosted by the equivalent of a parent-teacher association. While villagers mingled freely and danced with one another, the teachers and their spouses sat together and interacted mostly with one another. The husband of the director told me that he finds it "difficult to talk to these people." Barriers between the teachers and villagers are reflected in, among other things, the exclusive use of formal address and reference terms.

Although socioeconomic and prestige differences are important, the distance between teachers and villagers stems also from the perception most villagers share that the teachers are more powerful than they. This particularly applies to the director and her husband. Villagers assumed that the director, assistant director, and spouses were members of the PZPR. Politically aligned with the local bureaucracy, they are categorically "them" and not "us." Despite cleavages among farmers on a number of dimensions, fractions coalesce in the face of outside groups. Most villagers cultivate connections with those higher in the vertical power structure for varying reasons, yet social relations are constrained by class boundaries maintained both by deference and resentment. Connections with the teachers may be useful if one is trying to get a child into a desirable and crowded educational institution, such as the technical school for mine engineering or a university, an unusual but not unheard-of occurrence in the village, but such currying of favor is primarily directed toward the acquisition of privileged access to scarce commodities or services. Their help may be solicited in filling out the complicated paperwork associated with getting a passport to the United States or to help obtain more than the basic coal allotment. In exchange farmers may provide certain scarce commodities—meat in particular. It is difficult to judge how much power with the local bureaucracy the teachers in fact have, but as faculty in an unimportant village elementary school, they are surely low in the hierarchy, and one suspects their influence is limited.

One of the other two landless households in the village is that of an elderly couple without heirs to their farm who turned their land over to the State Land Fund in exchange for a tiny pension, an option available to all retiring farmers since the mid-1970s. The land of retiring farmers was originally supposed to have been merged into state farms but in fact has been made available for incorporation into the farms of the largest landowners, either through lease arrangements or outright sale (Wädekin 1982:89). Most villagers think this old couple was foolish to exchange their land for a pension amounting to less than half a month's salary. The Paluchs, among others, would have been happy to rent it from them. Even though many farmers, especially commercial farmers, buy land from the State Land Fund if they can meet the minimum qualifications (a farm of at least 5 hectares and an agricultural education), the elderly are under considerable village pressure not to give up their land. In fact, few of the elderly accept the pensions, preferring instead to make private and quasi-legal sharecropping or lease arrangements with kin or neighbors. Not only do the elderly often realize a larger income in this manner, they remain landowners—a status all are loathe to relinquish. There have always been more than a few who are willing "to arrange" something with those who are too old to farm themselves. And, given the fluctuations in agricultural policy in the past, they are not certain the state will continue to make purchasable land available. What the state gives, the state can take away.

The fifth landless household involves a couple who were separated. The woman continues to live in Wola Pławska but works in Mielec while her husband maintains the farm with the help of an unmarried son. Village sympathies were with the man. Divorce is still condemned in the villages, unlike urban areas, where it has become more commonplace. It is widely thought by men and women alike that women must accept whatever life has given them. Even the women who were widely known to be victims of spouse abuse had no thoughts of a separation, although their fortitude did not prevent them from making their plight public in an effort to shame their husbands into reforming— a tactic that did not seem to be working. "Where would I go? What would I do?" said one who had never worked at a wage job in her life.

The landless households fall outside the village hierarchy and agricultural relations. Yet the teachers are a prime channel for the funneling of socialist ideology into the village, being the only representatives of the state who regularly interact with almost all villagers. That socialist ideology did not penetrate very deeply into Wola Pławska is patently apparent. Even the young people who had the greatest exposure to it in school tended to follow their parents' example in scoffing (often unreasonably) at almost everything that appeared in the newspaper, for example, or on the television news. With its emphasis on individualism, both of salvation and of effort, the church was a major means by which socialist ideology was countermanded. I found no differences among the farming groups with respect to socialism; they were united in opposition to its ideology and to its practice.

In conclusion, the data for Wola Pławska do not, as a whole, support the hypothesized split between two "kinds" of agriculturists proposed by Polish theorists. That is, there are not, on the one side, the younger, well-educated, modern, professional farmers with large landholdings who are motivated by their work to produce for the commodity market and the socialist system and who should be supported by state policy and, on the other side, the old-fashioned, older, poorly educated, poorly equipped farmers without a socialist consciousness who produce only for their traditional subsistence and who should be either helped to change their production techniques and orientation or eliminated from the farming population altogether. The theorists also seem to be wrong about peasant-workers. Although some part-time cultivators fit the stereotype of "proletarians with land" who only produce for their own table, others manage thriving enterprises, raising swine and dairy cows on a commercial basis and selling substantial amounts of produce to the state in spite of their often smaller farms. The economic and political gaps among emergent strata that I have identified have been aggravated by policies based on the findings of these theorists.

In other words, though it is unlikely to be put this way, policy has helped farmers along the American road to differentiation. This is a process that was not only *already* under way during the 1970s in Wola Pławska but has its roots, as has been seen, in the sociocultural order of earlier centuries. Of course the irony is that, pace Lenin, this is taking place not in America but in a state that was long pleased to call itself socialist.

NOTES

1. The numerical data that support the statistical description and analysis were gathered in 1978 and 1979. More recent trips, especially one in 1990, indicate that the same relationships among groups pertain, though the actual figures were naturally different.

2. I have complete data for sixty-three of the seventy-five farming households consisting of the age of the head of household and the age, education, employment, and wage income of each household member. Farming data consist of the amount of land each household owns; the size of each individual plot; the number of cattle, swine, and poultry they have; whether the household owns a tractor; the amount of chemical fertilizer and lime they used per hectare of land in 1977 and 1978, and the gross farm sales per hectare to the state for both years. The receipt of money from a North American relative or a trip to the United States or Canada by any member of a household is also part of the statistical data, as are living standards as measured by ownership of an automobile and the size of the house, its construction (brick, concrete block, or wood), and the presence

or absence of running water. All the variables used in the statistical analysis are listed and further explained in Table A.1 of the Appendix.

3. The law limiting partible inheritance had only been in effect since 1967 (or for eleven years) when these data were collected. I assume, therefore, that even if the law were strictly enforced, its effects would not yet have made a significant impact on household structure.

4. See, for example, Harrison 1977 and especially Hann 1985, both of whom use this model, the latter to account for inequality in a Polish village in the 1980s.

5. Thanks to John Comaroff, who makes a similar point in his analysis of Barolong kinship (1980:93–94) and who pointed out its relevance to me.

6. In 1978 I used a figure of 30,000 or less złoty gross annually, a minimal amount barely sufficient to guarantee a coal allotment.

7. This positive aspect of foreign migrant remittances on agricultural or other kinds of income-generating infrastructure is quite unusual. For a review of the more typical neutral or negative impacts of remittances, see Kearney 1986.

8. The size of a farm accounts for 41 percent of the variance in the number of cows raised (see Table A.4, Equation 9), and, in fact, the number of cows, the number of workers in a household, and ownership of a tractor predicts 57 percent of the variance in landholdings (see Table A.4, Equation 10). Cows require a certain minimum amount of land, and large landholdings also imply ownership of a tractor. Moreover, dairy farming is labor intensive in a village in which only one household has an automated milking machine. Dairy farming thus requires more than the average number of workers.

9. Farmer-workers, for example, own an average of 8.2 hogs per household compared to 8.1 for commercial farmers. Some households are able to raise swine on a commercial basis whereas others with equal amounts of land, labor, and other means of production are not. It is possible that some are successful because the raising of swine, unlike dairy cows, does not necessarily require a lot of land if feed can be purchased commercially. Perhaps those with a favorable cash flow are better able to purchase feed, even though they may not have the 5 hectares that would entitle them to subsidized prices from the state.

8

Who Was
in Charge Here?

I N CHAPTER 6 I DESCRIBED the theory of control cum modernization that has long informed development. Development, of course, is defined as making farmers out of peasants, and inequality is assumed to be based on a combination of personal and behavioral characteristics. The issue of control versus ownership is a thorny one at both the theoretical and practical levels. There are homologous situations in Latin America, for example, in which some scholars have argued that certain small producers are "proletarians disguised as peasants" (Paré 1977:51, cited in Harris 1978:9–10). Luisa Paré has analyzed a special relationship between Mexican capitalist enterprises and family farming in which smallholding peasants produce sugarcane on their own land but are financed and organized by state capitalist sugar mills. The producers sell their sugarcane to the enterprise that has capitalized them for just sufficient remuneration to reproduce their labor power. Even though the peasants own their own land, the capitalist enterprise controls them, prompting Paré to call them (and sharecroppers and tenant farmers) semiproletarians. Their class character and ideological and political points of view, however, are not those of proletarians, according to this somewhat mechanical analysis, because of their continued attachment to the land and their reluctance to become totally dependent on wage labor (Harris 1978:9–10). This is, in fact, a widespread form of control. Another example of the same phenomenon are *ejidos*, communally owned property in village Mexico. Ejidos are actually largely controlled by the Mexican state and by Mexican (and sometimes foreign) capital. Some small North American farmers are seemingly in a similar situation in which they are so deeply in debt and so heavily contracted to major grain conglomerates that their production and distribution decisions are constrained by bankers and the capitalist enterprises (see Burbach and Flynn 1980).

Class and Control

Ownership without control is surely too formal a definition of class. Ownership of the means of production or lack of it is, however, the single criterion most frequently mentioned by virtually all Marxists, regardless of other differences among them. Marx never defined class in any systematic way, but it is clear that income or occupational differences do not constitute class in the Marxist sense but are reflections of it. The importance of control or lack of it is implicit in Marx's work, though not systematically elaborated. As important as either control or ownership is the division of labor in a society. Though palpably utopian in the ever increasing complexity of the modern (and postmodern) world, Marx did envision the elimination of specialization as a feature of the ideal classless society. In *Capital*, he argues that capitalist class relations determine the separation of factory work into workers and those who direct the work. This split allows both the concentration of knowledge and control into the hands of those who direct the labor process and also the apparent bifurcation of science and labor. According to Marx, capitalist class relations and class dominance are expressed in the very organization of the production and labor processes, a line of analysis well developed by Marxist scholars in the West (see Braverman 1974; Aronowitz 1978; Burawoy 1978, 1985). In short, class is constituted by a constellation of elements, including knowledge and control of the means of production, culture (Worsley 1984; Aronowitz 1982), consciousness (Thompson 1966), and capital in all its forms (Bourdieu 1986, 1988). By attempting to monopolize control over both production and distribution decisions and agricultural knowledge and to locate them in the Party bureaucracy, the PZPR-dominated state claimed it had negated the independent existence, even the actions, of landowning farmers.

Although ownership may be an overly formal criterion for class unless it is linked to control and knowledge, control and knowledge without formal ownership is also a problematic diagnostic. The very framework of class society implies that "peasant farming" is mediated by and controlled to a certain degree by those in a superior position. Control may be explicit and manifest in subtle but nonetheless overt force, as it sometimes was in socialist Poland, or it may be largely masked by cultural ideals, as in capitalist states. To argue that control by the state makes ownership irrelevant, however, is a mystification. What the theory of state control does not take into account is the dialectic between the control the state seeks to exert and the control taken by the farmers themselves, that is, practice at the village level—the part the farmers take in production and distribution decisions and how their knowledge and practice relates to, resists, and thereby modifies the control of the state. It was surely mechanistic, not to mention naively optimistic, to assume the efficacy of central control over production and distribution decisions and then to characterize small-commodity producers as having the class of proletarian but the occupation of "farmer."

Contrary to the predictions and prescriptions of Party bureaucrats, planners, and social scientists, it was not so much the state or Party institutions and bureaucrats that controlled production and distribution but the cultivators themselves, primarily through practices of resistance intended to circumvent restrictions on access to capital inputs, proscriptions limiting the use of nonfamily labor power, and production and sale for the profitable black market. Success in these legal and quasi-legal practices was not random but predicated upon the ability of some rural class fractions, the nucleus of which had been in place for generations, to use their cultural, political, and economic capital to manipulate other class fractions as well as, in some cases, the local Party hierarchy.

By the late 1970s, some farmers found themselves in a position to transform state programs designed to professionalize agriculture to their own advantage, to obtain increasingly scarce subsidized inputs, to increase both the size of their landholdings and their production, and to benefit from quota incentives. Thus, many of the goals of the socialist state were realized. But like the technology and reorganization of production characteristic of the sociology of development programs (such as the green revolution in Mexico in the 1950s and elsewhere in the decades since), the already more affluent prospered at the expense of the poor. By the 1980s, economic and political disasters at national and international levels caused the bureaucratic state to slacken whatever control or illusion of control it did maintain.

Farming Practice in Wola Pławska: Farmers 1, the State 0

As the statistics in Chapters 6 and 7 (and tabulated in the Appendix) show, though the land owned by a household in Wola Pławska had a significant relation to gross sales per hectare to the state ($r = 0.27$), it only predicted 5 percent of the variance in sales. The fifteen largest landowners in the village (the top 20 percent), all of whom had farms larger than 5 hectares, owned 40 percent of the village's arable land. This is the group that has had privileged access to relatively inexpensive credit and such capital inputs as feed grain and fertilizer through the state-controlled agricultural institutions. These fifteen farms were *not*, however, the most productive ones in the village as measured by gross sales to the state. The best combination of variables that predict gross sales per hectare is the number of swine owned, the amount of fertilizer used per hectare, and political/economic influence. Examining the fifteen most productive farms in terms of gross sales to the state, we find that they accounted for 37 percent of the sales to the state of the entire village, but they were not the *largest* farms. In fact, only four of them were over 5 hectares. Even though the villagewide correlation between the size of landholdings and sales is 0.41, there is no statistically significant association between landholdings and gross sales for the fifteen most productive farms. Furthermore, the same four farms that were larger than 5 hectares were the only ones in the commercial category (Group 4); all the others were farmer-worker or worker-farmer households (Groups 3 and 2)—those the state lumps together as peasant-workers. These farm proprietors, the bureaucrats say, are not sufficiently productive and should be eliminated from the farming population.

Because some of the apparently most successful farmers had fewer than 5 hectares, we can assume that socialist state policy limiting inexpensive capital tools to larger farms was not perfectly implemented and that farmers did not adhere to the dictates of the bureaucrats. Andrzej Korbonski (1984) asserts that the local apparatchiks, petty Party officials, often manipulated policy in order to realize their own selfish aims. In other words, they accepted bribes and were otherwise corrupt. There is ample evidence of nationwide duplicity on the part of bureaucrats and petty officials (and even on the part of the upper echelons of Party and state), but more can be added to Korbonski's explanation. My data suggest that farmers regularly circumvented institutional controls through distribution practices that paralleled the official system but were an unacknowledged part of it—the black market.

When Poland was in the international news on almost a daily basis between 1980 and 1982 and again in 1989, frequent references to black market practices were made. Goods and some services, including agricultural means, were limited and scarce and competition for them keen. As a result, chicanery and deception permeated all levels of society, ranging from the grocery store clerk who kept seldom-seen goods under the counter for customers who could provide some other equally scarce good or service to outright stealing from stores and factories for private sale on the black market. If almost everyone has the money to pay for the desirables of life but there is an insufficient supply to meet the wishes of all, then other, less equally distributed currency becomes the measure of success. In socialist Poland, the relevant media of exchange were U.S. dollars and contacts with influential people—those with access to anything perceived as desirable. Ordinary citizens were forced to participate to the best of their ability and to the limits of their resources in the marketplace of dollars and contacts. With the criteria of access to this marketplace unequally distributed by definition, inequalities were both created and reinforced.

Widespread fraudulence generated new linguistic meanings and forms of etiquette. The verb *załatwiać*, for example, which literally means to arrange or to transact, and *kombinować*, to combine or to speculate, came to refer almost exclusively to arranging something on the black market, often in exchange for dollars. The expression *na lewo*, literally, "on the left," meant to make some such arrangement "under the table," as we would say in English. It became socially acceptable, at least among villagers, to ask how much something cost but never how it was arranged or with whom, for overexploited resources often disappeared and people were compelled to protect their supply lines.

Western media focused primarily on the difficulties urban consumers encountered in acquiring the necessities, especially food. Analysts virtually ignored the farmers who supplied many of the black market commodities. Black market practices had already penetrated the economic structure of Wola Pławska by 1978–1979, well before the national economic situation reached crisis proportions and well before Poland captured international attention. The resources to manipulate the black market in the production realm were, to a certain degree, predicated upon one's position in the already existing village hierarchy. For example, returning to the problem of the fifteen apparently most productive farms in Wola Pławska, we find they had several things in common: Most of them sharply increased their farm sales to the state between 1977 and 1978, the two years for which I have complete data, two farms by as much as 53 and 42 percent, respectively. During the same period, the villagewide increase was only 12 percent. These fifteen farms accounted for not only 37 percent of the gross farm sales but 35 percent of the total swine owned, 25 percent of the cattle, 30 percent of the fertilizer purchased, 36 percent of the political/economic influence as measured, and 24 percent of the available labor power.

I should note, first, that, by agreement with my informants, all the data I collected and have used in the statistical analyses presented thus far are constituted by the same figures they gave to official recordkeepers in the gmina office. These figures are misleading in certain respects. The fifteen farms referred to above, for example, were the fifteen that sold the most to the state but were not necessarily the most productive in terms of their actual farm output. The figures for the most productive were uncollectible because a certain portion of what was produced was not marketed to the state but sold on the black market. Nonetheless, the methods used by those that sold the most to the state in order to gain access to various capital inputs are instructive. Let us look at hogs first because my data indicate that the correlation (Pearsons's r) between sales per hectare and the number of swine owned increased from 0.34 to 0.52 from 1977 to 1978, suggesting that swine were playing an increasingly important role in the profitability of farming.

The state had been strongly encouraging swine specialization for years in part to meet rising urban demands for meat but also to support export policies. (The continuities with the past are ironic; socialist Poland continued to export its food while some of its people went without.) Farmers never devoted all or even most of their acreage to growing feed grain for livestock. They purchase most of it on credit. However, because most of the fifteen households under consideration had farms of less than 5 hectares, all but four of them had to pay more for their feed grain and their credit, if they got it at all, than farmers with 5 hectares or more. How did the smaller farmers manage; how did they, in their own terms, *załatwiają sprawy*?[1]

There were at least two ways. With more people of working age in the household and smaller farms, several farmer-worker households had a large relative labor surplus vis-à-vis the requirements of the farm. With some members employed for wages, the household had greater cash flow and could better afford to pay more for credit and other capital inputs. In order to obtain credit, they had to sell their hogs to the state agency at a set price. This accounts for the large gross sales on paper. The costs, however, were high, and the profits correspondingly low. The second way to manage was to deal on the black market. In spite of producer increases paid to farmers in 1974 and 1976, selling meat on the black market was far more lucrative than selling to the state. In brief, farmers understated the number of hogs they were raising and sold the difference na lewo, for hard currency if possible. I knew of several families of worker-farmers and farmer-workers who used the contacts they established in the workplace to sell meat to city dwellers at between three and four times the price they would have received from the state. The smaller farms, though, with limited land and credit, were unable to fully exploit the black market. At least one woman in the village (there may well have been others) from a commercial household (Group 4) that owned a larger farm had a "meat route" in Mielec. She made rounds twice a week with a shopping bag full of homemade kielbasa and chickens, ducks, and occasionally geese, all dressed and ready for cooking.

For reasons that are no doubt apparent, no one was willing to provide me with all the figures and all the mechanisms by which they utilized the black market. Therefore, my data on this subject are anecdotal and unsystematic. Nonetheless, we know that the official figures pertaining to the number of hogs owned were deflated. The household of the meat woman, for example, listed only five hogs with the gmina office, so I used the same figure in the statistics—though I counted sixteen in the barn. Similarly, sales to the state for this household indicated that the farm was of average productivity. If black market sales were added to official sales, this household surely would have been one of the top in the village. The cultivation of pigs for the marketplace is today, after the restoration of capitalism on a national scale, highly relevant, as we shall see.

Although na lewo meat sales were probably the most lucrative in 1979, the private market in food was not confined to them alone. The farmers' market (both the daily *rynek* and the weekly *jarmark*) also had fresh fruits and vegetables available, even when they were absent from the state stores, but they cost two or three times what they would have in the state store, had they been available. At least one farmer who had 6 hectares and was also in the commercial group had an arrangement with a private greengrocer in Mielec—a middleman who bought produce from local farmers and, bypassing the state altogether, sold it in town at prices higher than charged by the official store. Another trio of farmers, also full-time producers, had a contract with a wholesale merchant in Kraków that depended upon a labor surplus. They grew a kind of dried bean similar to the navy bean especially for this buyer. An intensive application of labor, involving not only hand-harvesting but hand-sorting of the beans by size, rendered this crop unsuitable for families with labor shortages, in spite of its potential profitability. I spent a number of afternoons helping to sort beans while talking with members of one of these families. The three farmers shared the cost of transporting the sorted and sacked beans to Kraków.

This arrangement and the jarmark were not illegal in 1978 and 1979, though they had been earlier. The socialist state, faced with the fait accompli of an underground market, gave official sanction to what already existed because it could not prevent it, even if it wanted to, without resorting to outright force. Besides, the private market supplemented the official system in doing what it had thus far been unable to do: to provide sufficient and regular food supplies. Attempts to force farmers to bend to the will of the state and satisfy compulsory deliveries or to make contracts with the state agencies had caused farmers to cut back production in the past, producing additional shortages and political unrest. It would seem the farmers had taken a large measure of control in a domain the state sought to carve out for itself.

There were several ways of working na lewo in the production sphere. Although there was some mechanized equipment in the village, most farm work for most people was labor-intensive. A few farms, for example, had milking machines, but most households hand-milked two or three times a day, and whereas the hay, wheat, barley, and rye may have been mechanically cut by a tractor-drawn reaper, they were hand-gathered and tied with twine fashioned from a few stalks. A potato digger turned up the soil to expose the roots, but workers followed behind, gathering the potatoes into gunnysacks and hefting them into the wagon. The size of landholdings is not the sole determinant of wealth and class differences; the dependency of farmers on historically scarce draft power and farm equipment, either their own or hired, is also germane, as the data for Wola Pławska indicate.

One of the more notable practices in the production sphere had to do with labor exchanges among households. Given that the past and present sociocultural order connotes the independence of the household, it is not surprising that it is autonomous from the rest of the family as a production, distribution, and consumption unit. Nor is the related observation that, when larger cohorts of workers are necessary, reciprocal labor arrangements are made as the situation demands and not on the basis of kin obligations and as freely given "gifts." Most of the day-to-day work in the late 1970s and at present is done on an individual household basis. Those farms with the most efficient equipment, the combines, the hay mowers, and the potato diggers, are often able to compensate for labor shortfalls for the short-term, intensive tasks such as getting in the harvest by "loaning" their equipment to smaller farms in exchange for labor power. These are everyday occurrences in Wola Pławska and many households, such as that of Maria and Zosia described in Chapter 6, have long-standing work arrangements of this kind with others. Although these arrangements could be viewed as reciprocity among family and neighbors, the terms of labor exchange are susceptible to another interpretation, namely, the creation of surplus value through labor appropriation.

Another permutation has to do with the acquisition of needed agricultural inputs. Some households with small farms and an "excess" of labor power form alliances, preferably but not necessarily with kin who have larger farms and hence access to relatively inexpensive feed, fertilizer, credit, and other inputs. Extra amounts of these goods are resold to kin or neighbors, sometimes for cash but also in exchange for labor. In the case of loans, those with the smaller holdings also provide labor to their larger counterparts on demand, usually (but not only) at harvest or planting time. Industrial workers often take paid time off from their jobs to work on their own fields or those of neighbors to whom they owed favors. A less common way of paying back a loan in 1979 was with one or more piglets that, when grown, would probably be slaughtered, sold on the black market, and end up on the table of a family in town.

The activities of the Średniak family provide an example of how the process worked in 1979. There were six people in the household. Andrzej and Marysia were forty-two and forty years old, respectively. Marysia's widowed mother legally owned the house and lived with them. She and her husband gave about 2.5 hectares of land to Marysia as part of her dowry when Marysia was married in 1959. The youngest of the three children of the household, a girl of thirteen, was still in school; the older two boys, Jacek and Jan (nineteen and eighteen, respectively), had finished eight years of elementary school. Jacek also attended agricultural vocational school for two years. The household owned 3.8 hectares of land, just about the average for the village. A little less than half their land was in a single parcel, the rest scattered about the village in several small lots.

All members of the household participated to a greater or lesser degree in agricultural labor on the farm; the youngest daughter put in the least time. The Średniaks had a labor surplus—four full-time workers (Marysia, Andrzej, and the two sons) and two part-time workers (the daughter and the grandmother)—opening a number of options denied to labor-poor households. The grandmother, who was in good health, did all the housework and cooking; churned butter; fed the chickens, ducks, and swine; and milked the family's four dairy cows. Although Marysia worked part-time as a seamstress in a tailor shop in Mielec, she also did farm labor. Jan, however, usually worked on the farm of his father's brother and on that of a neighbor who was more distantly related. For this work, he was paid about Zł 100 for a day's work (the equivalent of Zł 2,500 a month for a six-day week), less than the minimum wage (which at the time was Zł 4,500 per month).

By all rights, the farm of the Średniaks should have been marginal. The uncle for whom Jan worked was the oldest in his family and inherited all his parents' land in the late 1960s. Combined with his wife's dowry, his farm totaled about 7.5 hectares. He raised about thirty hogs every year and also had a substantial dairy herd. The neighbor for whom Jan also worked raised about twenty hogs annually. In exchange for Jan's labor power, the neighbor and the uncle each bought extra feed grain, on subsidized credit, which they resold to the Średniaks at their cost. The Średniaks were thus able to raise a dozen hogs of their own on state subsidies. At marketing time, the uncle and the neighbor sold some of the Średniak's swine along with their own and gave the proceeds to them. The Średniaks slaughtered the rest and sold the meat privately.

Why did the uncle and the neighbor do this for the Średniaks? Aside from kin considerations, both households suffered labor shortages. The uncle was a widower with two young daughters, neither old enough to do farm work. His elderly father-in-law was also part of his household, but his health no longer allowed him to contribute substantially to the farm labor. The neighbor, on the other hand, had been working in the United States for several months. In his absence, the neighbor's wife experienced an acute but temporary labor shortage, and Jan's labor power was as necessary to the upkeep of this farm as it was to his uncle's. Although Jan's contribution to this household was temporary, increasing numbers of people were to migrate to the United States during the 1980s, making the opportunities to sell labor power more frequent and, to the degree that those who could not migrate were the sellers of labor, enhancing differentiation. On their side, the Średniaks were able to raise swine at a profit by using Jan's surplus labor power in order to gain access to inexpensive capital inputs they would otherwise be denied because of the smallness of their farm. The other two households (those of the uncle and the neighbor) obtained the labor power they needed to realize profits on their own farms. All households benefited from the arrangement. Andrzej wanted to buy more land to bring his farm to the 5-hectare minimum necessary to purchase his own capital inputs less expensively.

Thus, the black market in labor had the possibility of retarding differentiation as well as advancing it. These labor relations, however, have become less ambiguous as the policies of the capitalist state have effectively eliminated the black market and as national unemployment figures soar. But before we address the latest permutations of rural surplus extraction, we should examine the additional aspects of disguised labor appropriation in 1979.

A good example of how the larger farms parlayed their equipment into labor advantage during the late 1970s and early 1980s was the cooperative threshing group. Because the existing privately owned threshers were generally relatively primitive gas-powered machines, their operation required the effort of a number of workers. The most efficient threshing parties consisted of ten or twelve persons and therefore usually included at least three households, generally neighbors or kin who had threshed together for years. A schedule was made for all participating households, and on the appointed day all gathered at the barn of one and set to work. If the job took less than a day, they would move all the equipment to the second barn and so forth. Each household paid for the gasoline used in its own threshing but did not pay rent to the owner of the machine. All workers were fed by the host household and labored until everyone's grain was finished. Smaller households provided

TABLE 8.1   Differential Contribution and Consumption of Labor Power Within a Threshing Group

	(a) Days Needed to Thresh	(b) Percentage of Total Labor Power	(c) Workers Provided	(d) Workdays Provided (c × 3.5)	(e) Percentage of Labor Provided (d ÷ 38.5)
Farm A	2.0	57.1	3	10.5	27.3
Farm B	0.5	14.3	4	14.0	36.4
Farm C	1.0	28.6	4	14.0	36.4
Total	3.5	100.0	11	38.5	100.0

food for more workers and consumed less, a form of unequal exchange that is relevant to those who live close to the margins.

Let us take a typical example to illustrate how the larger farmer, usually the owner of the machine, had the advantage. Farm A owned the machine and had three workers. Because of the size of Farm A's landholdings, the crop would take two full days to thresh. Farm B, considerably smaller, had four workers and a half a day's work, whereas Farm C, also with four workers, required a full day. The threshing took a total of 3.5 days of work and eleven workers. Farm A contributed 10.5 labor days to the task (number of workers times 3.5) and Farms B and C 14 labor days each, a total of 38.5 labor days. Requiring 57 percent of the total labor time for its two days' work (2 divided by 3.5), Farm A contributed only 27 percent of the labor power (10.5 divided by 38.5). Farm B needed only 14 percent of the total time but contributed 36 percent, and Farm C, requiring 29 percent, also put in 36. Table 8.1 summarizes these relationships. Contributing the fewest labor days but requiring more than the other two combined, Farm A appropriated labor power from Farms B and C.

One might well ask if this example does not represent a demographic fluke. What would happen, for example, if Farm A had six workers and the others fewer? Empirically, this did not happen. The mean number of workers per household in the full-time farmer group, the commercial farmers (Group 4), where all the equipment was concentrated, was 2.1. In worker-farmer and farmer-worker households (Groups 2 and 3), from which clients were drawn, the averages were 2.7 and 3.5, respectively. Subsistence farmers (Group 1) had an average of but one worker per household.

Threshing groups were inherently unequal in composition as they required at least one owner of a thresher. Not surprisingly, none of the threshing groups in the village included more than one equipment owner, nor did any contain households with fewer than three workers. Kin were not necessarily included unless they had the prerequisite number of workers. Even allowing for the initial cost and the upkeep of the thresher, there was an imbalance of which all parties were acutely aware. The larger farmer rationalized by observing accurately that the smaller farms would not get all their grain threshed were it not for his machinery. Although a few very old farmers still hand-thresh with a flail, most of those under sixty do not even know how. One old man demonstrated the use of the flail to me while his son and grandchildren watched. The children stifled laughter when their father, inexperienced in the art of flailing, repeatedly knocked himself painfully on the shins. Before there were gas threshers, men spent most of the winter flailing and separating grain from chaff. In 1978 and 1979, however, worker-farmers and just as likely their wageworking sons and daughters took time off from their jobs to thresh. A major difference between farmer-worker and commercial farmers, of course, is that households tend to be in different stages of the developmental cycle of the family. In farmer-worker households, sons and daughters who work off the farm for wages can be drawn back onto it in times of labor-intensive activity, a regular occurrence with deleterious effects on local industry.

By 1990 most of the gas threshers had been phased out and replaced with far less labor-intensive combines. For the most part, these are owned by the same farmers who had threshers a decade ago. Rather than appropriate the labor power of neighbors and kin in large blocks only at harvest or planting time, patrons now claim their due over the course of the entire year. Moreover, their due has grown. Kasek, my host in 1990, watched his father, a mechanic now retired from WSK, join a small group of men preparing to service the tractors, trucks, and combine of Antoni, a farmer across the road whose land was within the limits of Rzędzienowice. Antoni was preparing for the upcoming harvest. His father, Kasek commented, used to work a few days a year for Antoni in exchange for a few hours of plowing and threshing services in the spring and again at the end of summer.

Now that Antoni has a combine, he no longer requires as much concentrated help at threshing time. But he still plows and harvests Kasek's, and Kasek's father's small pieces of land as well as that of a number of other small farmers and worker-farmers. In spite of his acquisition of a combine, Antoni no longer cultivates as much rye or wheat as he once did; large amounts of his huge (by local standards) farm are now planted in poppy seed, coriander, and other specialty crops that require intensive applications of labor during the growing season as well as at harvest time but are far more profitable than grains. Antoni calls on Kasek and his father and other clients far more often than he did ten years ago, often without warning, Kasek says.

I'll have worked all day [at WSK] and Antoni will waylay me as I walk home from the bus stop and oh-so-politely ask me if I could stop over that afternoon to help him with this or that. And of course, no matter what I have already planned to do, no matter how tired I am, I always say that yes, of course, I'll be there as soon as I've had my dinner. After all, he has the equipment, he is the owner [właściciel].

This was said with more bitterness than had been apparent among others ten years earlier. Then as now, however, small farmers really had no other choice. In 1979 threshers and small tractors suitable for use on private farms were in short supply. They were theoretically available for rent from the agricultural machine station, but there was an insufficient number to service everybody; the larger farms, as a matter of policy, had first call. The same applied to combines in 1990.

The outright sale of labor power in Wola Pławska was not widespread in 1979. Nevertheless, villagers reported that it had increased noticeably over the previous four or five years. The wives and school-age children of several of the poorer worker-farmer households worked part-time on the land of another large farmer in Rzędzienowice, one also described as a właściciel. Although I do not have specific data for Rzędzienowice, Wola Pławskans told me that this farm, like that of Antoni, was at least 50 hectares. (People tend to be evasive about exactly how much land they or others have. My figures are from official sources rather than self-reported. I make no claims for their correspondence to reality.) One of the few combines I saw in 1979 was in use on this farm, and Julian, the owner, hired several people from his own village to work on a seasonal basis. The hiring of agricultural labor was not illegal, but the tax on hired labor was high.

Some Western observers claim that the progressive land tax and that on hired labor made the costs of large farms run on this basis prohibitive and, because farmers hiring labor had to pay social insurance for workers, the development of agrarian capitalism was constrained under socialism (Lane and Kolankiewicz (1973:48–49). Taxes, however, are progressive in most parts of the capitalist world, and employers must pay benefits for their employees; this has not prevented capitalists from entering the market or from realizing profits. In any case, the larger farmers did not pay social benefits or a tax because they hired workers unofficially. Workers in turn did not publicly acknowledge receiving wages. This compact, like all na lewo arrangements, was strictly informal. But whether formal or informal, such practices promote social differentiation among the participants.

Those who owned mechanized means of production in 1979 were as aware as their nineteenth- and early twentieth-century counterparts must have been that they could make their machinery more profitable by loaning it and their services to other farmers during slack periods. Because fees, whether in cash or in labor exchange days, could be set with impunity, the potential for realizing high returns was enormous. It goes without saying that equipment owners serviced their own farms at the most propitious times. Therefore, farmers who had to await the availability of equipment often suffered losses in productivity because of sowing or harvesting delays. As the amount they marketed declined accordingly, it became more difficult yet to acquire the capital inputs that might maintain minimal levels of farm productivity and enable them to compete.

Without belaboring the point, I should emphasize that farmers with the equipment, and these were and by and large still are those with the larger landholdings, have a decided advantage to the point that the long-existent economic categories described earlier, which once were primarily differences of degree rather than of kind, have been transformed into class fragments. As the logic of the process works itself out, the result has been further accumulation of surplus and the acceleration of class fractionation. Given the economic crisis of the early 1990s and the new government's more immediate need to place national resources in other areas, it is unclear whether generally affordable agricultural machinery and other capital input shortages can be resolved in the short term under the new capitalist restructuring. As the supply eventually increases under a market economy, I have no doubt that only a small number of farmers who are already prosperous will be able to afford them, further accelerating the movement along the American road to agrarian capitalism that began well before there was a government intent upon rebuilding the overt manifestations of a capitalist state.

Not everyone in the village, by any means, agreed that class differentiation (by any name) was occurring, but as the old categories are transformed and evolve, consciousness of affinities within and of opposition between them is growing, as is elaboration of bourgeois ideology. Vertical integration was long manifest in patron-client relations between those with the largest landholdings, the machinery, and the access to capital inputs from the socialist state and those who were unable to acquire the means of production to compete. Even in 1979, horizontal links were not predicated primarily on family ties but on economic and political bonds that crosscut kinship. In other words, labor appropriation and the semiproletarianization of some small farmers was usually disguised as reciprocity as those without access to tractors, threshers, transport, and other machinery were forced to trade the family's labor power for them. This is not to suggest that there were and are no kinship links across emerging class divisions but simply to stress that lateral affiliations were then and still are formed on the basis of common class interest rather than primarily on kinship. Horizontal integration among proto-capitalists was manifest in, for example, marriage alliances that explicitly joined productive farms and the pooling of resources in order to corner the market in what were already especially profitable specialty crops and livestock.

Even those villagers who lacked the necessary resources to participate directly in the black market were accomplices to it in their expressed admiration of those who did break the spirit and letter of socialist ideology (and the law) and in their unwillingness to break class solidarity by naming active participants. There were many rural and urban Poles who could not play a part in all aspects of the legal economy prior to 1990 because they had too few salable resources, too little money or no other source of income (particularly a dollar income), lacked the labor power, or were in some other way handicapped in the competition for scarce resources. The black market was a consequence, and its social costs included an increasingly large alienated populace who were squeezed mercilessly by the two-tier system. During the 1970s and 1980s, the prices of many goods and services, including luxury foods, were typically quoted in dollars rather than złoty. The illegal black market and the officially sanctioned dollar economy imposed the rationing by price normally associated with the capitalist marketplace in which almost anything could be bought if one had the money. Both the black market and the dollar economy contributed to social inequities on an enormous scale and fostered farmer consciousness and action in opposition to the socialist state. They also contributed to the further class fragmentation within the farming population. Furthermore, the black market was instrumental in reducing respect for the social system itself and for law in general.

Wola Pławska and Rzędzienowice are insignificant little villages, and skeptics might well argue that what farmers in these villages do can hardly have an effect on the politics or the economy of the country as a whole. These villages, however, are no different from thousands just like them throughout the country, and there is no reason to think that people in Wola Pławska and Rzędzienowice are any different from those who live in the southwest, the northeast, or the central part of the country. According to all reports, na lewo practices I observed in Wola Pławska were only a microcosm of similar practices common throughout the Polish countryside and urban areas alike (see Steven 1982; Wedel 1986). The moral dominance of what the socialist state would have liked to be its organic ideology continued to slip as virtually everyone who could operated not only on the edge of the law but outside the parameters of the guiding principles of the socialist system. Antisocialist conscious-

ness, which stresses individual endeavor and which was actually encouraged by the system that has since failed, was sustained by resentment
of the powerful rather than by solidarity with powerless peers. As one
Pole put it:

> There is a cumulative effect of so much hardship during times of peace
> when the enemy is ill-defined and the issues intangible. The danger of
> moral disintegration is very real indeed. Only the most committed opposition
> activists or the most rigid party hard-liners have it easy. For them everything
> is so simple—the solutions to our problems so self-evidently obvious. For
> the rest of us, standing in line for the bare essentials, scrabbling around
> for that little bit of extra, just getting by, hoping that we'll make it through
> the next winter, are really all that concern us. When a proud people begin
> to feel like that, there is no knowing what they may do next to alleviate
> their sense of grievance (quoted in Steven 1982:86).

One might reasonably ask how and why the socialist state tolerated
extensive black market activities that flew in the face of all that should
be sacred to the socialist ideal. A simple answer is that the prime goal
of Polish economic policy between 1970 and 1980 was to finance its
ambitious plan for high capital investment based mostly on the import
of Western technology and to increase living standards by importing
feed grains to allow for the expansion of livestock herds. A central
objective had to have been to pay back the loans that were keeping
the country at the mercy of Western investment bankers. Poland needed
(and still needs) every dollar it can lay its hands on, and the black
market in goods, services, and commodities, paid for in hard currency,
provided many of those dollars. The state did not need to be an active
part of the black market, as Stewart Steven (1982) charged it was; by
nothing more than its silent complicity it became a major player in the
na lewo game.

We have come full circle back to the issue of control. Although few
theorists associated with the ideological project of the PZPR state would
likely claim that nationalization of the means of production unambiguously denotes socialism, most no doubt would argue that the socialization
of private property would constitute a first and decisive step in that
direction. Moreover, they certainly would argue that control over the
means of production is also a criterion of class location. Because the
Party presumed to have controlled many, if not most, of the decisions
of farmers, farmers, as constituent elements in an overall socialist political
economy, were also presumed to be qualitatively different from family
farmers in capitalist countries in terms of their ideology and political
consciousness. They were viewed as having been fully incorporated into
the socialist system in terms of Marxist ideology, proletarian conscious-

ness, and socialist practice. That they emphatically were not suggests the final paradox of Polish agriculture and indeed of the management of the socialist state: the ways in which people acted in their perceived interests to counteract the interests articulated by official state policy.

The ironic aspect of the actions of the farmers is not so much that they were behaving contrary to official policy (at several levels), though they were, but that their actions corresponded to an obvious but unstated goal of the entrenched bureaucracy—increased productivity to be sure, but increased productivity at any and all costs, including social costs. Those costs included contributing to and reinforcing tendencies toward rural differentiation that were already in place. As socialist theory, the formulation of state control as symptomatic of socialist relations of production failed on both empirical and theoretical grounds. What is more, rural resistance to the control of the state developed such that farmers themselves, by reproducing the social relations of family farming under conditions of the commodification of means of production, also reproduced the class relations of proto-capitalism. The contradictions implicit in the Polish paradox are not limited to "the agricultural sector"; even in 1978 and 1979, when this research was begun, it was clear that agriculture could not become "a little capitalist" without deep implications for the nature of the entire society. Without arguing that the social and material relations of proto-capitalism in the countryside *caused* the overall restoration of capitalism on a national scale, we can see that those implications have since become patently obvious.

In early 1990 Rural Solidarity, all branches of the Peasant party, and at least some members of the OKP, what was once the Solidarity faction in the Sejm, added their voices to farmer demands that remaining restrictions on the buying and selling of land and on private production activities be removed, that additional resources including technology and capital inputs be directed toward private farming, that there be an unfettered market in food, and that most aspects of food production and distribution be subjected to market rules. Rather than radical laissez-faire capitalism, however, they also demanded minimum procurement prices for their produce and a ceiling on prices for production inputs—special protection for farmers, in other words. These are the demands of small farmers in many parts of the world and are usually incorporated into the platform of agrarian populism. The Mazowiecki government quickly met some of the farmers' requirements—for example, food subsidies to consumers and remaining restrictions on land transactions and entrepreneurial activities were canceled—but, significantly, it left others untouched. No ceiling was placed on the costs of fertilizer, pesticides, and other inputs when general price increases were put into effect, so the price of these commodities rose in concert with those of other products. Moreover, administrative controls on procurement prices paid to farmers for their products remain far below the minimum farmers have demanded. Consequently, farmers are decidedly still part of the opposition, this time to the Mazowiecki government.

The potential of neocapitalist agrarian production raises the specter of overtly incompatible relations between emerging rural petit bourgeoisie and the rest of the farmers and between the farmers and the working class. For example, among the effects of production for profit and distribution according to even partial market principles—earlier manifest in the black market and the private market in food—is the fluctuation of prices implicit in free market distribution. One result of the black and private markets, of course, was even less food available in the state-subsidized market and higher consumer prices in the black and private markets. Thus, the poor members of society, rarely mentioned in most sources except in passing, were restricted from access even before market principles were put into effect. Consumer and producer subsidies of meat, cheese, milk, and bread were lifted at the end of July 1989 as part of the negotiated agreement between the PZPR and Rural Solidarity. Officials immediately raised the retail cost of those products by between 100 and 500 percent. The prices of other essentials were also raised. By the first of the following year, the price of coal, the major source of heat in all homes, was increased by 600 percent, electricity by 400 percent, the price of heating gas by 400 percent. The cost of municipal buses and trams, on which almost all Poles depend to get to work, rose 200 percent and intercity buses and railroads by 250 percent. Gasoline prices also doubled. Further price increases announced in mid-1990 added more costs to the consumers. Some families, it is reported, are subsisting on bread and potatoes. Significantly, Jan Szczepański, an eminent sociologist, said in January 1990 that in the short run Polish housewives

> have their own way of getting along. . . . Under Mazowiecki, households are as primitive as they were under Gomułka. Mazowiecki, however, has the support of psychological factors related to the role of the Catholic Church and the religiousness of the Poles. Although the latter does not interfere with their resourcefulness and underhand dealings, all the same it does help people to cope with difficulties. This makes them ready to support the government because Mazowiecki is a religious man and not a Communist.[2]

Szczepański adds, however, that people will not endure these conditions for more than a year without rebelling. The November 1990 presidential election in which Mazowiecki suffered a humiliating defeat proved him correct.

The intent of the dramatic restructuring clearly is to make the state-owned and -operated utilities and services self-sufficient. Less clear is just who is realizing the return on increases in food prices. Not all farmers are "sitting on bags of money" as some officials of the new government have charged as apparent justification for the squeeze put on farmers, that is, by keeping procurement prices low while raising retail prices to consumers and production costs to farmers. In practical terms, the policies of the new government mean that farmers receive next to nothing or in some cases actually lose money on every kilogram of wheat or every pig they sell. Sales of fertilizers, pesticides, and even seed grain were down by over 30 percent during the 1990 growing season. Sacks of them remained in warehouses because many farmers could not even afford the basic inputs needed to produce their crops, critics charged. It was indeed true that most farmers could not afford the capital inputs at the prices demanded by the "free market." As Kasek explained it to me in July 1990, one piglet costs Zł 350,000 (almost the minimum month's salary at that time) and an additional Zł 20,000 to feed it for five to six months, if all feed is purchased. Thus, there is a total cash investment of Zł 770,000, but the selling price is only Zł 1,000,000; the total return of Zł 230,000 (about the cost of a pair of shoes) must cover all other inputs, utilities, and so forth as well as remunerate labor. Over 400 farmers occupied the Ministry of Agriculture for six days in June and July 1990, demanding that producer subsidies and minimum procurement prices for milk, meat, and grains be restored. The procurement price paid for the two liters of cream needed to make a kilogram of butter, for example, is next to nothing, yet the retail cost of that butter is so high that there is a glut of butter on the market and, one would assume, cutbacks in milk and cream production. Aside from a minimal concession on milk, however, the government refused to back down. The minister of agriculture subsequently resigned because, he said, the government has failed to institute a coherent agricultural policy.

Small producers are leaving animal production in droves; others, the more affluent farmers who did relatively well during the late 1970s and even during the lean 1980s, are speculating in animal production and specialty crops. A man who lives at the border between Wola Pławska and Rzędzienowice, for example, is building a facility for 800 swine. Julian and Antoni, the właścicieli described above, have 500 and "hundreds" of pigs, respectively. It is clear that nobody raising just a few pigs can survive but that those who have many realize economies of scale; moreover, they can afford to wait until procurement prices are subjected to market forces and the return on their investment rises. Some villagers are predicting that before much longer the new rural entrepreneurs, the "green barons," as they are called, will be hiring parobcy—the decidedly derogatory term for field hands that was used to describe workers on the manors before World War II. (Green barons contrast with red barons, former PZPR managers who, it is charged, are the only ones who can afford to buy shares in the former state-owned enterprises.) Hard-line free market advocates in and out of the Sejm would actually like to see the small, "inefficient" farms absorbed by their ostensibly more productive cohorts and their owners become agricultural workers because it is the successful entrepreneurs, rural and urban alike, who must form the core of the "middle class" that they say the country desperately needs to become a truly capitalist state. Julian and Antoni are optimistic about their future; small producers are decidedly pessimistic.

Some editorials in major newspapers and journals praise the green barons, or "business farmers," as their fans prefer to call them. It is the business farmers upon whom the future of agriculture depends, according to Josef Kusmierek, a journalist specializing in economics who wrote extensively about farming for the underground press between 1978 and 1989 and whose articles are now found regularly in *Gazeta Wyborcza*, the Solidarity daily newspaper. Business farmers, Kusmierek says, are not traditional, "pure" peasants who have "kept modern agroscience at arm's length" but "educated people . . . who purchased dilapidated farms in the country and, with the original, very elderly owners, started their lives over from scratch" (Kusmierek 1990:10).[3] Ordinary peasants as well as workers and city dwellers in general, he continues, must put aside the suspicions of kulaks that were nurtured by the socialist state and rally to the support of these business farmers, who are also "potential partners in the meat and milk processing industries . . . in the future (authentic) cooperatives, in the farm machine industry" (Kusmierek 1990:10). I know of no such entrepreneurs who are newcomers to farming in Wola Pławska or Rzędzienowice, but I asked several small farmers if Julian and Antoni were green barons and was answered with a shrug. Few villagers are openly critical of neighbors and kin, especially if they seek to emulate the emerging bourgeoisie among them, as most do. Business farmers might well be innovative and highly productive, as Kusmierek claims and some evidence suggests, but to promote their interests at the expense of small farmers becomes a self-fulfilling prophecy as well as yet another version of the dualism of modernization theory discussed earlier.

It is difficult to imagine a future large-scale agrarian capitalism in Poland unless most of the land now incorporated into farms of less than 5 hectares is appropriated by those with the material resources and available labor power to farm it extensively—unlikely until all remaining state restraints are lifted and the forces of the market are allowed to wipe out the smallest farmers (subsistence cultivators, worker-farmers, or farmer-workers), as generally happens unless they are protected. Such reform along the lines of rural capitalization may solve some of the immediate production and distribution problems of Poland, but rural differentiation and inequalities throughout society are sure to intensify.

It is clear that one set of social costs under the socialist state, that is, insufficient supplies of readily available food to meet the demands of all the people, is being traded for another appropriate to capitalism. In the 1970s and 1980s, people complained bitterly that they could not buy all the meat in the quantities they liked, yet many observers noted that even during the crisis years of the early 1980s, meat seemed to be on most tables. In 1990, consumer prices had already risen far faster than cost-of-living increases. Long queues of people waiting to buy meat, cheese, eggs, butter, and fruit have disappeared. The shelves are full, but most people are still doing without, for few can easily afford even food, much less nonessentials. In June 1990 the average monthly salary for industrial workers in the state sector was Zł 890,000, but around Mielec, I was told, the typical salary was still around Zł 500,000–600,000, even less for people with the kinds of jobs villagers held. Minimum wages, in other words, were the norm. Unemployment benefits for the three-quarters of a million without jobs average Zł 127,000. To put this in perspective, at an exchange rate of 9,500:1, a salary of Zł 500,000 is about $52, and Zł 890,000 equals $95. A kilogram of tomatoes cost Zł 9,000 in July or about 50 cents a pound—not much less than in the United States, where the minimum wage of $3.65 an hour is almost 6.5 times the average in Poland. Put another way, the typical Pole must work one hour to buy a pound of tomatoes. Although not all food and food-related inputs are scheduled for immediate subjection to market forces, Harvard economist Jeffrey Sachs (mentioned in Chapter 2), whose advice the government takes, recommends that eventuality for the medium-term future. The full conversion of the economy to market forces took place in 1991. In late 1990 even village tables were set sparingly and guests helped themselves to only the tiniest portions. Farming households that, for the sake of convenience, once bought butter at the dairy and bread at the bakery now churn and bake their own. Workers simply make do with dramatically decreased amounts. Thus, in spite of the cohesion of farmers for the purpose of pressing their demands and their alliance with workers, intelligentsia, and other sectors of society prior to the change of government, agrarian capitalism is a contrary force at work, and it has uncomfortable ramifications for the entire society.

The explicit goal of the government is, of course, increasingly profitable production by larger than present farms and distribution based on adherence to free market forces. The costs, however, are high, at least in the short and medium term. The number of people who would be unemployed by the end of 1990 was revised steadily upward after the first of the year. From 2,000 to 3,000 of the 14,000 employees of WSK in Mielec had been laid off by mid-1990, and an additional 3,500 were subject to three weeks' leave at any time. This had already occurred twice since January. Correspondents who wrote to me in spring 1991 said that additional people had been laid off. People were becoming ugly, one employee of WSK told me; they were writing anonymous letters to shift bosses about the real or imagined laxity of fellow employees, hoping that others would be let go first. Youth who started courses at the various local and regional trade schools a few years ago with a virtual guarantee of employment when they finished are now unemployed and almost completely without prospects. Many cannot afford the bus fare to Mielec for an evening's recreation, and even the *klubs* in both Wola Pławska and Rzędzienowice, almost cost-free gathering places for young people a decade ago, are now locked and boarded. With the moribund industrial sector unable to provide full employment for city dwellers, with aid from the United States and Western Europe far more meager than hoped for, with fewer foreign capitalists looking for investments than expected, rural inhabitants as well as city dwellers are facing hunger and deprivation not known for two generations.

NOTES

1. Wedel (1986) discusses at length the phenomenon of *załatwiance spraw*, or arranging things.

2. Quoted in "Interview with Jan Szczepański," *Uncensored Poland* 2/90 (31 January 1990):18–20.

3. Kusmierek's original article, "Agriculture—the Key to a Prosperous Poland," appeared in *Gazeta International* 3 (15 March 1990) and is reprinted in *Uncensored Poland* 6/90 (31 March 1990):10–11.

9

Who Is in Control?

L AND PRODUCES CROPS and provides subsistence. Even half a hectare, a cow, a few chickens and ducks, and a pig or two defend one against the immediate hunger already being suffered in cities. No one in Wola Pławska or Rzędzienowice, including the smallest worker-farmers, will be letting go of their land willingly. If anything they are devising new ways of defending it against wealthier neighbors, or anyone else for that matter. But land is more than simply a means to live; it also allows farmers to resist, sometimes only in a limited way, the obvious encroachments of the state and to avoid the patent commodification of their labor power. Radical scholars have argued that the separation of the conception of work and its execution is characteristic of all class-based modes of production, state socialism as well as capitalism.[1] Some aspects of this idea may be problematic (e.g., such a separation may not be characteristic of mercantile versus monopoly capitalism). Nonetheless, in the division of labor characteristic of late capitalism in the West, the institutions of the state and the industrial economy, though organically linked, are formally separate, rendering their relationship opaque and making it difficult for workers to recognize and resist the source of their exploitation. Michael Burawoy (1985:122–208), however, explains that because the institutions of the state in state socialist nations such as Poland were formally *fused* with those of the economy, management had available the means of direct coercion and unambiguous domination of workers at its disposal—coercion and domination that were, until 1989, coterminous with Party and state. Management, Party, and trade unions (other than Solidarity), in other words, were direct extensions of the state into the factories; the power of the socialist state was transparent. Even the illusion of control was stripped away from Polish workers, making the appropriation of their labor painfully apparent to them.

In addition to the material embodiment of that which gives sustenance and provides an order of meaning and identity, then, the productive land of a farmer may also and as importantly be an icon, a signifier of control—the control workers seek to exercise over the disposal of their own labor power and its products and that they *and* farmers perceive the latter as possessing by dint of landownership. Even smallholders and sharecroppers were not as demeaned in their own eyes and the eyes of others as factory workers precisely because those who worked the land made the decisions about production, at least on a day-to-day basis. If the socialist state condemned the "peasant way of life" as barbarous, old-fashioned, and, sin of all sins in the advanced industrial world, inefficient, then the rest of society elevated it to a symbol of resistance to changes wrought by the state socialist organization of production, most of all the manifest loss of perceived autonomy. Just as the present state still condemns it, so too may urban workers continue to sanctify it.

Populism Prospers

Urban perceptions of "the country" are sometimes contradictory (Williams 1975). For certain purposes, it can be regarded as a bastion of ignorance, superstition, and backwardness. In times of particularly acute social disorganization, however, it can be envisaged as a repository of the good life, a place where traditional values of religion, family, an honest day's work, and above all else self-sufficiency are maintained. Polish farmers were the last remnant of socialist society that even *appeared* to have exercised any control over their productive lives, who seemed able to both conceive of and execute their own production and, by resisting its commodification, seemed able to dispose of their labor power at will. Thus, despite the potential and realized conflict between the interests of farmers, especially the emerging bourgeoisie among them, and those of the rest of society, and despite growing disparities in the countryside itself, farmers and the lifestyle they epitomize came to signify self-sufficiency and independence under the socialist state. In light of the continuities between the previous state and the present one, this is a relationship that is likely to continue.

What is more, in a world in which workers had no illusions about the domination under which they labored, in which the Soviet Union was widely recognized as the ultimate guarantor of the Polish state, and in which citizens believed that the fruits of their own labor power paid for their subjugation, the continued existence of private farmers conjured up a bucolic and largely imaginary version of the past—a collective memory of a former lifestyle, political independence, and organization of production that was, in reality, far from homogeneous, harmonious, and organic. In the popular imagination, pre-1945 society had been constituted mostly by socially conscious and beneficent aristocratic landowners, independent farmers, and just enough artisans and small-scale industry to provide for the nonagricultural needs of the population. This mythical rendition of history poses a certain appeal to contemporary workers but a generation or two removed from "the peasantry" themselves. First under the heavy and palpable hand of the socialist state and now under a new and to them foreign organization of production that is threatening their livelihood, workers are vividly aware of their lack of autonomy and control over their destiny. The invoked past is informed by the ideology of agrarian populism—a philosophy that was prevalent from the nineteenth century and whose adherents crosscut all classes. Nineteenth-century populists pitted peasants, emblematic of the undifferentiated people, against capitalists and socialists alike. Twentieth-century populists continued to oppose socialism but also regard big government as an adversary of the people, ignoring all other social divisions except those stemming directly and obviously from economic and governmental imbalances of power. Historic and contemporary divisions along class, ethnic, race, or gender lines have never been part of the populist agenda.

In Chapter 7 I critiqued neopopulism in the context of Chayanovian demographic differentiation and the functionalist sociology of development paradigms and suggested that the theory informing Polish agricultural development after 1956 had certain unmistakable affinities to them. To carry this analysis a step farther, we might look at that farm policy in the context of the control issue. We find that neopopulist prescriptions for "peasant" farming in the capitalist world and the Polish policy of the socialist decades are broadly similar. In neopopulist literature pertaining to agricultural development in both nonsocialist underdeveloped and developed capitalist countries, including those in Western Europe and North America, agricultural economists have long claimed that family farms are economically superior to larger agribusiness enterprises, especially in kinds of production that are susceptible to high labor inputs (Wortman and Cummings 1978; Hightower 1973; Rodefeld et al. 1978). Neopopulists argue on these grounds that capitalist enterprises should be prevented from replacing small, labor-intensive family farms, despite their superexploitation of family labor power. If we consider the Polish state farms the functional equivalent of capitalist enterprises in terms of their technical requirements and need for capitalist calculations, the debate between advocates of capitalist or capitalist-like farming and neopopulist proponents of family farming has an analog in Poland.[2] Comparison of statistical yearbooks for farming suggests that family farms did indeed outperform state farms in a number of branches of production—notably livestock and truck farming—areas that are labor intensive in Poland.[3] This was surely recognized if not always acknowledged by the social scientists who guided farm policy.

Contemporary Western European neopopulists such as Claude Servolin (1972) and Samir Amin and K. Vergopoulos (1974), note the threat that differentiation, under the pressure of the commodification of the means of production, poses to the persistence of peasant farming in France and Greece. They suggest that the state use the administrative means at its disposal to mitigate or retard differentiation by extracting the "excess" surplus some peasant farmers might ordinarily accumulate. The administrative measures they urge include establishing unfavorable terms of trade for agriculture by subsidizing cheap food for the urban population, so that cultivators are left with only enough surplus to reproduce themselves more or less unchanged, thereby preventing the inevitable process of differentiation from unfolding. This is the role they suggest the French and Greek states take to deliberately prevent the larger, more economically viable peasant farms from augmenting themselves by absorbing the small farms. Without such administrative controls to prevent the emergence of a rural bourgeoisie, they suggest, the resulting larger farms will eventually be organized on capitalist principles with hired labor power and family farming will be eliminated altogether.

The pre-1989 Polish state's analogue to the recommendations of neopopulists for Western European peasants was its attempt, also through administrative means, to limit the influence of the market by extracting surplus from its farmers. Administrative measures included compulsory deliveries from farmers and the subsidizing of food to consumers. Compulsory deliveries, however, failed to stimulate production sufficiently to meet demand. Production was inadequate in part because demand increased but also because some farmers withdrew from commodity production altogether. They were alienated by a system that, by denying them basic social benefits, had made them second-class citizens. Consequently, they preferred not to grow crops at all rather than be forced to sell their produce to the state at prices they claimed were extortionary.

The hated compulsory deliveries were abolished in 1972, to be replaced with a contract system that it was hoped would be a better stimulus to production. Free health care and social insurance were extended to private producers for the first time as the state sought to incorporate them more fully into the socialist system. The state began to buy from farmers on a voluntary but strictly contractual basis and also attempted to influence farmers by controlling selling prices of all agricultural products and access to all inputs as well as to all investments and credits (Duymovic 1980:187). Certain strings were attached to contracts with the state, such as the coal allotments, which were intended to provide additional incentives to sell to the state, but the major inducements were prices paid for products and inputs. Although a private market for some farm products, mainly fresh fruits and vegetables, was allowed by the late 1970s, the sale of grains, meats, and other commercial farm products remained legally controlled. Abolishing compulsory deliveries in favor of market incentives, however, did not prevent the private and black markets in agricultural produce, particularly meat, from emerging, as we have seen.

Food was subsidized at artificially low prices until January 1990, the overt principle being that all the necessities of life should be equally available to all citizens of the socialist state. By the mid-1970s, food subsidies amounted to 15 percent of the annual state budget (Duymovic 1980:190; Dziewanowski 1977:213). Subsidies to suppress surplus accumulation by primary producers, it will be recalled, is also a tactic of neopopulism. The state limited as much as possible the influence of the market, which, if left alone, would drive up prices paid to producers as demand increased. Presumably by underwriting the cost of food to the consumer, in other words, the socialist state retarded some of the surplus accumulation that might have ordinarily occurred. As Alain de Janvry (1980:158) points out, however, the terms of trade and surplus extraction that the neopopulists as well as in this case the socialist state depended on "cannot eliminate *all* the surplus of *every* peasant, even if it does so on the average. Surplus extraction may slow down differentiation but in no way cancels it." That this proposition has been found to be accurate in Poland has not prevented popular imagination from wistfully invoking an image of "the peasant" to signify a past that it portrays as actually devoid of any other conflict apart from the strife caused by popular opposition to the socialist state.

Beyond its appeal to Polish workers, the romantic ideal of the independent, autonomous farmer in full control of his labor power and his life, symbolizing a past that never was and a future that can never be, is part of the ideology of some spectrums of the contemporary political opposition. As recently as 1987, experts were saying that few Poles seemed to foresee or necessarily want a political economy organized along the lines of capitalism. Moreover, the left opposition that concerned itself with issues of class was subjected to particularly harsh restrictions (Feher and Heller 1986:41; Kavan 1987:3). The voice of the Left was and remains muted and its cause not taken up by large sectors of the population. The general reluctance to voice dissent in terms associated with the Left, that is, those of inequality or class, dates to the Stalinist period (1948–1956) but still pertains to a large degree today. Between 1948 and 1956 all political rhetoric, all identification with class and inequality, even the content of the terms *Left* and *Right* were appropriated by the state and given new meaning. Insofar as the later opposition figures who are now prominent members of the leadership concerned themselves with class and equality prior to their accession to power, they did so not in terms of a real or potential class struggle between the interests of, say, workers and emergent bourgeoisie, rural or urban, but only in terms of the struggle between state and Party and "the people."

The populism of the immediate past and the present emerges in part from the availability of the symbols of the discourse provided by the prewar Peasant party, the nationalism and chauvinism of the interwar National Democrats (see Chapters 3 and 4), and the availability of the Catholic church as an alternative forum to that of the PZPR. The language of what was until August 1989 the alternative civil society was particularly revealing. There had developed a central emphasis on "freedom and peace," words that became a code for resistance on the part of many dissidents and ordinary citizens alike and that united what might otherwise have been disparate strands of opposition.[4] The Soviet Union and the PZPR/state were the main enemies when freedom was invoked, but the term also was taken as emblematic of "the West," enthusiastically and uncritically embraced as a citadel of that attribute, especially but not exclusively by the young—an emblem that was (and still is) also symbolically as well as materially linked to the passion for Western goods and the sacralizing of free enterprise.

"Language," Anthony Giddens notes, "is intrinsically involved with that which has to be done; the constitution of language as 'meaningful' is inseparable from the constitution of forms of social life as continuing practice" (1979:4). With concern for internal class struggle and equality relegated to the category of Soviet propaganda, the content of much of the dissidence within Poland between 1980 and 1989 bore a remarkable resemblance to that of earlier populism. To be sure, insofar as the opposition concerned itself with issues of ecology, the environment, or nuclear disarmament, it was a left populism. Nonetheless, the larger part of samizdat literature published both in Poland and abroad identified with and supported without reflective comment the aspirations of farmers for the relaxation of remaining state controls over production and distribution.[5] With most social conflict reduced to a simple dichotomy between the *undifferentiated* people and the state, contemporary Poles created a unified and highly imaginary community (Anderson 1983), just as their populist predecessors had.

This consensus is, of course, unraveling in the cold light of the present as new conflicts emerge and new definitions are given to the categories of Left and Right. It is in fact hazardous to one's political career to be labeled a leftist, something Wałęsa clearly took into account in attempting to "clean the Solidarity house," as he put it in June 1990 when he fired some of his early associates in Solidarity and distanced himself from the former colleagues he now regards as leftists (e.g., Michnik and Geremek). This was Wałęsa's way of reasserting his importance in the shaping of the state, of announcing his dissatisfaction with the Mazowiecki government, of indicating his desire to be president, and of preparing the ground for the announcement of the Center Agreement, the titular leader of which is right-wing populist senator Kaczyński, but which is clearly Wałęsa's party.

Kaczyński is critical of the Left, characterizing it (them?) as ambiguous about the merits of private property and too willing to compromise with Communists and the PZPR (now renamed the Social Democracy of the Republic of Poland, further confounding the very meaning of socialism and, according to wags, giving democracy a bad name). Furthermore, the Left is, according to Kaczyński, anticlerical if not anti-Christian. Finally, it is mistrustful of "the people." The Right, on the other hand (of which Kaczyński is a self-styled spokesperson) is completely, unambiguously, and emphatically in favor of immediately turning all property over to private owners but not to former Communist managers. Kaczyński characterizes the Right as strongly against any alliance with the Communist party or any Communists or socialists, completely aligned with the values and practices of the Catholic church, and having absolute trust in the common sense of "ordinary people" (Ash 1990:52). With the exception of his allegation that Geremek, Michnik, and others in their camp are not entirely committed to the ideals of private property, a ludicrous charge in light of the policies they have helped formulate and implement, there may be some truth to Kaczyński's other points. To label a certain mistrust of the clergy and a healthy skepticism about populism as leftist, however, deprives the term of any possible political meaning.

During late summer 1990, Wałęsa had far less general public support than Mazowiecki. This quickly changed as the restructuring sputtered and faltered and as thoughts and then the reality of approaching winter made deprivations more cruel. The farmers were an exception; they favored Wałęsa from the beginning. When farmers marched on and occupied the Agricultural Ministry in July, it was Wałęsa who convinced them that they should return to their fields and trust him to look after their interests. Farmers with whom I talked in Wola Pławska and Rzędzienowice favored Wałęsa over Mazowiecki for president because, they said, Wałęsa is on the side of "the people." They were tired of waiting, they said, for the new government to take action on their behalf, to decrease the prices of capital inputs and increase those of their products, to make farming profitable in other words. They supported

Mazowiecki when he asked them in January to be patient and to make sacrifices. They *had* been patient for almost eight months, they said. They have tightened their belts and they have made more than their share of sacrifices. Now they think Wałęsa ought to be president, and they favor his calls for acceleration of the changes promised by Mazowiecki's government. This means lifting restrictions on the freedom and independence of farmers, they said, and of letting the market determine the prices their products bring. "Acceleration" also means the immediate elimination of all former Communist party members from positions of power, including, of course, President Jaruzelski but also tens of thousands of lesser members who manage factories and various enterprises. Where the experienced people to replace them are to be found in the short run has never been addressed. Moreover, Wałęsa has on several occasions publicly expressed his misgivings about the slowness and inefficiency of "the democratic process." Under Wałęsa's leadership, Poland is likely to be moving more emphatically to a right-wing populist stance. As for agriculture, he had not yet announced a concrete program as this manuscript goes to press but is unlikely to devise one dramatically different from that of the Mazowiecki government.

The ideological underpinnings of populism, both historical and contemporary, constitute invented tradition (Hobsbawm and Ranger 1983). Invented traditions are practices, often of a symbolic or ritual nature, that "seek to inculcate certain values or norms of behavior by [quasi-obligatory] repetition" (Hobsbawm 1983:1–2). Not imported as were British notions of monarchy to colonial Africa or fabricated from whole cloth as were Highland Scottish kilts and tartans, the populist theme in Poland nevertheless embroiders a set of symbols centering on the freedom and independence of the private producer, symbols that seek to disavow the existence, even the possibility, of class differences and conflict among agriculturists.

As in the past, virtually all contemporary farmers in Wola Pławska, even the poorest with the tiniest plots, share the populist aspirations and identify with and emulate the wealthiest in the community. This is the case even if they are informally employed on a larger farm or depend on it for the loan or rent of equipment. Politically active farmers, and for the most part these are the comparatively affluent, belonged in 1979 to the United Peasant party (ZSL), the socialist state–sanctioned heir to prewar populist parties. Today they are members of one or another branch of the Polish Peasant party (PSL), if not PSL-Odrodzenie, as the ZSL is now called, or one of several others. During its existence from the late 1940s to 1989, the ZSL used its platform, publications, and activities to promote the socialist state's plan to "modernize" farming, including the eventual demise of subsistence cultivators and the concentration of their land into larger, presumably more productive and presumably privately owned units.[6]

That the recipients of the newly freed land would be those with already large and technologically efficient farms went unremarked and therefore uncontested. The champions of this point of view had obvious arguments on their side. The performance of state farms—already being dismantled and sold off to individual entrepreneurs—was as unworthy of accolades as the rest of the command economy, and the tiny farms, whether those of subsistence farmers or worker-farmers, never really met the productivity requirements of the country. This argument, however, divorces the economic from the political and social. No matter that only a handful can ever hope to profit from modernization and the apparent loosening of state controls. As long as the ideal remains the well-off, independent farmer and that ideal seems even remotely attainable—as it increasingly does under today's conditions, but only for a few—and as long as farmers continue to enjoy the support of other sectors of the population, they will struggle for their freedom and independence. Freedom and independence, however, do not mean in this case unregulated private enterprise, but the establishing of special supports for farmers, including minimum procurement prices, guaranteed low-cost loans for production, and so forth. These are the same kinds of supports demanded and received by farmers elsewhere in the world, including the United States, where it has often been demonstrated that though they may be intended for small farmers, in fact such supports benefit the largest landowners and agribusiness far more.

Polish populism is a specific case of a general phenomenon in that it has constituted an ideological but not a political or economic alternative to both socialist and capitalist rural development for a hundred years or more, not only in Poland but throughout Europe and the United States. Western populism opposes the undifferentiated people to corporations; Polish populism places the state in place of the corporations but is otherwise broadly similar. Its anti-institutional polemics notwithstanding, populism in and of itself provides neither a theory of history nor a vision of the kinds of processes and infrastructures necessary to ensure social change along the lines many of its proponents envisage.[7] With its anticorporate or antistate bias and its emphasis on small-scale independent production and "traditional" values of family-oriented self-sufficiency, populist philosophy, like the concern with the maintenance of tradition, constitutes, to paraphrase Raymond Williams (1975), a highly selective reading of history. As such, its contemporary reemergence signals the reinvention of a tradition that was itself invented—an ideological constitution of history par excellence.

The paradox is that, flawed and atheoretical as it is, the ideology of populism in Poland more closely corresponded to the everyday reality of the 1970s and 1980s than did available alternatives. Therein, of course, lies its attraction. The populism of the immediate past was as much an historically constituted phenomenon as an ideological construction; the populism of the present is no different.

Control Versus Hegemony

Assumptions of fundamental differences between Polish farmers and petty commodity producers elsewhere in the world have been found to be unsubstantiated in Wola Pławska, at least where antisocialist, anti-Communist sentiments were already widespread in 1978 and 1979. If the subsequent return to capitalism cum right populism and the complete opprobrium of the Left does not represent a sudden, unexpected, and unexpectable turn of events, as I have argued it does not, how can we characterize the Polish social formation from 1947 to 1989? In various ways, most Poles, rural and urban, were saying throughout the 1970s and 1980s (and probably much earlier as well) that "if what we have in Poland is socialism, we don't want it." At the heart of much of the patent disillusionment was the official view, shared by Poland, the Soviet Union, and other Eastern European countries and explicit in all propaganda, that their societies were definitionally socialist. Yet even if one takes only the two most fundamental precepts of Marxism-Leninism shared by all Marxist-Leninists regardless of what other differences there may be among them, namely, that the Communist party represents the objective interests of the working class and of the entire nation and that the socialist state is part of an international proletarian movement, it would have been difficult to find anyone in Poland who believed the state, as dominated by the PZPR, fit that description. Most Party members themselves seemed not to believe it (see Jones et al. 1984).

By appropriating the bedrock assumptions of Marxism and distorting the socialist political and economic program in such a way that they were almost universally disbelieved, the state committed what Michael Szkolny terms "conceptual embezzlement" (1981:3). Conceptual embezzlement "is the primary function of ideology in state collectivist society; for by this gigantic intellectual fraud the ruling class succeeds in cutting off the entire population from the only source of ideas which represents a serious potential threat to the social order," that is, Marxist criticism (Szkolny 1981:3). Even though censorship—particularly of contemporary left scholarship—was imposed between 1948 and 1989, Szkolny goes on to point out that the formal suppression of radical commentary was rendered superfluous by the qualitatively different and more effective censorship constituted by conceptual embezzlement. Thus, most Poles proved impermeable to the inroads of socialist consciousness or practice, and Polish scholars to critical theory.

Marxists have set forth various models or definitions of Soviet-style societies. The minority orthodox Marxist-Leninist position is that ownership of means of production is directly linked to consciousness, everyday practice, and political action in a relatively unproblematic way. Hence, among the earliest revolutionary acts was the appropriation of privately owned productive means and their investiture in the hands of the state, which was supposed to act in the name of and for the benefit of all the people. Socialist consciousness was expected to follow in due course as workers, peasants, and intellectuals labored for the common good. The economic base or infrastructure, in other words, is said to determine consciousness and practice, at least "in the final instance."[8] From this perspective, the Soviet Union and, since the mid-1940s, the Eastern European countries were already state socialist, with the Communist party representing not only the working class but all citizens and ruling in their name. Whatever societal flaws could be discerned were the result of past mistakes, political dogmatism, and theoretical distortions. There is no class conflict in this model: Dissent is the work of reactionary forces both internal and external. This is the way in which the Polish state, the Soviet Union, and the other Eastern European nation-states long defined themselves. Yet some Western Marxists (Cliff 1956; Bettleheim 1975) have asserted that Poland and other Eastern European countries were state capitalist, that is, the state simply took over the role of the capitalist class. A different set of Marxists (for example, Sweezy 1980; Bahro 1981) theorized a transitional society in which aspects of both socialism and capitalism pertain, whereas a fourth (for example, Camiller and Rothschild 1979 and Singer 1981) postulated a new kind of social formation, sui generis—a postrevolutionary class society that was neither socialist nor capitalist.

The state socialist model denies even the possibility or the relevance of class or any other kind of structural conflict among its citizens and cannot be reasonably sustained by any but the most dedicated ideologues. Although since 1944 the Polish political economy had features of both capitalism and socialism, to reduce it to one or the other—theories of convergence—is to impose false and misleading uniformity. The seemingly more neutral dichotomy between command and free market economy likewise implies convergence and, in a command economy, gives the state—defined as nothing more than the set of official institutions—the role of primary societal actor. Moreover, it connotes an otherwise erroneous symmetry based solely on formal economic functions. Equally unsatisfactory is the unilinear view that the only possible successor to capitalism is socialism and that therefore all social formations not clearly capitalist must be transitional; "transitional" is a teleological category without analytic content. Postrevolutionary class society does not cover the terrain completely either—none of the Eastern European countries, including Poland, experienced a socialist revolution. Theorists of this school, moreover, like the others, sometimes imply that social change is primarily the result of imposed political and economic templates. However, as should already be clear, the concept of a transformed though not an altogether new form of a class-based social and economic organization comes closest to the point of view I adopt here.

Whatever other faults or merits it may have, each of these competing theoretical models, with the partial exception of the postrevolutionary thesis, assumes that the ruling class, be it composed of capitalists, proletarians, or apparatchiks, governs via the determining mechanism of a state apparatus. All reify the state by implicitly defining it as made up of a more or less determined set of institutions, or at best as a semiautonomous entity. And, except for the state socialist model, all posit the major societal conflict as between the working class and the bureaucratic Communist party as the executive of that state. Finally, all designate the state as the major actor in effecting social change.

Poland, of course, had socialism imposed from the top down more than forty years ago. Until 1989 it was avowedly governed by principles of Marxism-Leninism, and all Poles see their recent history in terms of a socialist state. The institutions and culture of the new regime in Poland like those of the Bolsheviks in the USSR did not arise from the conditions of late capitalism that had reached the limits of its expansion, as Marx would have predicted. The early attempts to collectivize land were not motivated by the need to move beyond the productive limitations of efficient smallholders, nor did workers take over factories to end their alienation. And it was not because capitalist market forces were unable to translate rising productivity into use values benefiting all of society that the institution of central planning was motivated. As Daniel Singer (1989:202–203) points out, "The system did not transcend capitalism; it acted as a substitute designed to perform capitalism's early tasks, including the dirtiest. And this strange social formation was being presented as a model of socialism."

We have reached a point where we must ask how the Soviet and Eastern European versions of socialism ended up in a maze of contradictions to which there was no exit. The policy shifts leading to the economic quandary that preceded the fall of the Communist party and the demise of the socialist state were not simply a matter of expediency in response to the pressure of external events over which the Party had no control. They were the conjunction of ad hoc decisions and the economistic and class reductionist theory of the state that the Party inherited from the Soviet Union via Lenin and Stalin.

Lenin's interpretation of the state has been one of the most influential in Marxism in terms of its impact on concrete political formations, having been put into effect in the Soviet Union and, with minor modification in Poland and the rest of Eastern Europe. The success of the Soviet Revolution caused the Leninist view, as embellished by Stalin, to become almost monolithic in Eastern European Marxist thought until the last twenty years. In *The State and Revolution* (1965), Lenin's major work on the topic, he defined the state as restricted to the set of repressive juridical institutions (the army, the police, codes of law, parliament) that enforce ruling-class domination of society. The state is the political order and is subordinate to civil society, where, in this essentialist and morphological version of social formation, the economic base and hence production relations are supposed to be located. The historical agencies of governmental oppression under capitalism, for example, are part of the "superstructure" of the capitalist mode of production that supports and enforces the economic base. The nature of capitalist exploitative relations of production, in other words, determines to whose benefit the repressive state apparatus will be put. There is a fundamental separation between the state and civil society, with the nature of the state ordained by and derived from the nature of civil society. Historical development and change, then, must first occur in civil society, that is, the economic base, which then and only then gives rise to a transformation in the superstructure, where consciousness and behavior are located.

It was Lenin's view that the capitalist state is a distinctly capitalist phenomenon, organized by and for the benefit of the capitalist class. As such, in its existing form, the state cannot possibly be taken over by the working class to its own advantage but must be destroyed and replaced with a different set of institutions organized by and for the proletariat. The dictatorship of the proletariat, referring as it does to a dictatorship of the working class over the capitalist was Lenin's alternative to the capitalist state. The dictatorship was to operate through popular decisionmaking bodies such as the soviet and workers' councils. He made it clear that "the withering away of the state" could not occur until after the transition to socialism was complete.

Philip Corrigan, H. Ramsey, and D. Sayer (1978) maintain that although Lenin's theory of the state overtly demands that the existing structures be destroyed, a capture analysis that rests on the assumption that the state is an autonomous element of the superstructure was implicit from the very beginning; Stalin only elaborated what was already there. When the Communist party vanguard captured the apparatus of the Russian state, it supposed that it could subsequently use the neutral structure as a means of transforming production and its relations, a thoroughly economistic notion of production. At least since 1920, therefore, the central strategy of the Communist party of the Soviet Union for socialist construction has been based implicitly on the conviction that the usurpation of leadership by a vanguard with advanced socialist consciousness and scientific knowledge of historical materialism allowed it to put the existing state structure to work developing the productive forces in the interests of all the people. Because most economic sectors and geographic areas of the new Soviet Union were underdeveloped by any account, the first and primary task the Party set for itself was based on "the assumption that modernization must come before socialism" and that technical change "must precede meaningful social change" (Corrigan et al. 1978:42). Similar conditions prevailed in Poland in 1947 when the new Communist party assumed control of the state. Not surprisingly, a similar program for development was instituted.

A major problem with what has come to be identified as Leninism is derived from the failure of pre-Bolshevik Marxist theory to predict socialist revolutions in underdeveloped countries, leaving planners unprepared to implement a principled agenda from the starting point of undeveloped socialism as distinguished from advanced capitalism. One of the first items on the Bolshevik development agenda was to modernize and expand its industrial base. By modernization, the Soviets came to mean increased production through the use of technology and even labor control on the capitalist model. Lenin, Trotsky, and Stalin all admired the principles of Taylorism and sought to introduce them to the Soviet Union, denying that the technological and organizational expertise characteristic of capitalism are tied to a capitalist class structure (Corrigan et al. 1978:42; Braverman 1974). The Bolshevik Revolution became heir to an impoverished, "vulgar and naive" conception of the economic base (Corrigan et al. 1978:28–29). Production was reduced to technology and the social relations of production to state ownership, theses that have their roots in the economistic, reductionist, and deterministic Marxism that dates to the Second International and that was transferred to the Polish state.

There is a major contradiction implicit in Lenin's theory, namely, that it at once supposes that the capitalist state must be destroyed and that it is ultimately capturable. The former premise was never put into operation; the latter, which was, entailed replacing the ruling capitalist class with what turned out to be an entrenched party of bureaucrats, technocrats, and intellectuals that only claimed to act in the name of ordinary people. The logical corollary of the Soviet and Polish emphasis on advanced technology in order to increase production, that is, modernization, was (after the initial promotion of less-qualified people) the inevitable reliance on highly educated "experts," drawn mostly from the intelligentsia. Although the Bolshevik party, for example, started as a party of workers, its original membership was decimated first by the civil war and then by the purges that began in the late 1920s and coincided with Stalin's rise. During the upheavals of the 1920s and 1930s (war communism, the New Economic Policy, internal divisiveness, the forced collectivization of agriculture), the new Party elite, the bureaucrats and technocrats, solidified their power, prestige, and perquisites as the gap between real income and money income widened and the hierarchical principle of one-person rule became entrenched. The "scaffolding of dedicated bosses, held together by discipline, privilege, and power, was a deliberate strategy of social engineering to help stabilize the flux" (Lewin 1976:172).

Thus, the division of labor into workers and those who direct the work, into those who produce and those who make decisions about what is to be produced and how it is to be produced and distributed, a division seemingly as necessary to socialism as to capitalism, came to be controlled by a nucleus of expert and ultimately bureaucratic Party and non-Party members—a vanguard core group. In light of the emphasis placed on technology, modernization, and increased production—top-down socialism, as it were—it was perhaps inevitable that the autonomous workers' councils and the soviets were subordinated to a centralized bureaucratic control and that the cultural and social capital of the country reverted to the remnants of the old intelligentsia, augmented, to be sure, by a "nouveau intelligentsia," drawn partially from the classes of workers and peasants that aligned themselves with the new Party, either officially or de facto.

Party bureaucrats were the first to appropriate material cultural goods, as such appropriation presupposed economic capital, which they now possessed in the form of control, if not ownership, of the means of production. As controllers of economic capital, they had to find ways of also appropriating embodied cultural capital of the intelligentsia in the form of, for example, the scientific, technical, and academic knowledge required to run their enterprises, to educate the technicians, to report on sociological phenomena, and so forth. The managers and intellectuals charged with shaping and overseeing the apparatuses of the state, coercive as well as consensual, had an ambiguous status, even if they were among those who regarded themselves as opposition. They could convert their own cultural capital into economic capital only by selling their services and knowledge—that which makes their cultural capital possible in the first place. In this sense, they are the least powerful segment of the dominant group in society. Nonetheless, to the degree that they also derive their profits at a more removed level from the use of the economic capital of the country, they are still part of the dominant group.

Finally, inherent in the view of the state that is identified with Lenin is the reduction of all levels of social reality, including that of the state itself, to the economic base. In this model, any and every change in the social system is caused or at least preceded by change in the base. It follows both that political action should focus on the economic and that a separate analysis of the state is superfluous (Clarke 1977:2–3). In terms of revolutionary action, the implication is that the final stages of the revolution will be made via the agency of the state, dominated by the vanguard, with its advanced socialist consciousness, acting in the name and interests of the proletariat and the new socialist mode of production (Clarke 1977:22). It is only when the economic order is completely reconstructed on socialist planes that popular consciousness can be entirely transformed to mesh with the already altered material conditions. At that point, the state, no longer necessary, will wither away. That the state has not disappeared, however, and was unlikely to disappear in the Soviet Union or socialist Poland is implicit in the very model the vanguard adopted. As Ludo Abicht puts it:

> In those countries where . . . vanguard parties have come to power . . . one cannot speak of a successful socialization of society. . . . The triumphant vanguard party has not succeeded in bridging the gap between its military or political victory and the freer socialist society it had inscribed on its banner and for which its members often heroically struggled. . . . In the structure of the liberating instrument itself, the ruling party, order had already been built in an unconscious and unchangeable way, and there was no mechanism to transfer that power to the people. On the path to the utopia of a communist society, the party of the new type collided with the wall of its own logic (1984:36–37).

If we agree that Poland was never the society envisaged by orthodox Marxist theorists and that the form of its Communist party and the socialist state was unlikely to lead the country toward a greater liberation of human energy, and that the actions of farmers, workers, and dissidents of all classes that were intended and did in fact overcome the control the Party sought to impose are manifestations of class struggle, then we must inquire as to the nature and location of that struggle. Part of the answer lies in a consideration of Antonio Gramsci's concepts of ideology, hegemony, and the emergence of counterhegemonies and their relations to state power.

Gramsci developed his analysis for application to capitalist states over seventy years ago in an intellectual milieu that, because of its charac- teristically essentialist and often teleological world view, is decidedly dated. Nevertheless, his work can still tell us something about the socialist state in Poland. Gramsci rejects the definition of the state as only a set of coercive institutions and argues that state domination is not simply given by structural determinants but is constantly being renegotiated in the light of changing historical circumstances and the critical agency of human action in both conforming to and resisting political and civil society (1971:244). Gramsci departs from the reified base/superstructure model and divides society conceptually into two parts, political and civil, stressing the dialectical relation between them. Political society, that which Lenin called the state, refers to the coercive institutions of administration whose primary though not sole function is based on the logic of force. Civil society, in contrast, is made up of those institutions, both public and private, that rely on shared symbols, ideas, and meaning rather than simply naked force to make the dominant ideology universal, while at the same time limiting opposition. Civil society is not without its coercive element, just as political society also implies the consent of the dominated, but the preeminence of one class over others is its defining feature. "Civil society exercises the hegemony of the dominant class via norms and values and political society through the juridical apparatus" (Gramsci 1971:12). The essence of Gramsci's theory is that a dominant class does not need to resort to overt force and control to maintain that dominance if it exercises hegemony (McLellen 1979:185).

For Gramsci, the primary issue in the acceptance of domination by "the people" is the hegemony imposed by a dominant class over the values and norms of all other classes. As an "ideological apparatus," the state legitimizes this hegemony, with the intelligentsia among its prime agents. Nonetheless Gramsci recognizes that dominant-class hegemony does not perfectly penetrate and enthrall the consciousness of popular classes. Alternative hegemonies or counterhegemonies arise from the philosophy, activities, and class struggles of what he calls organic intellectuals, grassroots intelligentsia who reflect norms and values of ordinary people. Gramsci's acknowledgment that popular consciousness is not simply a false, vulgar, and distorted reflection of ruling-class ideology (or scientific socialist knowledge) allows him to pose an anthropological/sociological theory of knowledge and a dynamic theory of the state. It is only when the consensus of capitalist development starts to break down, for economic reasons, to be sure, but also and as importantly as a result of the counterhegemony of alternative sets of values that derive from ethnic or racial minorities, from women, or from popular concerns with environment or human rights, that a society can transform itself. The same analysis presumably would apply to the development of a farming-class counterhegemony. According to this analysis, the principal crisis of capitalism is not economic but increasing hegemonic contradiction (which may, of course, be linked to economic contradictions). Similar principles can be applied to the transformation of state socialism in Poland.

By replacing the notion of dominant-class hegemony with that of the hegemony of the Communist party—which is more or less synonymous with the state—we can make several observations about the concrete situation in Poland. First, the widespread support of the popular uprisings of the 1980s is not so mute testimony that the state apparatuses did not exercise uncontested hegemony over civil society. Second, the activities of the underground press, the products of which were widely circulated, continued unabated right up until their legalization in 1989, as did unsanctioned lecture series and seminars, private poetry readings, and art exhibits. Many of these events were held in churches, and most of them were explicitly anti-Party if not antisocialist in their challenge to official cultural life. Power for a class rests not only on the economic level and on the simple capture or destruction (or both) of the state apparatuses but also upon the legitimacy that class has succeeded in establishing by virtue of successful ideological struggle in the cultural milieu of civil society. Among other things, this means preeminence in the struggle over definitions of the past and prescriptions for the future. Moreover, the failure of the socialist state's efforts through its repressive institutions to prevent these informal activities was also indicative of the tenuous nature of its legitimation project.

The activities of farmers, explicitly antisocialist and resistant to the political and economic control the socialist state sought to impose on them, and the saliency of a counterideology of populism, posed a significant threat to the socialist state. The social identity of "peasant" was coming unstuck as hoped, but that of "farmer by occupation in the service of socialism" was far more problematic. The political apparatus failed utterly to establish its control over even the mundane productive and distribution activities of the new "farmers." Hegemony and the longevity of a state imply each other; dominant-class control of the repressive institutions of a state without hegemony in civil society is inadequate to maintain long-term power. This is a project that requires intensive and extensive legitimation work so as to create a state so natural that it is but rarely subjected to sustained scrutiny as an ideological project. The possibility of contesting this ideological project, not through revolutionary violence against state institutions but through counter-hegemonies, may succeed in swamping dominant-class ideology and replacing it and the dominant class altogether—what Gramsci calls "surrounding the state" (see Carnoy 1984:72–73). In 1985 I suggested such a prospect for Poland, namely, that the counterideology of populism, private ownership, and individualism would surround the Leninist state (Nagengast 1985). These have since swamped it.

The Future

This study has been based on the assumption that Polish agriculture is incomprehensible outside of its national context. Conversely, to the degree that Poland is an agrarian society, the state of the nation-state is illuminated by the ethnography of a typical farming community such as Wola Pławska. Only by so elaborating a multilevel analysis, I maintain, is it possible to comprehend the Polish paradox. But the analysis cannot stop at the borders of Poland. Recent Polish history has been tightly interwoven with that of the Soviet Union. During the course of this study, this special relationship has been profoundly altered as the Soviet project in Eastern Europe has unraveled. But from a deeper historical perspective, what is most remarkable about Poland is not that it has emerged from the "socialist" camp but that it was, although ever so briefly, part of it in the first place. Viewed from the *longue durée*, the recent brief interlude under the influence of the Soviet Union is recognizable as a special case in which the history of Poland momentarily departed from a more typical trajectory. Indeed, the events of 1989–1991 demonstrated that Poland is well integrated into the capitalist West. Thus, seen from the larger context within which this study has been developed, the end of this doomed experiment should not be taken as evidence of a "capitalist" resolution to Poland's developmental problems. Rather, in light of what we have discovered through the historical dimension of this study, it would be more accurate to say that Poland's industrial economy is returning to the capitalist path of underdevelopment from which it briefly departed to follow a socialist road of underdevelopment. Agriculture is different. Farming throughout the putative socialist interlude remained structured essentially along proto-capitalist lines—atavistic to be sure, especially in terms of the form the expropriation of surplus labor took, but proto-capitalist nonetheless. It and farmers took a detour through a socialist experiment in name only.

In the West, the emergence of Poland from the Soviet orb is widely considered to be tantamount to its eminent "development." And indeed this was an assumption initially held by people in Wola Pławska. But Polish glasnost, which quickly went far beyond the reforms of the Soviet Union, is intensifying some of the disturbing trends that I discovered in 1979, especially social differentiation, which appears to have been accelerated by the new policies. Thus, whereas some in Wola Pławska are benefiting economically from conditions the new regime is creating, many more are losing ground literally and figuratively as a seemingly inexorable process of economic differentiation proceeds.

Although the former Communist government, in profound contradiction to its official ideals, itself promoted social differentiation by allowing and even promoting the sensibilities, identities, and practices conducive to capitalist production in the countryside, it did so with the end goal of a fully socialized economy. By the time all social benefits were extended to farmers in 1972, it also set forth social welfare measures that provided the bare essentials for everyone. In 1991 the façade of socialized and socializing agriculture was swept away and, with it, the social welfare programs and guaranteed benefits that cushioned those who were unable to be self-sufficient from farming. That Poland will be fully reinserted into world capitalism is no longer an issue; all that remains is to predict the form this new relation will take. If historical precedent is any guide, then the shape of this relationship over the past several centuries is instructive. From the eighteenth century, Poland's relationship to Western Europe was that of a peripheral, underdeveloped agrarian society, not unlike the structured relationship of combined development and underdevelopment that was also emerging between Western Europe and Latin America, later to be reoriented mainly along an axis between the United States and Latin America. Polish dependency on Western Europe dates from the fifteenth and sixteenth centuries, when it became the granary of the West, its magnates and szlachta converting free peasant land into folwarks dedicated to production for export and enserfing formerly free peasants as coerced labor. From the times of the British corn laws, the Napoleonic Wars, and the final dismemberment of Poland in 1795 to the invasion of Poland by Germany in 1939, and in innumerable forms of internationally structured asymmetry, Poland has been a poor cousin of Western Europe. With the end of the Soviet Union's direct and day-to-day influence in Poland, it now appears that this asymmetric relationship is being reestablished.

The first major steps on the slippery slope of this reinsertion of Poland as a peripheral dependency into the West preceded perestroika by some sixteen or eighteen years. In retrospect it is now possible to discern that the loans taken from the Western bankers and the World Bank in 1971, 1972, 1973—loans that were to have modernized Polish industry—have had and are having the effect of locking Poland into unequal relationships with Western Europe and the United States. In mid-1990, people in Wola Pławska expressed fears about such trends that were already apparent to them. Indeed some observed with trepidation that Poland was becoming more and more a Third World country vis-à-vis Western Europe, dependent on it for capital investment and with only basic commodities and abundant unemployed (and therefore cheap labor) to exchange.

Whereas the institutionalization of socialism in Poland entailed a displacement of control from the legal and social spheres of "traditional" Polish society to the political dominance of the Communist party, the establishment of the new capitalist relations entails a post-perestroika displacement of control to an even less human and humanitarian economic sphere, a terrain from which Poland has been removed for almost half a century. In mid-1990 people in Wola Pławska were becoming aware, and with no small sense of dismay, that they had emerged from the closed world administered by the Communist party into a different universe of possible opportunities but also one of possibly greater perils and contradictions.

Elzbieta, now nineteen, graduated from a technical school in December 1989. She was virtually guaranteed a job as a home economist when she started her studies three years earlier. Now she gets up at 9:00 a.m., sometimes 10:00, and complains daily of a stomachache. The doctor says it is nerves. She reads a lot and goes to Mielec once in a while to follow up on the rumor of a possible job, but the bus fare is expensive. Her chances of a job are slim. Nationwide there were only 20,000 job offerings in February for the half a million then officially unemployed. Half of the vacancies were in the provinces of Warsaw and Katowice (hundreds of kilometers from Wola Pławska) and most of them for either highly skilled or completely unskilled jobs. In many towns there were no vacancies at all for white-collar workers.[9] Not even the most optimistic forecast a decline in unemployment soon; if anything, it will continue to rise above the 1.3 million it reached at the end of 1990. Moreover, production is down dramatically; 20, 25, even 30 percent over 1989 in some areas. Of course 1989 had been an especially difficult year in which shortages and inflation helped to precipitate the overthrow of the PZPR. Hyperinflation has been brought under control, but retail prices continue to creep up by 4, 5, or 6 percent a month. Life has not improved for most people.

What political consequences will unequal reincorporation into the West as a poor country cousin bring? As former dependency on the Soviet Union gives way to a new dependency on the West, Polish nationalism may take new twists, as nationalism has in other nearby nation-states. Whereas the perceived appropriate form of nationalist opposition and resistance to the Soviets and their surrogate, the PZPR, was an idealization of liberal capitalism and conservative Catholicism, the expected form of Polish nationalism as a dependent underdeveloped country in the depths of depression within the Western orb could well be something more ominous.

NOTES

1. See, for example, Braverman 1974 and Burawoy 1985.

2. In fact, state enterprises did not calculate profits in the same way a capitalist enterprise would. However, economic reformers throughout Eastern Europe recommended capitalist calculation and the elimination of unprofitable enterprises long before the changes in government. There was an increasing trend is this direction, namely, in Hungary during the 1970s (Nove 1983), and International Monetary Fund loans are predicated on such reforms in Poland.

3. The small private plots of *kolkhoz* and *sovkhoz* workers in the Soviet Union are considerably more productive than the state farms or collectives in the same areas because of the more intensive application of labor. State farms are considered closer to communism than collectives because, in Marxist theory, relations of production are expressed above all in property relations. State farms assign the ownership of the means of production to the state, whereas on collectives ownership is held in common by all the members (Humphrey 1983:75, 93). Collectives have always been relatively insignificant in Poland, even at the height of the collectivization period. Since 1956 they have not made up more than 1 percent of the arable land.

4. An opposition group composed of students and young workers, which called itself Freedom and Peace, united around issues of demilitarization and the right of young people to avoid military service because of religious or conscientious objections. The leaders of Freedom and Peace in Kraków, long a stronghold of the most politically conservative Poles (in the U.S. and British sense of conservative), were especially vocal proponents of alliance with the West and especially egregious confounders of freedom and free enterprise. Some of them are now members of the Senate. Similar concerns and nuclear disarmament were also a central concern of Charter 77 in Czechoslovakia, according to Kavan 1987.

5. See, for example, Raina 1978, articles in *Poland Watch,* and the first two volumes of the journal *East European Reporter,* 1986–1987.

6. See, for example, issues of the ZSL publication *Wieś Współczesna* between about 1975 and 1988.

7. Just what processes, actions, and infrastructures are necessary and conceivable to ensure progressive change is hardly irrelevant but well beyond the scope of this book.

8. See, for example, the work of Althusser (e.g., 1969, 1971), once the leading theoretician of the French Communist party.

9. *Uncensored Poland* 6/90 (31 March 1990):7.

Appendix

TABLE A.1   Variables Used in Statistical Analyses

1	Stratification	Stratification group assigned to each household: 1 = subsistence farmers, 2 = worker-farmers, 3 = farmer-workers, 4 = full-time commercial farmers
2	House #	Address of each house in the village; used for identification purposes only
3	Age	That of head of household; usually the male who owns the house, occasionally a woman
4	Land	Total landholdings registered to members of household; usually one person but sometimes a man and woman
5	Average plots	Mean size of individual plots making up landholding
6	NPK per hectare	Average kilograms of NPK purchased in 1977 and 1978 divided by number of hectares owned
7	Lime 1978	Kilograms of lime fertilizer purchased in 1978 divided by number of hectares
8	Gross sales per hectare	Gross sales to the state divided by number of hectares
9	Tractor	0 = no, 1 = yes
10	Cattle	Number of cows, calves, and steers owned
11	Swine	Number of pigs
12	Poultry	Includes ducks, geese, and chickens
13	Consumers	Number of persons of all ages living in household
14	Workers	All able-bodied persons between ages of eighteen and sixty-five, regardless of whether farming or working for wages
15	Gross wages	Includes wage income of all members of household
16	Construction	Composite variable: 1 = wooden house without indoor plumbing, 2 = concrete block without plumbing, 3 = brick without plumbing, 4 = wood with plumbing, 5 = concrete block with plumbing, 6 = brick with plumbing
17	Auto	0 = no, 1 = yes
18	American connection	Trip to North America, visit from American relative, or receipt of money from an American in last fifteen years; 0 = no, 1 = yes
19	Lime 1977	Number of kilograms of lime fertilizer purchased in 1977 divided by number of hectares
20	Education	Composite variable made up of average of household: 1 = < elementary school, 2 = elementary, 3 = vocational/middle school, 4 = high school

TABLE A.2   Statistics for Cases Used in Regression Analysis (N = 63)

Variable	Mean	Standard Deviation (% of Mean)	Minimum Value	Maximum Value
1 Strat	2.774	35	1.000	4.000
2 Hs#	42.69	61	1.000	102.0
3 Age	52.69	22	30.00	75.00
4 Land	3.741	59	.8700	9.180
5 AvPl	.5255	46	.1900	1.280
6 NPK/ha	195.8	32	.0000	312.0
7 Lime78	33.53	127	.0000	170.0
8 GSale	.1986E 05	62	.0000	.5555E 05
9 Trctr	.1452	245	.0000	1.000
10 Cattle	5.226	90	.0000	28.00
11 Swine	6.742	111	.0000	35.00
12 Poultry	26.68	60	.0000	80.00
13 Cnsmr	4.516	46	1.000	13.00
14 Wrkr	2.645	51	.0000	7.000
15 GWage	.5118E 05	10	.0000	.2340E 06
16 Const	2.032	89	1.000	6.000
17 Auto	.1935	206	.0000	1.000
18 AmC	.9677E 01	308	.0000	1.000
19 Lime77	115.2	72	.0000	427.0
20 Educ	2.245	17	1.000	3.500

TABLE A.3　Pearsons's R Correlation Matrix

	1 Strat	2 Hs#	3 Age	4 Land	5 AvPl	6 NPK/ha	7 Lime78	8 GSale	9 Trctr
1 Strat	1.00								
2 Hs#	−.14	1.00							
3 Age	.16	−.23	1.00						
4 Land	.61	−.01	−.03	1.00					
5 AvPl	.34	−.16	.11	.42	1.00				
6 NPK/ha	.28	−.30	.21	.06	.02	1.00			
7 Lime78	.15	−.09	−.03	.23	−.01	.20	1.00		
8 GSale	.41	.02	−.14	.27	.19	.34	.41	1.00	
9 Trctr	.43	.19	−.09	.58	.36	.05	.13	.43	1.00
10 Cattle	.43	−.08	−.10	.64	.26	.24	.39	.27	.46
11 Swine	.28	−.08	−.14	.36	.32	.19	−.02	.44	.46
12 Poultry	.23	−.11	−.01	.38	.08	.13	−.20	−.04	.19
13 Cnsmr	.08	.04	−.23	.34	−.09	.08	.23	.16	−.01
14 Wrkr	.09	−.14	.06	.34	−.02	.19	.28	.09	.04
15 GWage	−.26	.04	−.03	−.04	−.28	.02	.20	−.16	−.29
16 Const	.05	.27	−.11	.08	−.02	.01	−.09	.01	.30
17 Auto	.07	.20	.15	.14	.01	−.00	−.02	−.00	.15
18 AmC	.02	.11	−.38	.16	.04	.05	.01	.22	.33
19 Lime77	.37	.03	−.14	.38	.16	.36	.30	.47	.45
20 Educ	.11	−.12	−.01	.16	.01	.32	.23	.22	.15

10 Cattle	11 Swine	12 Poultry	13 Cnsmr	14 Wrkr	15 GWage	16 Const	17 Auto	18 AmC	19 Lime77	20 Educ
1.00										
.22	1.00									
.25	.30	1.00								
.15	.09	.15	1.00							
.12	.18	.12	.72	1.00						
−.15	−.21	−.04	.62	.62	1.00					
.02	.23	.24	.04	−.06	−.03	1.00				
−.03	−.01	−.04	.12	.19	.24	.38	1.00			
.05	.38	.09	.10	.01	−.13	.33	.12	1.00		
.32	.23	.10	.09	.11	−.09	.13	−.02	.14	1.00	
.06	.17	−.08	.30	.38	.32	.15	.13	.05	.45	1.00

TABLE A.4 Regression Equations

Equation 1
1 4 14
R.Sq.=.358 Dep. Var.=1, Strat.

Variable	Regression Coeff.	"T" Ratio	Beta			
4 Land	.284	5.9	.65			
14 Wrkr	−.806E 01	1.0	.11			

	Other Variables				
Variable	"T" if in Eq.	Variable	"T" if in Eq.
2 Hs#	−1.4	3 Age	1.8
5 AvPl	.7	6 NPK/ha	2.5
7 Lime78	.3	8 GSale	2.6
9 Trctr	.8	10 Cattle	.3
11 Swine	.1	12 Poultry	.2
13 Cnsmr	−.7	15 GWage	−2.2
16 Const	.1	17 Auto	.0
18 AmC	−1.8	19 Lime77	1.5
20 Educ	1.4		

Constant=1.91 Std. Err. Est.=.773

Equation 2
1 14
R.Sq.=.000 Dep. Var.=1, Strat.

Variable	Regression Coeff.	"T" Ratio	Beta
14 Wrkr	.769E 01	.8	.11

	Other Variables		
Variable	"T" if in Eq.	Variable	"T" if in Eq.
2 Hs#	−1.0	3 Age	1.2
4 Land	5.9	5 AvPl	2.8
6 NPK/ha	1.9	7 Lime78	.9
8 GSale	3.3	9 Trctr	3.6
10 Cattle	3.5	11 Swine	1.5
12 Poultry	1.9	13 Cnsmr	.1
15 GWage	−3.5	16 Const	.5
17 Auto	4.0	18 AmC	−1.0
19 Lime77	2.9	20 Educ	1.4

Constant=2.57 Std. Err. Est.=.968

Equation 3
4 3
R.Sq.=.000 Dep. Var.=4, Land

Variable	Regression Coeff.	"T" Ratio	Beta
3 Age	−.547E 02	.2	.03

	Other Variables		
Variable	"T" if in Eq.	Variable	"T" if in Eq.
1 Strat	6.0	2 Hs#	−.2
5 AvPl	3.6	6 NPK/ha	.4
7 Lime78	1.8	8 GSale	2.1
9 Trctr	5.4	10 Cattle	6.4
11 Swine	2.5	12 Poultry	3.3
13 Cnsmr	2.8	14 Wrkr	2.8
15 GWage	−.3	16 Const	.7
17 Auto	1.1	18 AmC	.2
19 Lime77	3.1	20 Educ	1.6

Constant=4.03 Std. Err. Est.=2.21

(continues)

Table A.4 (*continued*)

Equation 4

1 4

R.Sq.=.357 Dep. Var.=1, Strat.

Variable	Regression Coeff.	"T" Ratio	Beta		Variable	"T" if in Eq.	Variable	"T" if in Eq.
						Other Variables		
4 Land	.267	5.9	.61		2 Hs#	−1.3	3 Age	1.8
					5 AvPl	.9	6 NPK/ha	2.3
					7 Lime78	.1	8 GSale	2.6
					9 Trctr	1.0	10 Cattle	.5
					11 Swine	.1	12 Poultry	.2
					13 Cnsmr	−1.2	14 Wrkr	−1.0
					15 GWage	−2.3	16 Const	.1
					17 Auto	−.1	18 AmC	−1.5
					19 Lime77	1.5	20 Educ	.9

Constant=1.78 Std. Err. Est.=.774

Equation 5

1 8

R.Sq.=.151 Dep. Var.=1, Strat.

Variable	Regression Coeff.	"T" Ratio	Beta		Variable	"T" if in Eq.	Variable	"T" if in Eq.
						Other Variables		
8 GSale	.320E 04	3.4	.41		2 Hs#	−1.3	3 Age	1.9
					4 Land	5.3	5 AvPl	2.4
					6 NPK/ha	1.3	7 Lime78	−.2
					9 Trctr	2.5	10 Cattle	3.0
					11 Swine	1.0	12 Poultry	2.1
					13 Cnsmr	.2	14 Wrkr	.4
					15 GWage	−1.7	16 Const	.4
					17 Auto	.6	18 AmC	−.6
					19 Lime77	1.7	20 Educ	.1

Constant=2.14 Std. Err. Est.=.889

Equation 6

1 4 8

R.Sq.=.412 Dep. Var.=1, Strat.

Variable	Regression Coeff.	"T" Ratio	Beta		Variable	"T" if in Eq.	Variable	"T" if in Eq.
						Other Variables		
4 Land	.236	5.2	.54		2 Hs#	−1.4	3 Age	2.3
					5 AvPl	.7	6 NPK/ha	1.7
8 GSale	.207E 04	2.6	.26		7 Lime78	−.9	9 Trctr	.1
					10 Cattle	.2	11 Swine	−.7
					12 Poultry	.6	13 Cnsmr	−1.5
					14 Wrkr	−1.1	15 GWage	−2.0
					16 Const	.2	17 Auto	−.0
					18 AmC	−1.8	19 Lime77	.5
					20 Educ	.4		

Constant=1.48 Std. Err. Est.=.740

(*continues*)

Table A.4 (*continued*)

Equation 7
1 3 20
R.Sq.=.046 Dep. Var.=1, Strat.

Variable	Regression Coeff.	"T" Ratio	Beta
3 Age	.153E 01	1.4	.18
20 Educ	.468	1.8	.23

Other Variables

Variable	"T" if in Eq.	Variable	"T" if in Eq.
2 Hs#	-.7	4 Land	5.7
5 AvPl	2.5	6 NPK/ha	1.5
7 Lime78	.8	8 GSale	3.4
9 Trctr	3.7	10 Cattle	3.8
11 Swine	1.8	12 Poultry	2.0
13 Cnsmr	.4	14 Wrkr	.0
15 GWage	-2.9	16 Const	.3
17 Auto	.1	18 AmC	-.2
19 Lime77	2.7		

Constant=.932 Std. Err. Est.=.943

Equation 8
4 9
R.Sq.=.323 Dep. Var.=4, Land

Variable	Regression Coeff.	"T" Ratio	Beta
9 Trctr	3.57	5.5	.58

Other Variables

Variable	"T" if in Eq.	Variable	"T" if in Eq.
1 Strat	4.3	2 Hs#	-1.2
3 Age	.2	5 AvPl	2.2
6 NPK/ha	.3	7 Lime78	1.5
8 GSale	.2	10 Cattle	4.7
11 Swine	.7	12 Poultry	2.9
13 Cnsmr	3.6	14 Wrkr	3.3
15 GWage	1.3	16 Const	-.8
17 Auto	.5	18 AmC	-1.0
19 Lime77	1.3	20 Educ	1.2

Constant=3.22 Std. Err. Est.=1.81

Equation 9
4 10
R.Sq.=.405 Dep. Var.=4, Land

Variable	Regression Coeff.	"T" Ratio	Beta
10 Cattle	.300	6.5	.64

Other Variables

Variable	"T" if in Eq.	Variable	"T" if in Eq.
1 Strat	4.2	2 Hs#	.4
3 Age	.4	5 AvPl	2.8
6 NPK/ha	-.9	7 Lime78	-.3
8 GSale	1.0	9 Trctr	3.5
11 Swine	2.0	12 Poultry	2.5
13 Cnsmr	2.6	14 Wrkr	2.9
15 GWage	.6	16 Const	.7
17 Auto	1.7	18 AmC	.4
19 Lime77	1.9	20 Educ	1.5

Constant=2.18 Std. Err. Est.=.169

(*continues*)

Table A.4 (*continued*)

Equation 10
4 10 9 14
R.Sq.=.568 Dep. Var.=4, Land

Variable	Regression Coeff.	"T" Ratio	Beta
10 Cattle	.206	4.6	.44
9 Trctr	2.24	3.8	.36
14 Wrkr	.440	3.2	.27

Other Variables

Variable	"T" if in Eq.	Variable	"T" if in Eq.
1 Strat	3.4	2 Hs#	−.1
3 Age	.4	5 AvPl	2.4
6 NPK/ha	−1.5	7 Lime78	−1.0
8 GSale	−.4	11 Swine	.6
12 Poultry	2.1	13 Cnsmr	1.4
15 GWage	−.6	16 Const	−.3
17 Auto	.6	18 AmC	−.0
19 Lime77	.5	20 Educ	−.1

Constant=1.18 Std. Err. Est.=1.44

Equation 11
4 7
R.Sq.=.035 Dep. Var.=4, Land

Variable	Regression Coeff.	"T" Ratio	Beta
7 Lime78	.116E 01	1.8	.23

Other Variables

Variable	"T" if in Eq.	Variable	"T" if in Eq.
1 Strat	5.7	2 Hs#	.0
3 Age	−.2	5 AvPl	3.7
6 NPK/ha	.2	8 GSale	1.6
9 Trctr	5.3	10 Cattle	6.1
11 Swine	2.7	12 Poultry	3.9
13 Cnsmr	2.4	14 Wrkr	2.4
15 GWage	−.7	16 Const	.8
17 Auto	1.2	18 AmC	.3
19 Lime77	2.7	20 Educ	1.3

Constant=3.35 Std. Err. Est.=2.16

Equation 12
7 8
R.Sq.=.156 Dep. Var.=7, Lime78

Variable	Regression Coeff.	"T" Ratio	Beta
8 GSale	.144E 02	3.5	.41

Other Variables

Variable	"T" if in Eq.	Variable	"T" if in Eq.
1 Strat	−.2	2 Hs#	−.8
3 Age	.3	4 Land	1.0
5 AvPl	−.7	6 NPK/ha	−.2
9 Trctr	−.4	10 Cattle	2.5
11 Swine	−2.0	12 Poultry	−1.4
13 Cnsmr	1.4	14 Wrkr	2.1
15 GWage	2.4	16 Const	−.7
17 Auto	−.2	18 AmC	−.8
19 Lime77	1.0	20 Educ	1.2

Constant=5.00 Std. Err. Est.=39.2

(*continues*)

Table A.4 (*continued*)

Equation 13

7 10

R.Sq.=.136 Dep. Var.=7, Lime78

Variable	Regression Coeff.	"T" Ratio	Beta
10 Cattle	3.51	3.2	.39

Other Variables

Variable	"T" if in Eq.	Variable	"T" if in Eq.
1 Strat	−.2	2 Hs#	−.5
3 Age	.1	4 Land	−.3
5 AvPl	−.9	6 NPK/ha	.1
8 GSale	2.8	9 Trctr	−.5
11 Swine	−1.0	12 Poultry	−2.5
13 Cnsmr	1.5	14 Wrkr	2.1
15 GWage	2.3	16 Const	−.7
17 Auto	−.1	18 AmC	−.4
19 Lime77	1.6	20 Educ	1.7

Constant=15.2 Std. Err. Est.=39.6

Equation 14

7 8 10 15

R.Sq.=.314 Dep. Var.=7, Lime78

Variable	Regression Coeff.	"T" Ratio	Beta
8 GSale	.130E 02	3.3	.37
10 Cattle	3.04	3.0	.34
15 GWage	.254E 03	2.9	.31

Other Variables

Variable	"T" if in Eq.	Variable	"T" if in Eq.
1 Strat	−.8	2 Hs#	−.8
3 Age	.6	4 Land	−1.0
5 AvPl	−.8	6 NPK/ha	−.9
9 Trctr	−1.1	11 Swine	−1.9
12 Poultry	−2.6	13 Cnsmr	−.9
14 Wrkr	.1	16 Const	−.8
17 Auto	−.9	18 AmC	−.3
19 Lime77	.5	20 Educ	.1

Constant=−21.1 Std. Err. Est.=35.3

References and Bibliography

Abicht, Ludo. 1984. "Loyola, Lenin, and the Road to Liberation," *Monthly Review* 36 (5):24–41.

Abrams, Philip. 1988. "Notes on the Difficulty of Studying the State," *Journal of Historical Anthropology* 1:58–89.

Althusser, Louis. 1969. *For Marx*. New York: Vintage Books.

_____. 1971. "Ideological State Apparatuses." In Louis Althusser, *Lenin and Philosophy and Other Essays*. New York: Monthly Review Press.

Amin, Samir. 1974. *Accmulation on a World Scale*. New York: Monthly Review Press.

Amin, Samir, and K. Vergopoulos. 1974. *La question paysanne et le capitalisme*. Paris: Anthropos.

Anderson, Benedict. 1983. *Imagined Communities*. London: Verso.

Anderson, Michael. 1972. *Family and Kinship in Nineteenth-Century Lancashire*. Cambridge: Cambridge University Press.

Anderson, Perry. 1974. *Lineages of the Absolutist State*. London: New Left Books.

_____. 1980. *Arguments Within English Marxism*. London: Verso.

Aronowitz, Stanley. 1978. "Marx, Braverman and the Logic of Capital," *Insurgent Sociologist* 7 (1-2):124–146.

_____. 1982. "Cracks in the Bloc: American Labor's Historic Compromise and the Present Crisis," *Social Text* 5:22–52.

Ash, Timothy Garton. 1985. *The Polish Revolution: Solidarity*. New York: Vintage Books.

_____. 1990. "Angry New Eastern Europe," *New York Review of Books* 37 (16 August):51–57.

_____. 1991. "Poland After Solidarity," *New York Review of Books* 38 (13 June):46–58.

Aubin, Herman. 1942. "The Land East of the Elbe and German Colonization Eastward." In J. H. Clapham and E. Power, eds., *The Cambridge History of Europe*. Cambridge: Cambridge University Press.

Bahro, Rudolf. 1981. *The Alternative in Eastern Europe*. London: Verso.

Bell, Daniel. 1962. "Crime as an American Way of Life." In D. Bell, ed., *The End of Ideology*. New York: Free Press.

Benet, Sula. 1951. *Song, Dance, and Customs of Peasant Poland*. London: Dennis Dobson.

Berend, Ivan, and G. Ránki. 1974. *Economic Development in East-Central Europe in the 19th and 20th Centuries*. New York: Columbia University Press.

Berger, John. 1979. *Pig Earth*. New York: Pantheon Books.

Bettleheim, Charles. 1975. *The Transition to Socialist Economy*. Hassocks: Harvester Press.

Bielasiak John, and M. D. Simon, eds. 1984. *Polish Politics: Edge of the Abyss.* New York: Praeger.

Bloch, Harriet. 1973. *Household Economy and Entrepreneurial Activity in a Polish Peasant Village.* Ph.D. dissertation, Columbia University.

Blum, Jerome. 1957. "The Rise of Serfdom in Eastern Europe," *American Historical Review* 62 (4):807–836.

Bodnar, John. 1987. *The Transplanted: A History of Immigrants in Urban America.* Bloomington: Indiana University Press.

Bourdieu, Pierre. 1977. *Outline of a Theory of Practice.* New York: Cambridge University Press.

———. 1984. *Distinction: A Social Critique of the Judgment of Taste.* Cambridge: Harvard University Press.

———. 1986. "The Forms of Capital." In J. G. Richardson, ed., *Handbook of Theory and Research for the Sociology of Education.* New York: Greenwood Press.

———. 1988. *Homo Academicus.* Stanford: Stanford University Press.

Braudel, Fernand. 1973. *Capitalism and Material Life, 1400–1800.* London: Weidenfeld and Nicolson.

Braverman, Harry. 1974. *Labor and Monopoly Capital.* New York and London: Monthly Review Press.

Brenner, Robert. 1977. "The Origins of Capitalist Development: A Critique of Neo-Smithian Marxism," *New Left Review* 104:25–92.

Brzóska, Marian. 1977. "Food Production in the Programme of the Socio-economic Development of Poland for 1976–1980." In *Village and Agriculture: Selected Publications from the Quarterly (Wieś i rolnictwo 1977–1978).* Warsaw: Polish Scientific Publishers.

Burawoy, Michael. 1978. "Towards a Marxist Theory of the Labor Process: Braverman and Beyond," *Politics and Society* 9 (1):89–130.

———. 1985. *The Politics of Production.* London: Verso.

Burbach, Roger, and P. Flynn. 1980. *Agribusiness in the Americas.* New York: Monthly Review Press and NACLA.

Cameron, J. 1980. "What the Bankers Did to Poland," *Fortune* 102 (22 September):125–126.

Camiller, Patrick, and Jon Rothschild. 1979. *Power and Opposition in Post-Revolutionary Societies.* London: Inklinks.

Carnoy, Martin. 1984. *The State and Political Theory.* Princeton: Princeton University Press.

Celt, Mark. 1972. "Another Round: Peasant and Party in Poland." In T. N. Cieplak, ed., *Poland Since 1956.* New York: Twayne Publishers.

Central Statistical Office. 1978. *Poland 1978: Statistical Data.* Warsaw: Polish Scientific Publishers.

Clammer, John. 1978. *The New Economic Anthropology.* London: Macmillan.

Clarke, Simon. 1977. "Marxism, Sociology, and Poulantzas' Theory of the State," *Capital and Class* 2:1–31.

Cliff, Tony. 1956. *Stalinist Russia: A Marxist Analysis.* London: M. Kidron.

Cohen, Stephen F. 1971. *Bukharin and the Bolshevik Revolution.* Oxford: Oxford University Press.

Comaroff, John L. 1980. "Class and Culture in a Peasant Economy: The Transformation of Land Tenure in Baralong," *Journal of African Law* 24 (1):85–113.

_____. 1982. "Dialectical Systems, History and Anthropology: Units of Study and Questions of Theory," *Journal of Southern African Studies* 8 (2):143–172.

_____. 1987. "Of Totemism and Ethnicity," *Ethos* 52 (3-4):301–323.

Concise Statistical Yearbook of Poland. 1983. Warsaw: Statistical Office of the Polish People's Republic.

Corrigan, Philip, H. Ramsey, and D. Sayer. 1978. *Socialist Construction and Marxist Theory.* London: Macmillan.

Corrigan, Philip, and Derek Sayer. 1985. *The Great Arch: English State Formation as Cultural Revolution.* Oxford: Blackwell.

Davidow, M. 1985a. "Agriculture: Problems and Progress," *Daily World* 17 (7 November):18–19.

_____. 1985b. "Marxism-Leninism in Polish Thought," *Daily World* 18 (5 December):14–15.

Davies, Norman. 1982. *God's Playground: A History of Poland.* Vol. 2, *1795 to the Present.* New York: Columbia University Press.

de Janvry, Alain. 1980. "Social Differentiation in Agriculture and the Ideology of Neopopulism." In F. H. Buttel and H. Newby, eds., *The Rural Sociology of the Advanced Society: Critical Perspectives.* Montclair, N.J.: Allanheld, Osmun.

Deutscher, Tamara. 1981. "Poland—Hopes and Fears," *New Left Review* 125:61–74.

Douglas, Dorothy W. [1953] 1972. *Transitional Economic Systems: The Polish-Czech Example.* New York: Monthly Review Press.

Duymovic, Andrew. 1980. "Poland's Agricultural Policies in the 1970s: Impact on Agricultural Trade with the United States." In R. A. Francisco, B. A. Laird, and R. D. Laird, eds., *Agricultural Policies in the USSR and Eastern Europe.* Boulder: Westview Press.

Dziewanowski, Marian K. 1977. *Poland in the Twentieth Century.* New York: Columbia University Press.

Enzensberger, Hans Magnus. 1990. "Europe in Ruins," *Granta* 33:113–139.

Feher, Ferenc, and Agnes Heller. 1986. "Eastern Left–Western Left, Part II: After 1968," *Socialist Review* 90:33–48.

Fejto, François. 1971. *A History of the People's Democracies: Eastern Europe Since Stalin.* London: Pall Mall Press.

Feldman, J. 1951. "The Polish Provinces of Austria and Prussia After 1815: The Springtime of Nations." In W. F. Reddaway et al., eds., *The Cambridge History of Poland.* Vol. 1. Cambridge: Cambridge University Press.

Foster, George. 1965. "Peasant Society and the Image of Limited Good," *American Anthropologist* 67:293–310.

Foucault, Michel. 1973. *Madness and Civilization: A History of Insanity in the Age of Reason.* Richard Howard, trans. New York: Vintage Books.

_____. 1977. *Discipline and Punish: The Birth of the Prison.* Alan Sheridan, trans. New York: Vintage Books.

_____. 1980. *The History of Sexuality.* Vol. 1, *An Introduction.* Robert Hurley, trans. New York: Pantheon.

Frank, André Gunder. 1966. *Capitalism and Underdevelopment in Latin America.* New York: Monthly Review Press.

————. 1977. "Long Live Transideological Enterprise! The Socialist Economies in the Capitalist International Division of Labor," *Review* 1:91–124.

Franklin, S. H. 1969. *The European Peasant.* London: Methuen.

Gałaj, Dyzma. 1965. "Attitudes of the Rural Population to the Part-time Farmers," *Polish Sociological Bulletin* 11 (1):117–122.

Gałeski, Bogusław. 1963a. *Chłopi i zawód rolniki* (Peasants and the occupation of farming). Warsaw: Państowe Wydawnictwo Naukowe.

————. 1963b. "Farmers' Attitudes to Their Occupations," *Polish Sociological Bulletin* 7 (1):57–68.

————. 1972. *Basic Concepts of Rural Sociology.* London: Manchester University Press.

Gałeski, Bogusław, and Anna Szemberg. 1982. "Village Typology in Poland." In H. Mendras and I. Mihailescu, eds., *Rural Community Studies.* Oxford: Pergamon.

Garnham, Nicholas, and Raymond Williams. 1980. "Pierre Bourdieu and the Sociology of Culture: An Introduction," *Media, Culture and Society* 2:209–223.

Geertz, Clifford. 1973. "The Politics of Meaning," In C. Geertz, *The Interpretation of Culture.* New York: Basic Books.

————. 1980. *Negara: The Theatre State in Nineteenth Century Bali.* Princeton: Princeton University Press.

Giddens, Anthony. 1979. *Central Problems in Social Theory: Actions, Structures and Contradictions in Social Analysis.* Berkeley: University of California Press.

Giroux, Henry. 1983. *Theory and Resistance in Education: A Pedagogy for the Opposition.* London: Heinemann.

Goodman, David, and Michael Redclift. 1982. *From Peasant to Proletarian.* New York: St. Martin's Press.

Goody, Jack. 1976. *Production and Reproduction: A Comparative Study of the Domestic Domain.* Cambridge: Cambridge University Press.

Gouldner, Alvin. 1970. *The Coming Crisis of Western Sociology.* London: Heinemann.

————. 1980. *The Two Marxisms: Contradictions and Anomalies in the Development of Theory.* New York: Seabury Press.

Gramsci, Antonio. 1971. *Selections from Prison Notebooks.* H. Hoare and G. Smith, eds. and trans. New York: International Publishers.

Green, Peter. 1977. "The Third Round in Poland," *New Left Review* 101/102:69–108.

Griffin, Keith. 1974. *The Political Economy of Agrarian Change: An Essay on the Green Revolution.* London: Macmillan.

Hakim, Catherine. 1980. "Census Reports as Documentary Evidence," *Sociological Review*, n.s., 28 (3):551–580.

Halpern, Joel M. 1969. "Yugoslavia: Modernization in an Ethnically Diverse State." In W. S. Vucinich, ed., *Contemporary Yugoslavia.* Berkeley: University of California Press.

Hann, Christopher M. 1980. *Tazlar: A Village in Hungary.* Cambridge: Cambridge University Press.

————. 1985. *A Village Without Solidarity: Polish Peasants in Years of Crisis.* New Haven and London: Yale University Press.

Harman, Chris. 1974. *Bureaucracy and Revolution in Eastern Europe.* London: Pluto Press.

Harris, Richard. 1978. "Marxism and the Agrarian Question in Latin America," *Latin American Perspectives* 5 (4):2–26.

Harrison, Michael. 1977. "The Peasant Mode of Production in the Work of A. V. Chayanov," *Journal of Peasant Studies* 4 (4):323–336.

Hewitt de Alcántara, Cynthia. 1978. *La modernización de la agricultura mexicana, 1940–1970.* Mexico City: Siglo Veintiuno Editores.

Hightower, James. 1973. *Hard Tomatoes, Hard Times.* Cambridge, Mass.: Schenkman.

Hobsbawm, Eric. 1962. *The Age of Revolution: 1789–1848.* New York: Mentor.

————. 1983. "Introduction," In E. Hobsbawm and T. Ranger, eds., *The Invention of Tradition.* Cambridge and London: Cambridge University Press.

Hobsbawm, Eric, and Terrence Ranger, eds. 1983. *The Invention of Tradition.* Cambridge and London: Cambridge University Press.

Humphrey, Caroline. 1983. *Karl Marx Collective.* Cambridge: Cambridge University Press.

Hunek, Tadeusz, and Jan Rajtar. 1977. "The Development of Food Economy in Poland." In *Village and Agriculture: Selected Publications from the Quarterly (Wieś i rolnictwo 1975–1976).* Warsaw: Polish Scientific Publishers.

Hunt, E. K. 1979. *History of Economic Thought: A Critical Perspective.* Belmont, Calif.: Wadsworth Publishing.

Jackson, George. 1966. *Comintern and Peasant in East Europe, 1919–1930.* New York and London: Columbia University Press.

Jones, T. Anthony, D. Bealmer, and M. Kennedy. 1984. "Public Opinion and Political Disruption." In J. Bielasiak and M. D. Simon, eds., *Polish Politics: Edge of the Abyss.* New York: Praeger.

Kavan, Jan. 1987. "The Renewal of Charter 77: Prague's Kamikaze Icebreakers," *Nation* 244 (24 January):78–82.

Kay, Geoffrey. 1975. *Development and Underdevelopment: A Marxist Analysis.* London: Macmillan.

Kazin, Michael. 1986. "Populism's Perilous Promise," *Socialist Review* 89:99–106.

Kearney, Michael. 1986. "From the Invisible Hand to Visible Feet: Anthropological Studies of Migration and Development," *Annual Review of Anthropology* 15:331–361.

Kearney, Michael. N.d. *Reconceptualizing the Peasantry.* Boulder: Westview Press, forthcoming.

Kersten, Krystyna, and T. Szarota. 1970. *Wieś Polska 1939–1948.* Warsaw: Państowe Wydawnictwo Naukowe.

Kieniewicz, Stefan. 1969. *The Emancipation of the Polish Peasantry.* Chicago: University of Chicago Press.

Klank, Leszek. 1978. "Changes in Acreage and Their Impact on the Effectiveness of Private Farms," *Wieś współczesna* (Modern countryside) 2 (252):14–16.

Kochanowicz, J. 1983. "The Polish Peasant Family as an Economic Unit." In R. Wall, J. Robin, and P. Laslett, eds., *Family Farms in Historic Europe*. Cambridge: Cambridge University Press.

Kolankiewicz, George. 1980. "The New 'Awkward Class': The Peasant-Worker in Poland," *Sociologia Ruralis* 201 (1-2):28–43.

Kolosi, Tamas, and E. Wnuk-Lipiński, eds. 1983. *Equality and Inequality Under Socialism: Poland and Hungary Compared*. Beverly Hills: Sage Publications.

Konrad, George, and Ivan Szelenyi. 1979. *The Intellectuals on the Road to Class Power*. New York: Harcourt Brace Jovanovich.

Korbonski, Andrzej. 1965. *Politics of Socialist Agriculture in Poland, 1945–1960*. New York: Columbia University Press.

———. 1984. "Agriculture and the Polish Renewal." In J. Bielasiak and M. Simon, eds., *Polish Politics: Edge of the Abyss*. New York: Praeger.

Kostrowicki, Jerzy, and Roman Szczesny. 1972. *Polish Agriculture: Characteristics, Types and Regions*. Budapest: Akademiai Kiado.

Kula, Witold. 1976. *An Economic Theory of the Feudal System*. London: New Left Books.

Kusmierek, Josef. 1990. "Agriculture—the Key to a Prosperous Poland," *Gazeta International* 3 (15 March). Reprinted in *Uncensored Poland* 6/90 (31 March):10–11.

Laclau, Ernesto. 1971. "Feudalism and Capitalism in Latin America," *New Left Review* 67:19–38.

Laclau, Ernesto, and Chantal Mouffe. 1985. *Hegemony and Socialist Strategy: Towards a Radical Democratic Politics*. London: Verso.

Lampland, Martha. 1987. *Living the Plan*. Ph.D. dissertation, University of Chicago.

Lane, David, and G. Kolankiewicz. 1973. *Social Groups in Polish Society*. New York: Columbia University Press.

Lappé, Frances Moore, J. Collins, and D. Kinley. 1981. *Aid as Obstacle*. San Francisco: Institute for Food and Development Policy.

Lenin, V. I. [1898] 1956. *The Development of Capitalism in Russia*. Moscow: Progress Publishers.

———. 1965. *The State and Revolution*. Beijing: Foreign Language Press.

Lewin, Moshe. 1968. *Russian Peasants and Soviet Power*. New York: W. F. Norton.

———. 1976. "Society and the Stalinist State," *Social History* 1 (May):172–173.

Lindsey, J. O. 1957. "The Social Classes and the Foundations of the States." In J. O. Lindsey, ed., *The New Cambridge Modern History*. Vol. 7, *The Old Regime, 1713–63*. Cambridge: Cambridge University Press.

McLellen, David. 1979. *Marxism After Marx: An Introduction*. New York: Harper and Row.

Mączak, Antoni. 1968. "The Social Distribution of Landed Property in Poland from the 16th to the 18th Century." In *Third International Conference of Economic History*. Paris: Mouton.

Majkowski, Władysław. 1985. *People's Poland: Patterns of Social Inequality and Conflict*. Westport, Conn.: Greenwood Press.

Malowist, Marian. 1958. "Poland, Russia, and Western Trade in the 15th and 16th Centuries," *Past and Present* 13:26–39.

_____ . 1959. "The Economic and Social Development of the Baltic Countries from the 15th to the 17th Centuries," *Economic History Review*, 2d series, 12 (2):177–189.

_____ . 1966. "The Problem of the Inequality of Economic Development in Europe in the Latter Middle Ages," *Economic History Review*, 2d series, 19 (1):15–28.

Margolick, David. 1989. "Basia Johnson: Lech's American Angel," *New York Times Magazine*, 8 October, 28–31.

Martin, Emily. 1987. *The Woman in the Body*. Boston: Beacon Press.

Michnik, Adam. 1981. "What We Want to Do and What We Can Do," *Telos* 47:66–77.

_____ . 1985. *Letters from Prison and Other Essays*. Maya Latynski, trans. Berkeley: University of California Press.

Morrison, James F. 1968. *The Polish People's Republic*. Baltimore: Johns Hopkins University Press.

Mouffe, Chantal. 1990. "Radical Democracy or Liberal Democracy?" *Socialist Review* 90/2:57–66.

Nagengast, (Marian) Carole. 1982. "Polish Peasants and the State," *Dialectical Anthropology* 7 (4):47–66.

_____ . 1985. *Poles Apart: Polish Farmers and the State*. Ph.D. dissertation, University of California, Irvine.

_____ . 1990. "Populism and the Polish State," *Socialist Review* 90/2:80–101.

Nagengast, Carole, and M. Kearney. 1990. "Mixtec Ethnicity: Social Identity, Political Consciousness, and Political Activism," *Latin American Research Review* 25 (1):61–91.

Narkiewicz, Olga A. 1976. *The Green Flag: Polish Populist Politics, 1867–1970*. London: Croom Helm.

National Foreign Assessment Center (CIA). 1980. *Handbook of Economic Statistics*. Washington, D.C.: U.S. Government Printing Office.

Nove, Alec. 1983. *The Economics of Feasible Socialism*. London: George Allen and Unwin.

Orvis, Julia Swift. 1947. "Partitioned Poland, 1795–1914." In B. Schmitt, ed., *Poland*. Berkeley: University of California Press.

Ostrowski, Krzysztof, and A. Przeworski. 1967. "Preliminary Inquiry into the Nature of Social Change: The Case of the Polish Countryside." In J. Wiatr, ed., *Studies in Polish Political Systems*. Wrocław: Zakład Narodowy im. Ossolinskich.

Oxaal, Ivan, T. Barnett, and D. Booth. 1975. "Editors' Introduction: Beyond the Sociology of Development." In I. Oxaal et al., eds., *Beyond the Sociology of Development*. London: Routledge and Kegan Paul.

Polonsky, Antony. 1972. *Politics in Independent Poland: 1921–1939*. Oxford: Clarendon Press.

Portal, Roger. 1962. *The Slavs: A Cultural and Historical Survey of the Slavonic Peoples*. New York: Harper and Row.

Raina, Peter. 1978. *Political Opposition in Poland, 1954–1977*. London: Poets and Painters Press.

Rakovski, Marc. 1978. *Towards an East European Marxism.* New York: St. Martin's Press.

Ratajczak, Klemens. 1978. "The Possibilities of Raising Farming Efficiency," *Wieś współczesna* (Modern countryside) 3 (253):8–9.

Reymont, Władysław. [1918] 1924. *The Peasants.* New York: Alfred A. Knopf.

Robinson, George T. 1960. *Rural Russia Under the Old Regime.* Berkeley: University of California Press.

Rochester, Anna. 1942. *Lenin on the Agrarian Question.* New York: International Press.

Rocznik Statystyczny. 1973. Warsaw: Główny Urząd Statystyczny.

———. 1978. Warsaw: Główny Urząd Statystyczny.

———. 1980. Warsaw: Główny Urząd Statystyczny.

———. 1982. Warsaw: Główny Urząd Statystyczny.

———. 1984. Warsaw: Główny Urząd Statystyczny.

———. 1988. Warsaw: Główny Urząd Statystyczny.

Rodefeld, Richard, J. Flora, and D. Voth, eds. 1978. *Change in Rural America.* St. Louis: C. F. Mosby.

Romanowski, J. 1977. "Prospects for the Future of Polish Agriculture." In R. D. Laird, J. Hajda, and B. A. Laird, eds., *The Future of Agriculture in the Soviet Union and Eastern Europe: The 1976–80 Five Year Plans.* Boulder: Westview Press.

Roxborough, Ian. 1979. *Theories of Underdevelopment.* London: Macmillan.

Rutkowski, Jan. 1950. "The Social and Economic Structure in the Fifteenth and Sixteenth Centuries." In W. F. Reddaway et al., eds., *The Cambridge History of Poland.* Vol. 1. Cambridge: Cambridge University Press.

———. 1956. *Studia z dziejów wsi polskiej XVI–XVIII w wyboru dokonał i wstępem opatrzyl Witold Kula* (Studies of the history of Polish villages from the sixteenth to eighteenth centuries, selected and introduced by Witold Kula). Warsaw: Państowe Wydawnictwo Naukowe.

Ryan, William. 1976. *Blaming the Victim.* New York: Random House.

Sanford, George. 1981. "Polish People's Republic." In B. Szajkowski, ed., *Marxist Governments: A World Survey.* New York: Saint Martin's Press.

Schoffer, I. 1959. "The Second Serfdom in Eastern Europe as a Problem of Historical Explanation," *Historical Studies: Australia and New Zealand* 9 (33):46–61.

Servolin, Claude. 1972. "L'absorption de l'agriculture dans le mode de production capitaliste." In Yves Tavernier, ed., *L'univers politique des paysans dans la France contemporaine.* Paris: A. Colin.

Shanin, Teodor. 1979. "Defining Peasants: Conceptualizations and De-conceptualizations Old and New in a Marxist Debate," *Peasant Studies* 8 (4):38–60.

Shoup, Paul. 1981. *The East European and Soviet Data Handbook.* New York: Columbia University Press.

Singer, Daniel. 1981. *The Road to Gdańsk.* New York: Monthly Review Press.

———. 1988. "Diamonds and Ashes," *Nation* 246 (9):300–305.

———. 1989. "The Specter of Capitalism," *Nation* 249 (21–28 August):202–205.

Skocpol, Theda. 1976. "France, Russia, China: A Structural Analysis of Social Revolutions," *Comparative Studies in Society and History* 18 (1):175–210.

———. 1979. *States and Social Revolutions.* Cambridge: Cambridge University Press.

Skorowidz Gminy Galicyji (Statistical abstracts of Galician gminas). 1907. Vienna.

Skreija, Andris. 1973. *Boguty: A Village in Poland.* Ph.D. dissertation, University of Minnesota.

Słomka, Jan. 1941. *From Serfdom to Self-Government: Memoirs of a Polish Village Mayor, 1842–1927.* London: Minerva Publishing.

Staniszkis, Jadwiga. 1984. *Poland's Self-Limiting Revolution.* Princeton: Princeton University Press.

Starski, Stanisław. 1982. *Class Struggle in Classless Poland.* Boston: South End Press.

Stavrianos, Leften Stavros. 1981. *Global Rift.* New York: Morrow.

Steven, Stewart. 1982. *The Poles.* New York: Macmillan.

Subtelny, Orest. 1986. *Domination of Eastern Europe: Native Nobilities and Foreign Absolutism, 1500–1715.* Kingston and Montreal: McGill-Queen's University Press.

Sweezy, Paul. 1980. "Post-Revolutionary Society," *Monthly Review* 32 (6):1–13.

Szczepański, Jan. 1973. *Odmiany czasu terazniejszego* (Change in the present time). Warsaw: Państowe Wydawnictwo Naukowe.

Szelenyi, Ivan. 1977. "Social Inequalities in State Socialist Redistributive Economies: Dilemmas for Social Policy in Contemporary Socialist Societies of Modern Europe." Manuscript.

Szkolny, Michael. 1981. "Revolution in Poland," *Monthly Review* 33 (2):1–21.

Taylor, John. 1979. *From Modernization to Modes of Production: A Critique of the Sociologies of Development and Underdevelopment.* London: Macmillan.

Tazbir, Janusz. 1968. "The Commonwealth of the Gentry," In A. Gieysztor et al., eds., *History of Poland.* Warsaw: Państowe Wydawnictwo Naukowe.

Thomas, William I., and Florian Znaniecki. 1918–1920. *The Polish Peasant in Europe and America.* 5 vols. Boston: Richard G. Badger, Gorham Press.

———. 1927. *The Polish Peasant in Europe and America.* 2 vols. New York: Alfred A. Knopf.

———. 1984. *The Polish Peasant in Europe and America.* E. Zaretsky, ed. Urbana: University of Illinois Press.

Thompson, Edward P. 1966. *The Making of the English Working Class.* New York: Vintage Books.

Thorner, D., B. Kerblay, and R. Smith, eds. 1966. *Theory of Peasant Economy.* Homewood, Ill.: Richard D. Irwin.

Tomczak, Franciszek, and J. Niemczyk. 1977. "Intensification and Changes in the Agrarian Structure of Agriculture." In D. Gałaj and J. Rajtar, eds., *Village and Agriculture.* Warsaw: Polish Scientific Publishers.

U.S. Department of Agriculture. 1981. *Agricultural Situation, Eastern Europe: Review of 1980 and Outlook for 1981.* Eastern Europe and USSR Branch, International Economics Division, Economic and Statistics Service, Supplement 3. Washington, D.C.: U.S. Government Printing Office.

Vaughan, M. 1971. "Poland." In M. S. Archer and S. Giner, eds., *Contemporary Europe: Class, Status and Power.* New York: St. Martin's Press.

Wädekin, Karl-Eugen. 1982. *Agrarian Policies in Communist Europe: A Critical Introduction.* Totowa, N.J.: Allanheld, Osmun.

Wallerstein, Immanuel. 1974. *The Modern World-System: Capitalist Agriculture and the Origins of the European World-Economy in the Sixteenth Century.* New York: Academic Press.

_____. 1979. *The Capitalist World-Economy: Essays.* Cambridge and London: Cambridge University Press.

Wandycz, Piotr. 1974. *The Lands of Partitioned Poland, 1795–1918.* Seattle: University of Washington Press.

Warriner, Doreen. 1964. *Economics of Peasant Farming.* London: Frank Cass.

Wedel, Janine. 1986. *The Private Poland.* New York and Oxford: Facts on File Publications.

Wesołowski, Włodzimierz, and K. Słomczyński. 1977. *Investigations on Class Structure and Social Stratification in Poland.* Warsaw: Państowe Wydawnictwo Naukowe.

Wesołowski, Włodzimierz, K. Słomczynski, and B. Mach, eds. 1978. *Social Mobility in Comparative Perspective.* Wrocław: Ossolineum.

Willetts, Henry. 1968. "Poland and the Evolution of Russia." In H. Trevor-Roper, ed., *The Age of Expansion.* New York: McGraw-Hill.

Williams, Raymond. 1975. *The Country and the City.* New York: Oxford University Press.

_____. 1977. *Marxism and Literature.* Oxford: Oxford University Press.

Willis, Paul. 1977. *Learning to Labor: How Working Class Kids Get Working Class Jobs.* New York: Columbia University Press.

Wolf, Eric. 1982. *Europe and the People Without History.* Berkeley: University of California Press.

Woodall, Jean, ed. 1982. *Policy and Politics in Contemporary Poland.* London: Frances Pinter Publishers.

World Almanac and Book of Facts. 1985. New York: Newspaper Enterprise Association.

_____. 1990. New York: World Almanac.

World Bank. 1979. *World Development Report.* New York: Oxford University Press.

_____. 1980. *World Development Report.* New York: Oxford University Press.

Worsley, Peter. 1981. "Marxism and Culture: The Missing Concept," *Dialectical Anthropology* 6 (2):103–121.

_____. 1984. *The Three Worlds: Culture and World Development.* London: Weidenfeld and Nicolson.

Wortman, Sterling, and R. Cummings. 1978. *To Feed This World.* Baltimore: Johns Hopkins University Press.

Woś, Augustyn. 1976. "Current Problems of the Socio-Economic Reconstruction of Polish Agriculture," *Zagadnienia Ekonomiki Rolnej* (Problems in agricultural economics). Warsaw: Państowe Wydawnictwo Naukowe.

Zauberman, Alfred. 1964. *Industrial Progress in Poland, Czechoslovakia and East Germany.* London: Oxford University Press.

About the Book
and Author

PREDOMINANTLY A RURAL NATION, Poland is most often depicted with urban scenes: steelworkers, trade unions, Communist party members, and Solidarity meetings. In contrast to this industrial vision, *Reluctant Socialists, Rural Entrepreneurs* views historical and recent changes and their agrarian consequences.

During her many years in the Polish countryside, Dr. Nagengast has observed, studied, and worked side by side with farmers and other members of the agrarian class. Here she provides a first-hand perspective on the monumental failures of the Polish version of socialism, which were largely due to decisions that led the nation-state down a distinctly capitalist path to agrarian development. On the basis of her extensive research, Nagengast makes chilling forecasts about the impact of the accelerating development of capitalism on the culture, politics, and economy of Poland.

This book will be useful to anthropologists, sociologists, and scholars interested in Eastern European and socialist studies.

Carole Nagengast, research anthropologist and chair of Amnesty International, U.S.A., 1991–1992, teaches at the University of New Mexico in Albuquerque.